LONG LIVE QUEER NIGHTLIFE

love

LONG LIVE QUEER NIGHTLIFE

How the Closing of Gay Bars Sparked a Revolution

AMIN GHAZIANI

PRINCETON UNIVERSITY PRESS
PRINCETON & OXFORD

Published by Princeton University Press
41 William Street, Princeton, New Jersey 08540
99 Banbury Road, Oxford OX2 6JX

press.princeton.edu

Library of Congress Cataloging-in-Publication Data

Names: Ghaziani, Amin, author.
Title: Long live queer nightlife : how the closing of gay bars sparked a revolution / Amin Ghaziani.
Description: Princeton : Princeton University Press, [2024] | Includes bibliographical references and index.
Identifiers: LCCN 2023020786 (print) | LCCN 2023020787 (ebook) | ISBN 9780691253855 (hardback) | ISBN 9780691253862 (ebook)
Subjects: LCSH: Gays—Social aspects. | Special events. | Nightclubs. | Gay business enterprises. | Intersectionality (Sociology) | BISAC: SOCIAL SCIENCE / LGBTQ+ Studies / Gay Studies | SOCIAL SCIENCE / Sociology / General
Classification: LCC HQ76.25 .G497 2024 (print) | LCC HQ76.25 (ebook) | DDC 306.76/6—dc23/eng/20230902
LC record available at https://lccn.loc.gov/2023020786
LC ebook record available at https://lccn.loc.gov/2023020787

British Library Cataloging-in-Publication Data is available

Editorial: Meagan Levinson & Erik Beranek
Production Editorial: Ali Parrington
Text Design: Chris Ferrante
Jacket Design: Katie Osborne
Production: Erin Suydam
Publicity: Kate Hensley
Copyeditor: Karen Verde

Jacket: (*Front*) Photo by Manu Valcarce, model: Camille Leon, courtesy of Gayzpacho; (*back*) Photo courtesy of Hungama; (*front flap*) The Cocoa Butter Club featuring Jada Love, Wesley Dykes, Niash Fortune, Romeo De La Cruz, Mark-Ashley Dupé, Zaki Musa, Cleopantha, and Sadie Sinner, photo by Aimee Mcghee.
Page ii: Photographer: QUEERGARDEN / Beliza Buzollo. Model: Finn Love.
Page vi: Topographic / Road map of London, England. Original map data is open data via © OpenStreetMap contributors. Courtesy of iStock / lasagnaforone.

This book has been composed in Dover Serif Text, with Monotype Grotesque Bold Extended and Mānuka Condensed Bold for display

Printed in the United States of America

10 9 8 7 6 5 4 3 2 1

Tired of London, Tired of Life

—Samuel Johnson

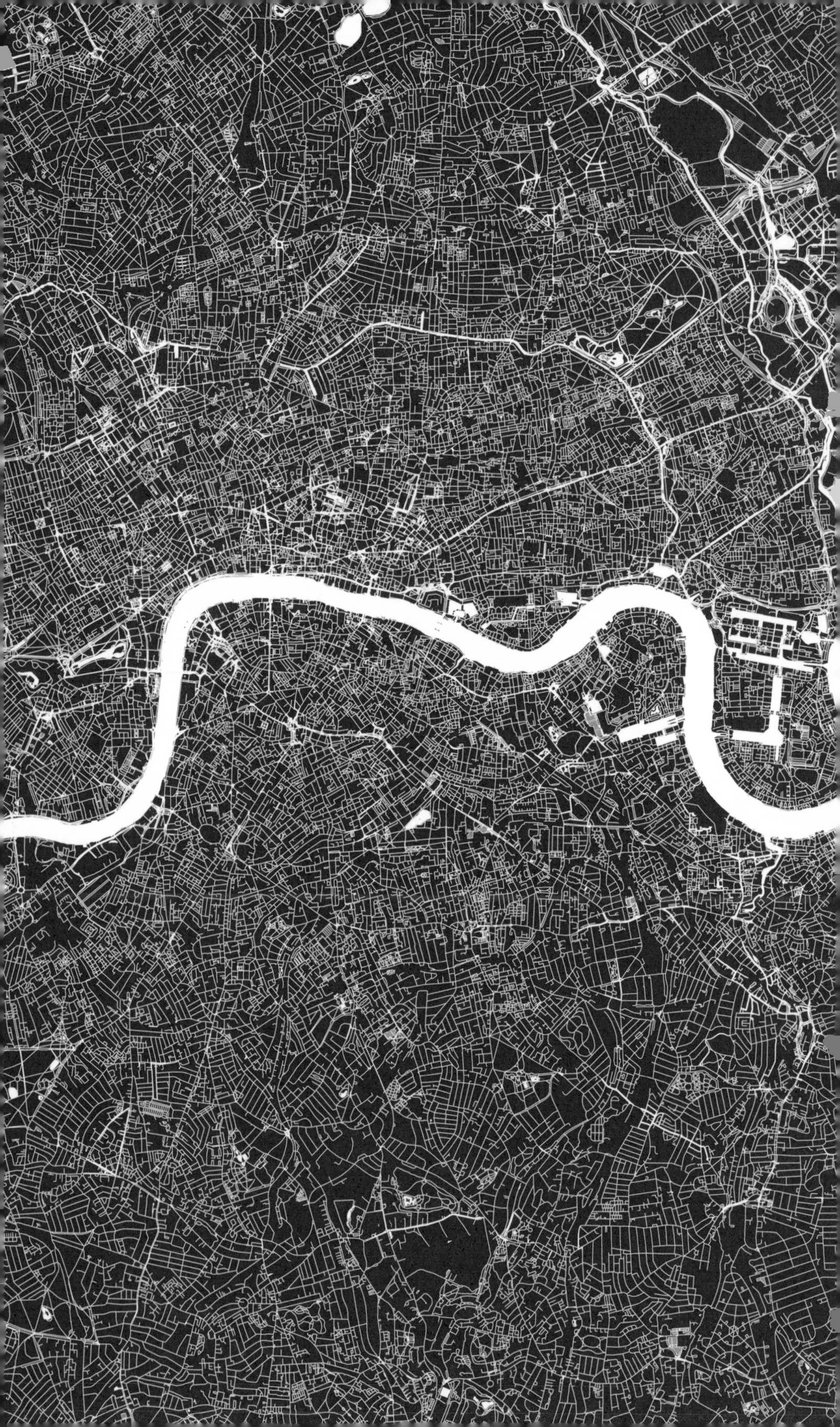

Contents

Preface

Buttmitzvah

Troxy

I had become habituated to hibernating during the pandemic. But here I was in London once again in 2022, bubbling to the brim with excitement. I was *going out*. For the first time in I don't know how long. My friend Ryan and I were headed to East London, a neighborhood once described to me as "a glorious mixture of otherness," for an occasion near and dear to any fabulously queer Jewish person. That's right: we snatched a pair of tickets to the biannual bash known as Buttmitzvah!

The Instagram post promised a Chrismukkah extravaganza ("the best of the holiday seasons—think Christmas stocking but filled with pickles and fishballs. Deeelicious.") and listed ticket prices in order of scarcity. Grab them fast, in the first release, and it would cost you £15.50 (US$20) (*oy vey!*). Think about it longer, and the price rose to £19.90 (US$25) for the second release (*oy gevalt!*), £23.20 (US$30) for the third release (*mazel tov!*), and £26.70 (US$35) for last chance tickets (*L'chaim!*). Final entry into the venue—the iconic art deco theater cum event space called Troxy—was at 11pm. Arrive after that, and we'd lose the chance to party our *punims* off.

Meet Matt, a matzo-munching member of the Buttmitzvah family.
Photo courtesy of Mike Massaro.

The deadline ensured that Ryan and I were timely. We got off the subway at Limehouse around 10:30 and made our way to Troxy, where we met up with our mate Matt, a member of the Buttmitzvah family (*mishpacha*) and one of the most vivaciously Jewish friends either of us has ever had. Gloriously dragged up with irony and blasphemy in roughly equal measure, Matt was resplendent in a golden harness, short-shorts, and *tefillin* (Jewish prayer straps) that wrapped around one arm. "It represents bondage to God!" he quipped, fully aware of the entendre, as he swept us inside London's irreverently queer Jewish club night.

Troxy is massive. Originally constructed in 1933, the former cinema, now converted into a live events space, can hold three thousand people. Its stage is 40 feet deep, and the ceiling looked as distant to me as a starry night. For the moment, however, we were busy being greeted by the mishpacha, a spirited group dressed in pickle outfits and brightly colored faux fur coats. "Welcome to Buttmitzvah!" they exclaimed as someone, in the grand tradition of Jewish parents everywhere, added, "Here's a bagel." Surrounded by donut-shaped pool

▸ Serving up bagels—and lewks/looks—at Buttmitzvah. Photo courtesy of Mike Massaro.

floaties, helium balloons shaped like dreidels and Stars of David, and people noshing on pickles ("it's a very Jewish food," I overhear), the mishpacha asked Ryan, "Have you met the family?" This was an immersive, theatrical welcome, complete with a snack table of pickles, bagels, and boxes of matzo crackers. I chuckled. *At what kind of queer party are you fed as you walk in?*

Following the music, Ryan and I found ourselves on a wildly packed dance floor in Troxy's main room. There were more bodies here than I had seen in years, and more kinds of bodies too. Every shape and size, all genders and races, the people thronging the room were dressed for the occasion—more than just a few of them were wearing black suits. "It's a bar mitzvah," Matt nudged as I took notice. Indeed, the DJ was skillfully controlling the floor with a glorious mashup of traditional Jewish tunes ("Hava Nagila" stood out), Israeli dance ("Offer Nissim"), and British pop ("Girls Aloud"), tossing in a little Dua Lipa and some Beyoncé for good measure. "Klezmer music gives me life!" screamed a reveler, throwing their hands in the air as if being showered with the entire exuberant, glittering, schmaltzy celebration.

Wide-eyed and overstimulated, Ryan and I felt not underdressed but wrongly dressed. We both wore some version of the typically anodyne, dark, well-enough-fitted attire for a night out at a gay bar, but we were bereft of the icons of fun-loving Judaica our fellow partiers sported. Two people were reading a comically oversized Talmud, another was wearing a home-made belly shirt adorned with the handwritten, all-caps message, "PART ME LIKE THE RED SEA," and there were yarmulkes everywhere.

For the most part, I couldn't discern the differences between respect, cheek, and cultural appropriation (I was inexperienced at specifically queer Jewish parties). Still, as the crowd became ever more boisterous, several Jewish-identifying attendees assured me that it was all in good fun. They weren't bothered by the Yiddishisms, they said in sometimes-shouted small talk, or the Jewish iconographies in liberal use by all the "*goy* gays" dancing the night away. Matt, drunk on excitement, gave me one bear hug after another, each time with a bigger grin. "Isn't this amazing?" he gushed. I leaned into his ear to ask over the throbbing din, "But are you okay with all this?" Matt pulled back, tilted his head, and looked sweetly into my eyes. Then

A Buttmitzvah partier with Abrahamic appeal: Part me like the Red Sea.
Photo courtesy of Mike Massaro.

he screamed, "It's all about *having* fun, not *making* fun! And for me, being Jewish is fun! Being gay is fun! This entire scene is coming from a place of celebration."

The unmistakable joy in the air was what made Buttmitzvah's ultra-flashy but never exclusive parties unique. A drag performer laughed hysterically under a "*Mazel tov* on your Buttmitzvah" banner. The mishpacha hoisted partiers on chairs as the crowd danced the hora, holding hands and swirling in circles that looked, to me, like a flash mob. The party, Matt said, intentionally queers Jewish traditions, inviting everyone to join in the fun. "It's a constant changing of experience. It's this immersive theater where you are a participant, think you're at this party, and think that you're just dancing to a DJ—and then all of a sudden, every half hour, there are random performances that may or may not be related to Jewishness or queerness." All the mishpacha's performances, erupting on stage from midnight to 2am, brought elements of tradition to the party, but it was like seeing them through a queer kaleidoscope—I felt invited to think and talk about everything happening around me, imagining telling friends the next

Menorah . . . but make it fashion! Photo courtesy of Mike Massaro.

morning, "I went to this really weird party where people were dressed as pickles and threw donuts at us!" For Matt, this is the desired effect. "What better way to combat anti-Semitism than bringing the strange with humor, and then making people feel comfortable?"

I'll never forget one scene, a nativity performance told from the point of view of a fictional twelve-year-old bat mitzvah celebrant named Becky and featuring her closeted toilet salesman father Mervin Rimmer and mum Gae Rimmer, a drag queen. Every Buttmitzvah party, I learned, was imagined as Becky's bat mitzvah and all the partygoers as her guests. Each time the organizers put on another event, it was also associated with a storyline celebrating a Jewish holiday, whether Hanukah, Passover, or Rosh Hashanah. The night I attended, the mishpacha combined Hanukah and Christmas into "Chrismukkah," and so Becky began her vignette musing about the Hanukah gifts she hoped for and the story of Jesus' birth.

Soon enough, I was heaving with laughter. Gae Rimmer and the angel "Gaybriel" made full use of a 70cm dildo the performers called "the schlong of Hashem" (translation: God's penis), then Gae gave birth (through her butt!) to Becky, who emerged with Nutella smeared on her face. This, at least, was how Becky imagined the divine birth. As I doubled-over in hysterics, a king and two queens came onto the stage to shower baby-Becky-Jesus with pickles, donuts, and vouchers to John Lewis, a British department store. "I don't want that!" mewled Becky. "All I want for Christmas is—" at that precise cue, dancers rushed out, joining Becky in song: "All I want for Christmas—is Jews!" Mariah Carey's campy classic blared, its lyrics rewritten with Jewishisms of all sorts.

And then—wedding music? Performers leapt from the stage and began dancing the hora with the crowd. Confounded and delighted, I again asked Matt to be my interpreter. The point of this cultural collision, he said, was "to bring together the bizarre and hilarious into a theatrical, immersive experience around Jewishness and queerness in an accessible space for a wide variety of people." *It looks intentionally irreverent*, I noted. "That is very much British humor," Matt explained. "Like, that is what British humor has always been about." *Which is what?* "Pushing the boundaries of what is socially appropriate to a ridiculous level that is laughed at and not found uncomfortable." Matt contrasted this with American humor: "The United States is

Dancing the hora. Photo courtesy of Mike Massaro.

Queer joy takes center stage. Photo courtesy of Mike Massaro.

politically incorrect. Like, it references race in a way that makes it uncomfortable, whereas I think in this instance, British humor is self-reflective. It is self-defaming in a way that you just have to laugh, and you just don't want to think about it for too long. It's irreverent. It's ridiculous."

Going further, Matt connected Buttmitzvah to the larger constellation of club nights, this vibrant form of queer nightlife that I had fast fallen in love with: "A bar setting is often about the individual, and it focuses on how you feel in that space. Buttmitzvah makes it about the community. It makes it about you with everybody else, not just you alone finding your two friends or the person you want to hook up with. The point is to be there with other people. That is why Buttmitzvah exists: to create a Jewish queer atmosphere that connects everyone who wants to come." As if settling any remaining discomfort I might have with what seemed like subtle though cheeky blasphemy, he added, "The religion is flexible enough to allow for this kind of experience."

Before I knew it, an hour had passed and an announcement rang out, "Ladies and gentlemen, it's time for the Macarena!" The mid-'90s

Spanglish hit song started to play as a video, syncopated so it looked like a pair of rabbis, arms flung around each other, danced to the beat, while live performers on stage began demonstrating the moves. Suddenly, we were all dancing along, an almost electric laughter running through the ebullient, temporary collective of people, abuzz with the absolutely silly and adorable—and so much fun it was! We dipped, swiveled, made the hand motions, and laughed with wild abandon.

Buttmitzvah was still going strong when Ryan and I decided to call it a night, traipsing to the tube station and asking in shared wonder, *What in the world was that?!?*

The Closure Epidemic

"The gay bar is in trouble."

The sentence stumbled off the pages of *The Guardian*, as if in a drunken lament. Precise figures are hard to pinpoint, the journalist wrote, but the moral of the story is clear: gay bars around the world are closing in alarming numbers.[1]

Now imagine that I have handed you a copy of the *Boston Review*, an independent, nonprofit, literary magazine and forum for public reasoning about the most pressing ideas of our times. As you scan this periodical from across the pond, your eyes, like mine, linger on another distressing headline:

"The Death of the Gay Bar."

Reading the essay makes me wonder about nightlife: what it means, why it matters, how it's changing. "In a world in which queer people are ever more accepted and rigid identity categories make less and less sense, what is the purpose of gay bars? Do we still need them?"[2]

A dour tone is widespread these days, as the media catches on to a global epidemic of closures. Where the *Washington Post* is almost blasé, noting that the number of gay bars has "dwindled," *The Economist* sees them as "under threat." *Bloomberg* hits harder, labeling them an "endangered species." *i-D*, an LGBTQ+ media channel, goes further still, asking if the entire "gay scene"—meaning all of nightlife—is "dead."[3] And these headlines generally describe trends that were underway before the pandemic.

By April 2020, 57 percent of the human population—that's 4.4 billion people—would be under some form of lockdown. *The Conversation* confirmed what I could see as I walked the lonesome streets of my neighborhood at home: all kinds of businesses, including gay bars, were "shuttered by the coronavirus" and, as *Reuters* pointed out, "scrambling to avert collapse." These beloved gathering places of ours had been struggling for a while, but the pandemic shut down the party, putting gay bars "on life support."[4]

I personally noticed the crush of closure coverage around the time I moved to London. For a sabbatical, my friend Ryan invited me to join him at the London School of Economics and Political Science, where he was a member of the faculty. There was no particular reason why I needed to be there, although I have been drawn ineffably to that city for as long as I can remember. I happily accepted the invitation—five months in London sounded like a dream—deciding in the spirit of serendipity to follow my feelings and see what would happen.

I arrived in January 2018, untroubled by the grey skies and rainy days (Vancouver, where I live, is much the same). It was easy enough to establish a routine, walking along Kingsway to and from the university from my nearby flat, picking up a cortado and copy of the free daily paper by the Holborn tube stop. That's when I first noticed it. *Extra! Extra!* A few months earlier, University College London (UCL) published a bombshell report about nightlife. Ben Campkin and Lo Marshall startled the entire city with their findings: between 2006 and 2016, 58 percent of bars, pubs, and nightclubs that catered to LGBTQ+ people shuttered. Once upon a time, there were 125 places to go, but by 2016, only fifty-three remained—a colossal loss. An audit by the Greater London Authority (GLA) found that 44 percent of all nightclubs, 35 percent of all grassroots music venues, and 25 percent of all pubs had closed too. All nightlife venues were suffering, clearly—and yet, LGBTQ+ spaces were suffering disproportionately.[5]

It was around this time that Samuel Douek, an architect turned film director, coined the term *closure epidemic* to describe the scene sweeping London—and in America, Australia, Belgium, Canada, Denmark, France, Netherlands, New Zealand, and Sweden. In the United States, Greggor Mattson documented a 37 percent decline in gay bars between 2007 and 2017, roughly the same time period covered by the UCL study. Some groups were harder hit: the number of lesbian bars fell by 51 percent, and places serving people of color plummeted by 59 percent. The rate of decline was just as astonishing. In the United States, an average of fifteen gay bars closed *every year* from 2008 to 2021. Writing for *Bloomberg*, Richard Morgan put these numbers into perspective "In 1976, there were 2,500 gay bars in the United States; today, there are fewer than 1,400 worldwide."[6]

The people I met in London were obsessed with these studies—and for good reasons. The city's bounty of entertainment options contributes to its status as a global hub of finance, culture, and creativity. Its workforce at night consists of 1.6 million workers—33 percent of all jobs—and nightlife industries contribute £26.3 billion (US$33.2 billion) to the overall economy. Forty percent of the country's £66 billion (US$83.4 billion) nighttime economy is represented by London alone, and the mayor projects additional growth of £2 billion (US$2.5 billion) per year through 2030. Expanding our view, the United Nations estimates that the creative economy, which includes nightlife, had a global valuation of £780 billion (US$985 billion) in 2023, and it will represent 10 percent of global GDP by 2030. Clearly, there is an urgency to understanding what happens in the hours after the sun sets, and when cities light up.[7]

Economic and cultural values matter a great deal, of course, but that's not why we go out. Going out is *fun*—and that quality makes it powerful. Because life is sometimes hard, having a place where we can feel joy, where we can move our bodies to blissful sounds rather than the monotones of the daily grind—these are things of beauty. If the walls feel like they are closing in on you, enjoying fellowship in a bar with your friends or dancing in a club offers a way out. At night, we find other worlds we can inhabit, even if only for a moment—but those moments matter a lot. After I graduated from college, my then-boyfriend Aaron, best friend Jon, and brother Aziz all traveled to London for a summer of self-discovery (or so we told our parents). What we found was the dance floor. I can still see twenty-one-year-old me moving my body at G-A-Y (Londoners pronounce each letter), based then at the two-thousand-person-capacity London Astoria on Charing Cross Road. The bass is thumping, and the floors are sticky from spilled sugary drinks. I'm scream-singing along to "Feel It" by the Tamperer. It's a thin slice of time, a sweet flash of my life that has stayed with me all these years. I still smile when I think about it, feeling an everlasting connection between me then, me now, and everyone else who spent time in that iconic space. It closed in 2009, sadly, when Crossrail, a £5.5 billion (US$6.9 billion) railway project, tore through it. But still, that night, I had so much fun—and I'll never forget it.

Fun is a gateway drug. That's how Ben Walters describes it. Ben is a writer, researcher, and campaigner who champions LGBTQ+ spaces in London. Fun, he tells me, "models and rehearses ways of feeling, understanding, acting, and relating." We'll get to know Ben later, but he makes a point we need to hear from the start. "Fun is important. Fun does things. Fun builds muscles. Fun offers a window into potential futures, including queer futures." I nod and smile, as Ben adds cheekily that "fun don't get no respect from society—or the academy."[8]

I have lost count of the number of studies I have read over the years about suffering and social problems, about hardships and inequalities—depictions of life for minorities as full of misery. Those arguments are accurate, and absolutely essential for guiding us toward a more just future. And yet, having fun and feeling joy is what sustains us while we grapple with the tough stuff. stef m. shuster, whose name is intentionally lowercase, and Laurel Westbrook, both sociologists, describe my discipline's tendency to dismiss such matters as a "joy deficit." When we singularly focus on what makes life miserable, the problems and the pain, all the things that make it pleasurable vanish from view. Put differently, negative experiences are only part of the picture, never its whole.[9]

I think we need to insist on joy. When we go out and have fun with our friends, important things are happening. Those moments, especially at night, create a shared emotional energy that promotes spontaneous, unscripted conditions for group pride, communal attachments, and feelings of belonging. Joy brings us closer together, and as it does, we model positive relationships with each other. And so, what might appear as a trivial thing is in fact a crucial foundation for collective life. This makes nightlife momentous, profoundly meaningful, and fabulous, as cultural critic madison moore, who also does not capitalize their name, would say. Those moments can bloom into a broader politics that propel us beyond "the negative and toiling in the present." These words, which I borrow from performance studies scholar José Esteban Muñoz, move us from deficit—assertions that nightlife is dying—to asset and joy. "We must dream and enact new and better pleasures," Muñoz says. Nightlife is where this happens.[10]

When I spoke with people about why they love nightlife, they used exuberant words: euphoria, ecstasy, freedom, sanctuary, romance, and especially utopia. Kat, the organizer of a party called Femmetopia, likes that word. "I was thinking about the club space as a kind of utopia," she told me. It happens by "flipping your minority status on its head." Inside a gay bar or nightclub, "we're the majority, and it's our space—that's what makes it so amazing." This is a great explanation for why nightlife can feel joyful: a small group can numerically take over a place in a way that is much harder to do with the institutions in which we exist by day.[11]

At night, we are the architects. "That's what's utopian about it," Kat explains. "It's about being in the majority and feeling—and the relief of that." Exhaling frees LGBTQ+ people to experiment with new ways of being ourselves and being in the world. Sometimes, as I will show you, the night frees us to imagine entirely new worlds. "You walk through the doors into a different reality," Kat adds, "in which the mundanities and prejudices of the everyday world become a distant memory." In these places, we unravel and rebuild, rebel and resist, protest and play, and widen the horizons of what it means to be human. This makes nightlife an experimental realm, a collection of places and moments when we stride toward our own spectacular self-creations. All this is why what's been called the closure epidemic demands our attention: places where we can pursue cultural experiments and engage in grander projects of worldmaking make life worth living.[12]

Let's begin then with the same observation as others have made: gay bars are closing in disquieting numbers. But loss is not the whole story. Looking for creative ways that people find joy will fill in the blanks. The image of nightlife as besieged by an epidemic of closures obscures what else is happening—and the pursuit of that *what else* will guide us to places less traveled. To do that, we need to follow a different map. Rather than ask the immediate if well-rehearsed question—why are gay bars closing?—we are setting out to answer something else, something more elusive: *How is nightlife changing? How is it persisting? Where do new joys await?*

Making Sense

Those first five months that I lived in London I interviewed eighty-eight people, like Ben and Kat. I asked questions as a sociologist would, inquiring about the characteristics of neighborhoods with LGBTQ+ reputations, cultural viewpoints about sexuality, economic pressures that people experience in the city, and perceptions about local and international nightlife scenes. When I returned home in the summer, I immersed myself in more than 1,500 pages of transcripts chock full of surprises. Later in the book, I will introduce you to Lewis, the founder of a fierce underground party called INFERNO. Lewis, who uses they/them pronouns, cautioned me against relying on numbers about bar closures to reproduce a narrative of doom and gloom. People who say nightlife is dying are wrong, Lewis assured me. And then they added with a grin, "I would laugh in their face!" I'll never forget what Lewis said when I asked why. "I *hate* these academics and these scholars that sit on panels with three or four other academics, and they're like, 'Oh yeah, nightlife is dying.' Bitch, I haven't seen you in a nightclub once! How *dare* you sit there on your little chair, on this little panel, under the spotlight and claim that nightlife is dying when you haven't been out to even support it or to see what it's even like right now? How *dare* you make these allegations, these sweeping statements?" I flinched at Lewis's words, feeling hot under my collar then and as I do again now as I recount them for you. Lewis never said it directly, but they didn't need to: *I* was an academic asking questions about nightlife!

I'm in no position to say how many people who write about nightlife have set foot inside a bar or nightclub (I have, around the world), if they had fun (I did, abundantly), or how they grapple with explanations other than the common trope that "nightlife is dying." What did occur to me in revelatory moments like the one with Lewis—and there were many, *many* others like it—was a detail that I think people miss. A joy deficit is the default assumption in too many conversations about nightlife. We hear repeatedly that LGBTQ+ nightlife was once better—gay bars as far as the eye can see!—but the situation now is bleak. I think that we need to resist the impulse to think about nightlife in such dismal ways, to feel only a sense of loss. It is true that a lot of gay bars are closing, but bars are not the sum total of nightlife, are they?

Researchers and public commentators are adamant about the numbers, about counting gay bars in travel guides like *Damron*, neighborhood listings on *Yelp*, archival records, newspapers, and in magazines. This is a fine strategy—we need so-called "hard data" to make sense of big-picture trends—but counting bars will offer us conclusions only about bars. And that will lead to assessments about a landscape that is inexorably shrinking, not a horizon that is changing, maybe even growing. When I was in London, the glass looked half full. This is not just a matter of semantics. To appreciate what I mean, we need to find another point of view, other ways of seeing.[13]

There are collectives and visionary individuals, like Lewis, who are producing underground parties in London called *club nights*. Once I started to meet these people, form relationships with them, and attend their events, I recognized a truth seldom shared: nightlife—the way it looks and feels—is evolving, not dying. A key driver for these changes today comes from what Kimberlé Crenshaw, a critical race theorist, would describe as the intersectional failures of gay bars, in which one form of difference, like sexuality, overrides the others, especially race and gender.

Over the years, gay bars developed a reputation as places that appeal mostly to gay men, and White gay men, at that. A lot of other people feel left out—though not defeated or disempowered. Instead, they are producing or attending a scene of radically inclusive club nights. From ongoing events that celebrate Jewish identities, Spanish heritage, Bollywood, or cultures of femininity to one-off parties in hidden locations, this form of nightlife is episodic and ephemeral. Club nights are scattered across the city and throughout the year, and they last for unpredictable amounts of time, from a couple of months to a few years and sometimes longer than a decade. Many of them cater to individuals who identify as queer, trans, Black, Indigenous, and people of color (QTBIPOC)—precisely those groups who have felt unwelcome or excluded in gay bars. Nightlife is transformative for people who are marginalized by multiple vectors of power, as it enables unique ways of seeing and being in the world. And what worlds are they building? Rather than only asking glum questions about gay bars, like nearly everyone else, I wanted to peek beneath the surface, where a riotously queer nightlife is *thriving*.[14]

The more I thought about what Lewis said, words that were harsh though honest and wise, the more I knew I had to go back to London. During my second and third visits in 2019 and 2022 (the pandemic forced me to take time off), I connected with twenty-four more people, all of whom were producing club nights like INFERNO—or Buttmitzvah, where we went earlier, and Femmetopia, where we'll go later. From them, I began to put together the pieces of an intriguing puzzle. In total, the 112 interviews and forty-two club nights that comprise the bass-heavy, beating heart of this book bring to light the significance of nightlife, the search for belonging in it, and how experiences of exclusion and the pursuit of joy inspire people to act creatively—whether in the service of protecting gay bars or reinventing what fellowship looks like at night.

Into this medley of voices and places I added viewpoints from dozens of planning reports published by the mayor's office and independent policy centers. These documents describe how city officials in London from the late 1990s onward have reframed nightlife from the embodiment of crime, anti-social behavior, and conflicts to one of the most prized expressions of urban culture. Flipping through hundreds of pages, I learned about the creative industries, the economics of nightlife, the manifold threats that nightlife venues face, how bars and clubs are like theaters and museums, and I discovered a unique mayoral charter that details specific ways to protect LGBTQ+ venues.[15]

My many moments at club nights, and the years I invested studying them from near and afar, have made my spirit sing—but they also baffled my mind. Although I spoke with more than a hundred people from every facet of nightlife scenes, scanned pages of dense reports, and even though I sweat my way through so many parties, the particular worlds where we are going hold little of that hard data I mentioned earlier. I cannot tell you exactly how many club nights happen every month or every year in London, or in any other city, for that matter—even though I can say with certainty that they exist all around the world. I also cannot tell you what percentage of club nights are run by people of color, trans folks, White gay men, or lesbians; what the profit margins are of a "typical" club night (as if there is such a thing); or present a precise distribution of the types of venues in which these parties occur or their preferred neighborhoods. This is a world that thrives on improvisation, that favors mobility and intermittence over permanence, and that is synonymous with the underground, both as a metaphor and a material place of gathering. Due to these unknowns, club nights are really hard to quantify—but I don't think that matters much. Club nights are intentionally inchoate, purposely undefined, and joyfully celebrated as such. The people who produce and attend these events are there to imagine new ways of being and new worlds of belonging—not new ways of counting.

I want us to capitalize on this uncertainty. Creativity plays with both the known and the unknowable, after all—and this potent mix is why I think the world of club nights is so irresistible. In the pages to come, I will foreground feelings and experiences as ways of knowing, and I will modulate between evidence and inferences we can reasonably derive from ambiguity. This is not a tour guide, not a memoir, not an exposé of some scandalous scene. During my visits to London over three years as an urban ethnographer of nightlife, I collected a massive amount of data. With it, I will broaden and deepen what we will learn, introducing you to people who are creating utopian forms of urban culture, those who are trying to manage it, and everyone in between—above ground and especially below it.

But First, Some History

The gay bar has a long and storied past. One of the earliest records we have comes from the White Swan on Vere Street, Clare Market, in London—more than two hundred years ago! The criminalization of homosexuality back then created a need for secrecy, which places like the White Swan provided. On July 8, 1810, the Bow Street Runners, an early version of the British police, raided the molly house (that term, from the eighteenth and nineteenth centuries, described meeting spots for homosexuals). Nearly thirty men were arrested, six were convicted of sodomy, and two were hanged a year later at Newgate prison. Thomas White was only sixteen years old, and Joseph Newbolt Hepburn, forty-two, was an ensign in a West India regiment. The fate of these men, condemned by the media as "monsters," created collective trauma, and it remains one of the most brutal exemplars of the public punishment of homosexual men in British history, though molly house raids remained common until the latter half of the twentieth century.[16]

Across the Atlantic, there were as many laws as states. Formal bans on selling or serving alcohol at establishments that openly hosted homosexuals, however, date to the repeal of Prohibition in 1933. Once alcohol became legal again, lawmakers created agencies to regulate its sales. In 1939, the State Liquor Authority (SLA) of New York shut down Gloria's Bar & Grill for "permitting homosexuals, degenerates, and undesirable people to congregate on the premises." When the bar refused to deny service, it lost its liquor license. Gloria's sued the SLA, arguing that state officials could not ban serving alcohol to homosexuals as long as they were behaving in an orderly fashion, but they lost at trial and again on appeal. For the next twenty-five years, SLAs across the country closed hundreds of bars that catered to, or even just tolerated, homosexuals.[17]

Post-prohibition liquor laws in nearby New Jersey banned serving alcohol to all "persons of ill repute," a category that lumped homosexuals, deemed a "nuisance," with criminals, gangsters, racketeers, pickpockets, swindlers, and prostitutes. The same year as Gloria's was targeted, a tavern in Newark was shut down for a month after a man "made up with rouge, lipstick, mascara and fingernail polish" asked for a drink in a "very effeminate voice." State officials were ruthless. As late as 1955, a saloon owner in Paterson, New Jersey, lost her liquor license after plainclothesmen reported fifteen male couples "dancing and sitting with heads close together, caressing, and giggling," and in 1956, a gay bar in liberal Asbury Park was fined for serving men who "rocked and swayed their posteriors in a maidenly fashion." The *New York Times* reports, "From the end of Prohibition in 1933 through 1967, when a State Supreme Court ruling finally outlawed the practice, New Jersey, like many other states, wielded its liquor laws like bludgeons to shutter gay bars." As context, remember that sodomy laws were still on the books in forty-nine states (Illinois was the first to decriminalize homosexuality in 1962). This, as Nick

Sibilla writes in *Reason* magazine, made the gathering of a group of gay people in public "practically a criminal conspiracy."[18]

It was the same on the West Coast of the United States. The Black Cat, a historic gay bar in Los Angeles, endured years of mistreatment by the California Department of Alcohol Beverage Control. In 1948, Sal Stoumen, the (straight) bar owner, had his liquor license suspended because the establishment was classified as a "disorderly house," a designation given to places frequented by homosexuals, since they were "injurious to public morals." Stoumen fought the police and liquor control inspectors for the right to serve anyone he pleased. Three years later, in 1951, the State Supreme Court ruled it illegal to close a venue simply because "persons of known homosexual tendencies patronized said premises and used said premises as a meeting place." The case, *Stoumen v. Reilly*, inspired a national conversation about the importance of gay bars.[19]

Because liquor licenses functioned as mechanisms of state surveillance and control, gay bars across the country became symbols of resistance. Here we can think of the Stonewall riots in 1969—or the "sip-in" some years earlier. On April 21, 1966, three men tried to break the stigma around homosexuality by presenting themselves as clean-cut citizens. Dick Leitsch, Craig Rodwell, and John Timmons knew that drinking while being openly gay was illegal. But inspired by civil rights activists who were engaging in sit-ins to desegregate diners in the American South, the three men intended to use the simple act of ordering a drink as their protest. They would wait to be denied service, and then sue. The first place they went, a nearby restaurant, was the perfect spot; it displayed a sign in the window with the stinging message, "If you are gay, please go away." Alas, it was closed that day. Eventually, the trio walked into Julius's Bar at 159 West 10th Street in New York (now a historic landmark). As the bartender brought over their first drink, the men revealed themselves as homosexuals—at which point the bartender covered the glass with his hand and refused to serve them. "I think it's against the law," he said. A flurry of legal cases ensued after the *New York Times* covered the event in a story entitled, "3 Deviates Invite Exclusion by Bars." A year after the sip-in, a state court ruling declared that evidence of "indecent behavior" needed to be "more than same-sex cruising, kissing, or touching."[20]

Rulings like these emboldened proprietors to open gay bars in greater numbers. That process had been accelerating since the Second World War, as more lesbians and gay men concentrated in port cities. Nightlife is "where queer life has happened for all kinds of historic, contingent, post-war reasons," Ben, who we met earlier, tells me. Indeed, foreclosed from the opportunity to participate in the social world on queer terms, LGBTQ+ people used nightlife to craft a world in their own image. Ben adds, "In the absence of being able to partake in mainstream society and culture on queer terms, more of it has happened in nightlife than anywhere else." This made gay bars a central institution, if not *the* single most important and visible expression of LGBTQ+ lives. As more networks formed around them, recognizable urban gay districts, or "gayborhoods" as I call them in my other work, emerged in the United States and in countries around the world. Even today, gay bars tend to cluster in these areas (although not exclusively).[21]

Early observers of this world, academics like Nancy Achilles, recognized the difficulties of creating communities in and around gay bars. "The bars come and go," she writes, "like a chain of lights blinking on and off over a map of the city." When Achilles made this poetic observation about San Francisco in the 1960s, she conceded that "the gay world" comprises a "galaxy of social types"—but she stuffed that entire galaxy into bars. There were and are different types, to be sure—"leather bars," others for "effeminate queens," and some for "lesbian clientele"—but when it comes to LGBTQ+ nightlife, what observers saw then, and still seem to focus on now, are bars.[22]

A decade later, drawing on a national sample from the United States, Joseph Harry replicated Nancy Achilles's findings about the "diversity of gay life-styles" expressed in different kinds of bars, which included establishments that catered to people who liked to dance, lesbians, hustlers, older people, dressy people, leather enthusiasts, and Black gay men and lesbians. Another decade after that, in the 1980s, Stephen Israelstam and Sylvia Lambert expanded the list of countries with vibrant bar scenes to include Canada, South Africa, Brazil, Mexico, and the United Kingdom. Slowly and methodically, researchers broadened their coverage of gay bars from one city, to one country, and then to many countries.[23]

Do you notice any patterns? When it comes to nightlife, pioneering researchers acknowledged the diversity of *social types* but not *organizational forms*. The gay world was vast, containing galaxies of difference—and yet, there was only one place, the gay bar, for everyone to go. Even recent work from the 2020s describes nightlife in terms of the ever-increasing varieties of bars: bear bars for hirsute gay men, leather bars for fetishists, lesbian and dyke bars, Black bars, drag bars, suburban gay bars, and even "post-gay" bars. Across seven decades of research, scholars have talked a lot about the bars, presenting variations on a recurring theme. To be fair, researchers have described different forms of LGBTQ+ social life, including house parties, bookstores, record companies, and music festivals, but nightlife remains curiously basic in this body of work.[24]

Disruptions

Gay bars are hugely important, both historically and currently. Places like the Pulse Nightclub in Orlando and the Admiral Duncan in London have prompted international conversations, protests, and vigils.[25] These and other gay bars provide vital, arguably safer places, but they often (though again, not always) center particular groups. Let's revisit that statistic from London: of its LGBTQ+ nighttime venues, 58 percent closed in the most recent decade. But notice what happens when we take a closer look: closures were most pronounced in the city center, including in Soho. Like other gayborhoods, this area is where we find clusters of bars that, as I mentioned earlier, draw mostly White gay men. If we prioritize them in our narrative about nightlife, we will miss the fact that QTBIPOC individuals—those who face multiple forms of oppression by existing at the intersections of racism, transphobia, and queerphobia—can have painful experiences of exclusion *in those same places*. Conclusions about the decline of nightlife hinge on the erasure of these groups and their cultural creations—and this I absolutely cannot and will not do.[26]

Picture it: you are in a gay bar in Washington, DC. Mostly pop music is playing, but when the rapper Juvenile's "Back that Azz Up" comes on, a group of Black and Latinx men start to dance around a set of tables. Some jump up on the benches in the booths that surround those tables. Nearby White men slowly step back, cautiously watching the scene unfold. The episode, a real-life example, shows how Black and Latinx gay men carve spaces of belonging for themselves, even if those spaces are fleeting. Mere minutes later, the DJ plays some Meghan Trainor, and the moment vanishes. Still, what the scene shows us is that the "same space"—a gay bar full of White men—can operate as a "different place" for QTBIPOC groups when they claim it and center themselves in it. Those moments are full of possibility, sometimes creating cultural ruptures, even glorious ruptures. Consider that, during the United States' Jim Crow era, African Americans were excluded from "White-only" music clubs. But that exclusion led to the emergence of Black-only cultural venues, like those in Newark, New Jersey, which became "a mecca for Black jazz in the thirties and forties" as Black patrons were turned away from Philadelphia's bars and music halls.[27]

These modified approaches to studying nightlife, in which we attend to the creation of different cultural centers in the same space or the rise of entirely new places, still don't get us very far beyond the bar—but they do capture a critical insight: when people feel excluded from society in some way, they manifest bursts of creativity. This resistance, I think, is asset-based thinking at its finest. The closure epidemic will provide for us a similar opportunity to explore power, agency, and intersectional achievements while embracing a prismatic vision of nightlife. Thus, it is now precisely the right time to ask: under what conditions do which people create forms of fellowship beyond gay bars?[28]

To answer that question, I will import a concept from organizational, social movement, and cultural studies into our reflections about urban nightlife, arguing that gay bar closures today are a kind of *disruptive event*. The phrase describes an unsettled moment of time, either anticipated or unexpected, that alters our routines and the ideas we take for granted. Recent examples include economic recessions, terrorist attacks, pandemics, mass shootings, union strikes, natural disasters, and wars. Our response to disruptions can create more upheaval, change begetting change as people question how things used to be, imagine how things could be, and mobilize toward those other outcomes.[29]

Sometimes, disruptions exacerbate existing inequalities—like racial profiling, which increased following the September 11 attacks in the United States, or the "individual freedoms" backlash against public health responses to the COVID-19 pandemic. These reactions occur because disruptions feel urgent; those of us who are affected feel compelled to respond right away. The problem with rapid responses, however, is that they target survival, they seek a return to the familiar, and they attempt to restore stability.

Consider again the closure epidemic and the responses to it that cropped up in London. In 2016, Mayor Sadiq Khan appointed Amy Lamé as the UK's first mayor-of-the-night, or "night czar" (the name "night mayor" was also considered, but the possibilities for puns were endless). The role represents a form of urban governance that promotes nocturnal vibrancy. "I think the nighttime economy is important, and the particular kinds of venues that we are trying to *save* are important because they build resilient communities," Amy Lamé told me personally. Mayors of the night liaise between bar owners, planning authorities, government representatives, and citizens. "[W]e need to make sure that we have spaces that exist in order for communities to thrive and *survive*," she added.

The appointment of a night czar and her statements, emphasizing words like "save" and "survive," highlight a relationship between disruptions and the prototypical protective responses to them. Lamé's mandate is to address a threat as quickly as possible and get things back on track. This makes the response prone to a cognitive trap that organizational researchers call *isomorphism*: the tendency to reproduce a similar form, to think about the thing that is most familiar or most common while overlooking other possibilities. To wit: the mayor and the night czar, like the media and many researchers, focus on gay bars, whether that's protecting them, promoting them, or encouraging new ones to open.[30]

In those same moments of widespread disruption, some of us will reevaluate rather than reproduce. And so, once something is interrupted or disarranged, new possibilities arise, sometimes revolutionary, for how we might put the pieces back together. When you hear that word, *revolution*, it is easy to picture something big and dramatic, impossible to miss—upheavals and transformations on a massive scale! But subtle revolutions are also possible. A single act or simple choice can change lives and entire political orders, switching the tracks down which history travels.[31]

To see how all this happens, these unexpected and complex things that escape notice by people who are preoccupied with survival and sustainability, we need to keep tweaking our questions: let's ask not (only) why gay bars are closing but (also) how people are responding. Squeezed out of the gay bars that catered to limited groups well before they began to shutter in large numbers, culture creatives found ways to cultivate joy in other ways and in other places. Join me as we next explore the experiments occurring in urban nightlife. Who is creating them, what is motivating them, and where are they happening?

Follow Me Underground

The night offers an opportunity to put people and places together in boundlessly creative ways. To examine these connections between our identities and the places where we go out, I want us to adopt a wide-angle lens and see nightlife as something expansive, like a field with both formal and informal rules and a bunch of actors whose varying degrees of power can enable and legitimize some while marginalizing and excluding others. Close your eyes for a moment and say that word out loud: *field*. What do you see?

When I hear it, I picture a vast, open space. To extend the metaphor, nightlife as a field is abundant with opportunities other than bars. There is room for many more types of people and places, experiments and experiences. Sure, we can still see the bars—it's ill-advised to ignore them—but other things now come into view as well. I want us to see gay bars *and* struggles to create other options in the field. By imagining nightlife in this way, we heed calls by Kareem Khubchandani, a humanist, to embrace a "more capacious" style of thinking, and what David Grazian, a social scientist, describes as a "larger landscape" of the city after dark. But where are these other places?[32]

In London, the closure of gay bars was a disruption as well as an inciting event in the field. As I noted earlier, an inventive and daring spirit is flourishing in an underground scene of club nights. There, the city's artists, audiophiles, and other culture creatives are fighting issues like gentrification and redevelopment which threaten the bars while ensuring that nightlife remains vibrant and marked by far more variety. By blending pleasure and politics, celebration and spatial acts of resistance, organizers are drawing on a long legacy of using episodic events to craft moments of fellowship in the midst of social occlusion—and they are revolutionizing nightlife along the way.

Unlike gay bars, club nights occur only occasionally, they are located in places beyond the gayborhood, and they can exist without a permanent institutional home (although some have residences). With dwindling numbers of bars in the limelight, public commentators overlook these other expressions of nightlife. Researchers—social scientists more often than humanists, I might add—misattribute events like club nights as "epiphenomena," or secondary gatherings that orbit the bars rather than unique worlds and sovereign centers of nightlife. No wonder we know so little about them! Ritualistic gatherings, even if they are only occasional, must occupy the center of our attention and analysis. When I take you to these parties, we will see people discovering themselves and each other anew in the course of what Jonathan Wynn describes as "effervescent moments of copresence." In the worlds that LGBTQ+ people create at club nights, they imagine something grand, like structural change, but enact it on the dance floor.[33]

While the specific parties we will visit in this book are on the newer side of things—and they may not even exist by the time you read these words—the general format of temporary or occasional gatherings outside of gay bars has a proud history. Matt Houlbrook, an authority on British queer history, found a hundred-year-old letter from Bill, who was making plans to go out one weekend. "Honey Bunch," Bill writes to his lover Bert in 1927, "I will be outside Lees Hall at 8 o'clock on Saturday, and we can easily find a dance." From Bill's tone, it seems that they had options. "We have fixed nothing for Saturday yet, but there are plenty of dances so don't forget to come." The handwritten letter is an astonishing artifact. It was penned forty years before the Sexual Offences Act of 1967, which partially decriminalized sex between men in England and Wales—yet there was Bill, between the world wars, with plenty of places to dance the night away with his honey bunch.[34]

We don't know where Bill and Bert ended up that night. Houlbrook guesses that they went to the Adelphi Rooms, a place for short-term boarding on Edgware Road. Leslie Kinder, a local waiter, would rent out spaces for fortnightly dances, selling tickets through friends and acquaintances. His events attracted up to three hundred men—clerks, cabinet makers, a coach painter—who would come, as Houlbrook describes, "painted and powdered . . . [wearing] earrings and low-necked dresses." If not the Adelphi Rooms, then maybe Bill and Bert went to the Caravan on Endell Street, Billie's on Little Denmark Street, or Betty's on Archer Street. These were not gay bars but venues where larger numbers of homosexual men would occasionally gather. The specific places came and went then as they do today—in Achilles' words, we can picture "a chain of lights blinking on and off over a map of the city."[35]

London's queer scene was extensive, although the places where people partied were not always public. The meaning of words like "public" and "underground" are far from fixed. The "public world" that Houlbrook describes consisted of streets, cafes, and urinals. Nightlife places, like the Adelphi Rooms where Leslie threw temporary parties, were "a quasi-private world in which to relax, meet friends, have fun, and know that one was not alone." While you needed to be an insider to find them—"not everyone knew about such places," Houlbrook says—they were anything but epiphenomenal. "Far from clandestine," Houlbrook continues, "venues like the Adelphi Rooms were tightly woven into the fabric of London's commercial nightlife. This vibrant social world . . . was an integral part of it."[36]

New York had a similar scene. Gay bars opened after the repeal of Prohibition, as I mentioned earlier. Most of these places only lasted a few months before police raids shut them down (again, blinking lights). Many men avoided the bars for fear of being caught, arrested, and revealed. This concern, the American historian George Chauncey suggests, was "an especially powerful threat to professionally successful men." Those who had "greater wealth and social status" turned to less visible places, like businessmen's bars in hotels or the opera house, further alternatives in the field of nightlife. These places welcomed "multiple audiences" and "multiple cultural meanings," Chauncey says, which allowed gay men to socialize under the radar—and without requiring a gay bar.[37]

As nightlife opportunities were expanding for gay men and lesbians, so too were social gatherings for people who felt marginalized by both their sexuality and their gender. The most popular events were called masquerade balls, or "drags." One of the earliest occurred in Washington, DC, on New Year's Eve in 1885. The *Washington Evening Star* reported that one participant, named "Miss Maud," was arrested while returning home the following morning. Genny Beemyn, a historian, draws us into the drama: "Dressed in 'a pink dress trimmed with white lace, with stockings and undergarments to match,' the 30-year-old, male-assigned, Black participant was charged with vagrancy and sentenced to three months in jail, even though the judge, the newspaper reported, 'admired his stylish appearance.'" Roughly a half century later, by the 1930s, drags drew hundreds of cross-dressers and spectators, though mostly White, who attended in Chicago, New Orleans, New York, Baltimore, Philadelphia, and other cities.[38]

Events like these were a product of their time. The Pulitzer Prize–winning author Michael Cunningham describes them as "merely drag fashion shows staged by white men two or three times a year in gay bars." People of color rarely participated, and even when they did, they were told to "whiten their faces." Pepper LaBeija, one of the stars of the circuit in New York, reflects, "It was our goal then to look like white women. They used to tell me, 'You have negroid features,' and I'd say, 'That's all right, I have white eyes.' That's how it was back then."[39]

Fed up with the racist scene, Black queens in Harlem in the 1960s began organizing their own ritualized performances, called "balls." These events were flamboyant dance competitions between "houses," or surrogate family structures led by "mothers" and "fathers." Like club nights, balls also created their own worlds by refusing the power of mainstream representations (no more whitening your face). As the queens put together more extravagant looks, their parties attracted more spectators, first by the dozens and then the hundreds. It was these Black and later Latinx queens who made ballroom an "underground sensation," Cunningham says, "undreamed of by the little gangs of white men parading around in frocks in basement taverns" in earlier decades. The 1990 documentary film *Paris Is Burning*, which took its title from the name of an annual ball organized by Paris Dupree, popularized the scene for mainstream audiences.[40]

Temporary gatherings at night have been a cornerstone for queer women of color as well, even though, once again, social scientists have said little about them. The oversight, Rochella Thorpe argues, happens because we assume that bars are "the center (both theoretical and actual) of lesbian communities." In her study of postwar Detroit, Thorpe finds separate social environments for Black lesbians, who would throw "rent parties," and White lesbians, who were the ones hanging out in the bars. Women of color hosted their own parties because racism made it nearly impossible for them to socialize in those same bars. "White women in the bars were very prejudiced," one woman shared with Thrope. Rent parties took place in private homes, and people found out about them through word of mouth. The hosts provided food, music, and alcohol "for a fraction of the admission charge at high-priced clubs," Thorpe adds, and used the profits to subsidize the high rents of Harlem apartments—hence a rent party. Ruth Ellis and her partner Babe threw some of the best. "All the gay people would come to our house," Ruth remembers. "That was known as 'a house where queers go.'"[41]

Bars that catered specifically to Black lesbians did open in later decades, but house parties remained more popular. Ronnie, a local bartender, explains the economic motivation: "What it really is about [is] Black people not havin' very much." House parties provided an alternative for people who aspired to open their own bar but did not have the financial means. In the 1970s, women called them "after-hours parties" or "blind pigs," in reference to the unlicensed sale of alcohol, and Black lesbians flocked to them. The blind pigs were much larger and far more anonymous than the rent parties thrown by Ruth and Babe, and they provided spaces in which to drink and dance well past closing time at the bars.[42]

Black women in Washington, DC, continue the tradition today. Nikki Lane calls these gatherings "scene spaces," which she defines as a "transient group of events"—from house parties to happy hours in commercial venues. The events are popular because "there are no Black lesbian bars or clubs in the city," Lane observes. The biggest parties are thrown by event promoters who rent spaces for one-off gatherings. In common, writings by Thorpe and Lane highlight how intersectional profiles can inspire parties that prioritize the "desires and experiences of Black women."[43]

Club nights today are a manifestation of a long-standing tradition. While they are not unique, per se, I think they are uniquely important, uniquely meaningful, and uniquely revelatory in many ways.[44] For starters, club nights refashion nightlife in opposition not just to a straight mainstream, as did the drags, balls, and rent parties that came before, but also—and possibly for the first time—to an established gay mainstream. And so, rather than serving as a refuge from homophobia, like earlier scenes, they are intentional expressions of inclusion that respond to experiences of exclusion at gay bars. Club nights thus provide an alternative to those bars, existing concurrently with them. But that does not make club nights interchangeable with gay bars. If you walk by a gay bar, you will recognize it by the rainbow flags that surround it, the large numbers of White men inside, or the popular music spilling out the doors. Club nights, as we will see, refuse those flags, attract a very different crowd, and often feature experimental sounds. Parties are promoted by word of mouth or on social media platforms (they are not publicly marked). You have to be in the know to go, hence the idea of an *underground* where parties feel hidden and secret.

Gay bars are fixed and emplaced, often located in areas with discernible LGBTQ+ communities, or a place with a liberal reputation. You can go to your favorite bar any night of the week (if it hasn't closed). Not so with club nights. They are irregular and nomadic, a series of related but discontinuous events. Club nights share this feature with the house parties that happened earlier in history, like Ruth and Babe's place, but they are more structured than those gatherings. Club nights are organizationally distinct, in other words: more formalized than house parties but less standardized than gay bars. The temporary format they use enables some clever economic experiments, a third quality that, as we will see in detail later, hints at how nightlife can thrive even as many bars close. For these reasons, it feels like club nights can pop up anywhere in the city at any time—and they are not to be missed.[45]

Club nights have many more standout features. Most parties are queer, not gay—a cultural and semantic shift that has sizable implications for what power looks like and how it operates. A fifth feature: many club nights prioritize gender politics, especially trans and nonbinary representations, in ways we have seldom seen. These parties are adamantly inclusive and broadly intersectional, much more than gay bars and earlier iterations of itinerant gatherings. Finally, while gay bars emerged in greater numbers in a permissive climate, following the repeal of laws against indecent behavior, club nights are gaining ground in a constrictive context of a closure epidemic in capitalist cities like London. Emerging in the thick of a large-scale disruption and responding to the shortcomings of gay bars are a collection of club nights that are remarkably diverse and differentiated, keenly self-aware and articulated.

So many events and scenes all over the world! From drags in the late 1880s to wherever Bill and Bert ended up that night in 1927, from postwar house parties for Black lesbians in Detroit to club nights in London today: all these places capture an entanglement between the mainstream and the underground, where some of us come alive in defiant celebrations and reclaim the humanity others try to steal, whether through the criminalization of gay sex, laws banning people from wearing the clothes of another gender, or racism. That defiance takes on a distinctly joyful quality in nightlife. Bill sounded excited in his note to Bert, despite the risks involved, and I'm sure Miss Maud had a fabulous time at the ball, even if she was arrested—and Ruth and Babe's house of queers sounds like it was a blast. Are you curious yet? If so, then it's time to look beyond the dimly blinking lights on Achilles' map and see each other, *really* see each other, under the bright strobes of nightlife beyond just the gay bar.

What Next—or *Where* Next?

There is a cache associated with time-limited events. Many of us reflect on our life by remembering the moments, and we string those moments together in an effort to define who we are. Flashes of time are life's highlights, like colorful lasers on a dance floor that come and go, and they light up the grey skies of daily life. Each gathering at night is an opportunity to meet up with old friends, make new ones, and create longer-lasting impressions. We love events, and we look forward to them, for this exact reason: because they are infrequent and uncommon. Events feel special. Those moments at a club night will pass in a heartbeat. But it doesn't matter. What does matter is that the moment existed at all. To be present in a place that prioritizes you, finally, feels like a revolution, a universe away from being invisible night after night in other places.[46]

In the chapters to come, we will see how people are reimagining nightlife and what it means to do so underground; we will explore economic models that champion creativity despite the devastations of capitalism; we will encounter soul-crushing reflections on racism; we will learn how people reclaim nightlife, and reorient it, in response to those experiences of exclusion; and we will pay thoughtful attention to naming practices—from *gay* bars to *queer* nightlife—that gesture toward greater visibility and more voices. Richard Morgan, the journalist from *Bloomberg* we met earlier, offers a memorable turn of phrase to synopsize these themes: "In an LGBTQ+ world, bars that are merely gay can seem anachronistic."[47]

At every party I attended, I felt an intimate mingling of rebellion and joy. That dance created a sensation of belonging for the people who took part in it. I was there too, and I experienced it as the cultural core of club nights. All of us need to connect, after all, and we do it by seeking meaning-rich interactions with each other. Because belonging is such a big idea, I don't want us to think about it in a casual or abstract sense. We form attachments with other people as we hang out with them here at a gay bar, or there at a club night. Place matters.

Now, finally, we come to a crescendo about the book's title. The expression "long live queer nightlife" is a play on quintessential Britishness, but in relation to royalty, it implies the preceding assumption that "gay nightlife is dead." The pairing of these delicate declarations, metaphors of continuity, transferal, and triumph, gives us a lot to work with! So, grab a cup of coffee (or a flask) and turn the page—it's time to go out.

1

Ways of Seeing

Statistics about bar closures abound in the press, resulting in a vision of nightlife as impoverished. But on the streets, people's experiences are much richer. "I think that journalists just quote this figure. They say, '58-percent of venues closed,' and then they say, 'queer nightlife is dying.' It's very easy to write a story based on that." Laurie, who tells me this, organizes The Chateau, a party that occurs in an obscure, once-religiously-themed cocktail bar. Laurie was twenty-eight when we met, and he invited me to join him one weekend on site. I traveled about an hour from Central London, where I was living, to Camberwell in South East London. A nondescript entryway leads to a door that beckons me to a basement. I walk down a flight of stairs and discover a low-ceilinged room adorned with brightly lit stained glass windows. This place looks more like a church crypt than a gay bar, I think to myself. Laurie walks over, smiles, and introduces himself. We chat for a moment, but he is eager to dive in: in a matter of minutes, Laurie cautions me against interpreting bar closures as evidence of decline, despite the appearance of a logical link. "It's lazy."

Public discussions, centered on gay bars and their closures, often look through a lens of deficit. And so, I can understand why some people are quick to conclude that nightlife is dying. But not Laurie. "We're constantly being told that queer spaces are closing," he sighs, "like, 'oh my god, no, it's terrible.'" In the first two decades of the 2000s, more than half of LGBTQ+ nighttime venues shuttered in London. That much is true. Less obvious is how people make sense of these numbers as they go about their nightly lives. Hence, a question to warm us up: how do people—from city officials and party producers to revelers and activists—acknowledge the closure epidemic? And how does their response to it, or our response, shape the way we imagine the future of nightlife?[1]

The Troubled Gay Bar

All revolutions require a trigger, a disruption, and for us that comes from the gay bar. Nearly every political and cultural formation in LGBTQ+ life from the 1960s onward was born from those bars, even if they have been rife with tensions. Problems and all, they were still the place so many of us went to imagine and articulate who we are. With a cultural significance so massive, we must grapple with why these places matter, and why they are struggling to survive.[2]

In the mayor's office, where I began looking for clues, I found a Venn diagram that identified five "adverse underlying conditions" pressuring nightlife in the capital. In no particular order, these are: land values (while land has become more expensive, businesses like gay bars operate on small profit margins), the national planning system (with permitted development rights, it has become easier to convert gay bars into shops and small supermarkets without being subject to the full planning process), business rates (set by the government, taxes on gay bars are now almost as expensive as their rents), licensing restrictions (conflicts around opening and closing hours arise when new homes are located close to bars that generate noise and crowds), and funding reductions (public and grant funding for leasing buildings at no or low cost, as well as managing them, is now harder to access). When these risk conditions overlap, they create a "perfect storm." Amy Lamé, who identifies as a lesbian, is London's night czar, the person responsible for protecting places like gay bars. She explains the imagery to me: "The combination of these things has created a situation in

London where it's very difficult for small, independent venues to survive and thrive."[3]

The UCL study first publicized statistics about closures in London, as we know. That report also adds more threats to the mayor's list, including the challenge of negotiating with landlords and local councils (who are elected local representatives) over rent increases, refurbishments, lease renewals, and licensing disputes. Both reports, one from a university and the other from the mayor's office, agree that the most common culprit is *redevelopment*. Ben Campkin, the lead author of the UCL study, clarifies the point: "It was clear that many spaces that were deemed safer spaces for our respondents had closed or been sold, or been converted to other uses, often when they were apparently quite vital businesses." His last point is important, as it refutes common misconceptions that gay bars are closing due to a lack of demand or declining revenues. "It wasn't that they were businesses that had gone into decline," Ben emphasizes. "It was actually that the land was more profitable as something else, or that the building was more profitable as something else." Amid these concerns about land values, "one of the things that was striking," Ben adds, "was the link to development, and large-scale development in particular."

Over the last decade, London has experienced some of the highest land value increases of any city, especially for parcels that can be redeveloped for residential purposes. "The cost of land is expensive in London," remarks Dwayne, a local DJ who identifies as Black British. He shares a startling rhetorical question: "Why would you safeguard a place where you make X when you can sell it for millions?" Considerations about land values have increased the probability that nightlife venues will be demolished and redeveloped into flats, often luxury units. "Let's get rid of this scrappy old pub, knock it down, and turn it into something else, like luxury flats or luxury bars," Greygory, the owner of a trans-friendly hairdressing service, explains.

The exploitation of land has an ignominious history. "There are examples all over the world where capitalism and its foot soldiers steal and murder people for land," Dan Glass says. Dan is a celebrated activist and author in London who is regularly profiled in the press for his social justice work. "It's an age-old route of inequality. In a queer context, it is no different in terms of how space is stolen from queer people." Tom, an Irish gay man, has lived in London for a decade. He also thinks about the politics of capitalism: "Reflecting right now—not sure that 'straight washing' is the right word for it—it's 'economic washing.' Up the rents so only massive chains can actually afford to be there." Manuel, a nonbinary-identifying Spanish gay man, offers a similar viewpoint: "What's worrying is when bars are closing not because of lack of use, not because there's not people that want to use them, but actually because of things [the venues] being made into luxury flats. There's an economics which I think is really troubling."

Nearly everyone I met raised concerns about land values. Jon, a forty-five-year-old Basque gay man, recommends that we extend protected status to bars, like we do for churches: "It's sad that they can do that, that they can just raise their rents like that. But again, it's all a business, isn't it? We live in a capitalist society. Some other places are protected, like churches are protected, and gay bars aren't." Protection is important because once we change something, we can't always undo it. Simon produces Duckie, a popular weekly party that had a twenty-seven-year residence at a bar called the Royal Vauxhall Tavern, where we will go later. He thinks deeply about these matters. "It's a bit sad though, because once a pub—or let's call it a public social resource—is privatized into residential, it's very hard to undo it and make it a pub again."

Land values and redevelopment priorities are two of brightest stars in the constellation of economic factors affecting nightlife. We met Samuel in the introduction, the one who coined the term closure epidemic. He and I talked about how austerity measures impact public goods. "Everyone was talking about it," Samuel remarks in reference to the closing of bars. "Everyone was talking about how much it was affecting the community, how many places were closing down, and it was part and parcel of the legacy of austerity that came out of the recession [in 2008]." What happened, I ask? In the aftermath of the global financial crisis, Samuel explains that "the UK government bailed out—the taxpayers bailed out—the three main banks that were about to collapse." The event "created a huge deficit in the budget," he adds. Something similar occurred in places around the world and, as a result, "a lot of countries implemented austerity." They reduced government deficits through spending cuts or raising taxes rather than, Samuel continues with disappointment, "fining the bankers."

The British government reduced public spending to tackle the deficit, a now familiar government policy. The impact was swift. Samuel says that it felt like the government "put its hand around the necks of the people who were most affected." A vivid visual, but for the sake of clarity, I ask him to explain what he means. Instead of addressing tax evasion or increasing the tax rate for high earners, the government reduced welfare spending, and this constricted people's economic capabilities. "Between the period 2010, which is when the Conservative government was elected, to 2014, you really felt that no one was spending money . . . A lot of people were made redundant [laid-off]. That, I think, had a direct influence on the amount of creativity and culture" in the city. And thus began the "age of austerity," as Conservative Party leader David Cameron described it in *The Guardian*.[4]

Austerity measures reconfigured the balance of political power. Dan Beaumont, a bar owner and club night organizer, elaborates, "In some ways, financial interests now operate above the heads of authorities, because they're more powerful, really, than either national or local government in a lot of ways." In what ways exactly? "That is mainly seen through the commodification of lands," Dan replies, "through gentrification, and through pushing out communities by making places unaffordable. That's where London is now." This pattern, which emerged from the recession, is bigger than any one city on either side of the pond. "That's where Berlin is heading," Dan adds. "And that's where New York has been." All these places are experiencing the consequences of similar pressures. "It's definitely a response to larger forces squeezing out places to exist that are not necessarily commercially driven but driven by culture and community."

The more people shared their points of view, the more I realized that the closure epidemic has layers of complexity and emotional depth—far more than statistics by themselves can convey. London-based artists and lesbian duo Rosie Hastings and Hannah Quinlan share these feelings in a "moving image archive of gay bars in the UK." Entitled *UK Gay Bar Directory*, the project presents more than one hundred gay bars across fourteen cities. By filming the bars when they were empty, the artists draw our attention to "the rapid closures of LGBTQ venues," as described in a brief.[5] Rosie tells me about the locations they selected. "They were all really popular, loved, historical gay bars." Why were such beloved bars closing? "They were closing because of reasons that seem linked to external forces to the gay scene, rather than internal forces like assimilation, or because people aren't going to gay bars as much. We didn't believe that narrative, so we wanted to find out what it really was." What did you discover? Rosie's response echoed UCL and mayoral reports. "In every case in London, it was because the lease was ending, because the council had revoked a license, because the council wanted to redevelop the area, they wanted to turn the gay bar or the sex club into a luxury hotel, or luxury flats, or a retail zone—make it a more 'palatable' area"—Rosie uses air quotes—"for tourists or for families."

Ben Walters, an independent researcher and journalist, takes a deep dive into demand, offering another challenge to the idea that bar closures are a function of declining enthusiasm for going out. "There's a rhetoric that circulates when the closure of queer venues comes up for discussion that is premised on the idea that these places are less popular than they used to be, or that they're less socially, culturally useful than they used to be, and so their time has come." Ben, like Rosie, doesn't buy it. "It's *not* that these places are less popular. It's *not* that they're not still serving a function. They *are* still popular. They *are* still very busy. They *are* still very packed. There *is* still a huge appetite." What's your answer, I ask Ben, for why bars are closing? He links demand with redevelopment and a reappraisal of land values. "The threat they face is economic, around essentially the price of square footage of London real estate. That's really what it boils down to." From here, Ben brilliantly explains why even financially successful gay bars struggle to survive: "It's not a question of whether it's commercially viable; it's a question of whether it's maximally profitable."

Running a gay bar will probably never represent a maximally profitable use of square footage—I think Ben's right about this—even if the number of people who will patronize the place is large in a city like London. "It's always going to make more money if it's put to use as chain retail, or chain restaurants with accommodation on the floors above," Ben adds. His viewpoint, a calculation of *commercial viability* against *maximum profitability*, is foundational for how we understand, and hopefully protect, nightlife venues. “If the question is, are these places commercially viable, nine times out of ten the answer is yes. If the question is, is this the maximum profit that can be wrung from this central London square footage, then the answer may be no—and that’s where the threat comes in.” This logic, put forth by developers seeking to demolish the site of a gay bar, reduces venues to commodities, and it prioritizes price over something perhaps more ambiguous though arguably more important: the priceless expressions of culture and creativity. “The city is there to make money, and we are there to spend and to earn. To be in the city is just to be an economic agent, and to compete and measure your value against other people.”

Although they do not make similar distinctions between commercial viability and maximum profitability, city officials generally agree with arguments about demand. When I met him, Edward Bayes was the culture-at-risk officer. As a twenty-six-year-old, heterosexual, White British man, he was responsible for supporting the mayor in developing policies to protect London’s cultural assets, including its nighttime venues. “The demand is there,” Bayes told me. “The need is there as well.” Bayes and the night czar both predict that demand for places to go out at night will actually *increase* as London’s population reaches 10.8 million by 2041, up from 8.8 million in 2017. London is among the most visited cities in the world (a point we’ll return to again later), and demand for visitor accommodations is projected to reach 196.4 million nights by 2041, up from 138.5 million nights in 2015.[6]

Money talks. That much is clear—but in a city like London, the interactions between supply and demand are many-sided. Richard, a thirty-eight-year-old diplomat, frames nightlife as a unique market. “It will always be economic for some gay places to exist.” Why is that? “It will always be profitable,” he replies matter-of-factly. “I think the market’s there, and it’s always going to be there. It may not be to the same degree as it was ten or fifteen years ago, but I think it will always be profitable to have a few gay venues, and as some close, others will open.” Richard pauses, and then he gifts me with a memorable analogy. “Just in terms of the size, London can sustain quite a bit of—I don’t know, you can buy an egg from Russia here.

So, if you can buy an egg from Russia here, there must be a market for a gay bar somewhere in the city. It's just so big a market." I echo the phrase back to him: if you can buy a Russian egg, and there's a market for that, there must also be one for gay bars. Richard looks pleased. "It's true," he says. "I mean, you can get all sorts of crazy stuff here. The big cities are not the places that are going to have trouble sustaining these things. I think life in the regions may change. But I don't at all see it as bad. If people want these kinds of things, they'll create them, and it'll be profitable. And if people don't want them, they're unprofitable, and they won't exist."[7]

If cities are places for people to live a meaningful life, to experience the sublimity that comes from cultural contact, and to have fun and feel joy along the way, then our risk analysis should be a point of departure, not a destination. LGBTQ+ lives are about more than markets, spending, and square footage, after all. Equipped with a better understanding of why so many bars are closing, let's next inquire into how cities are trying to protect their at-risk cultural assets.

The Night Czar

There are 1.6 million people working at night in London. Of that total, 168,000 people work in fields related to culture and leisure. Meanwhile, two-thirds of Londoners are active at night, doing everything from running errands to socializing to enjoying facilities like theaters and music venues. Consider as well that London is the third most-visited city in the world for international tourists, and that four out of five visitors say that access to culture and heritage sites is the main reason for their trip. The value of London's nighttime economy, recall, is estimated at an astounding £26.3 billion (US$33.2 billion), a figure that is expected to rise an additional £1.5 billion (US$1.9 billion) by 2026. Forty percent of the estimated £66 billion (US$83.4 billion) for the total UK nighttime economy is represented by London alone, and Mayor Sadiq Khan expects £2 billion (US$2.5 billion) in additional growth of nighttime industries each year through 2030. From these figures, the economic rationale for protecting nighttime venues is as clear and compelling as a stash of cash.[8]

In May 2016, the mayor addressed members of the creative industries at City Hall, where he acknowledged that the economically rich nightlife sector was vital for "London's well-being." He promised to make cultural life, in which he now included nightlife, a "top four" priority alongside housing, security, and clean air. Imagine that you were there at City Hall, listening to the mayor, and consider the implications of his words: nightlife is as important as the air we breathe![9]

In November, six months after his announcement, Khan made good on his promise and revealed the creation of a brand new role: night czar. After reviewing hundreds of applications, he introduced Amy Lamé, whom we met earlier, as the UK's first-ever night czar. Born in New Jersey but living in the UK since she was twenty-one, Lamé was already well-known in London as a Labor activist, broadcaster for BBC Radio, and mayor of Camden from 2010 to 2011. "It's a privilege to be London's very first Night Czar," she said. "I can't wait to hit the streets and have loads of ideas of what I can do for revelers, night-time workers, businesses, and stakeholders. For too long, the capital's night-time industry has been under pressure."[10]

Khan was inspired by similar initiatives in Amsterdam. The role he created in London signals the importance of what Mirik Milan calls "culture at night." A former club promoter, Milan became the world's first "Nacht Burgemeester" (the term Amsterdam uses for night czar) in 2014. The hours that begin after the day ends are critical for building "culturally diverse and socially inclusive cities," Milan says in his explanation for the importance of an official position. Individuals like Lamé and Milan have "convening power," or the ability to create conversations between public and private entities, including local planning authorities, who can come together and explore different ways of seeing. Convening power might sound soft, but it is a crucial asset that enables night czars to provide an opportunity for experts to share what works.[11]

After Khan made his announcement, London became the biggest city in the world to appoint an ambassador for the city after dark. And then, soon after London, Mayor Bill de Blasio of New York appointed Ariel Palitz as the first "nightlife mayor." More than forty cities have since followed suit with their own politician-of-the-night, including Berlin, Budapest, Geneva, Madrid, Paris, San Francisco, Sydney,

Tokyo, Toronto, Zurich, and others. Lamé, Milan, Palitz, and others are manifestations of a new form of urban governance that is gaining international recognition: mayors of the night prioritize culture as an engine of urban economic development.[12]

Both the mayor and the night czar are responding to closures as if they are a clear threat to London's cultural health. On this matter, the numbers are impossible to ignore. LGBTQ+ venues: in 2017, there were 53, down from 125 in 2006. Grassroots music venues: in 2016, there were 94, down from 144 in 2007. Nightclubs: in 2017, there were 570, down from 880 in 2001. Pubs: in 2017, there were 3,530, down from 4,835 in 2001. City officials are trying to protect existing establishments and help new ones to open. "I don't want young and creative Londoners abandoning our city to head to Amsterdam, to Berlin, to Prague where clubs are supported and allowed to flourish," Khan said in a 2016 interview with *The Independent*. "We can save London's iconic club scene, which draws thousands of visitors to the capital, generates jobs, and helps ensure our city remains prosperous, vibrant and dynamic." Lamé offered something similar in an interview with the BBC that same year. "I need to stem the flow of those closures," she asserted. "That will be one of my top priorities—it's never too late."[13]

I interviewed Lamé and Bayes in 2018 in their office at City Hall. "I understand that nightlife contributes about £26 billion to London's economy, and it employs one in eight people in the city," I note as we get comfortable sitting around a circular table. "Clearly, the nighttime economy is important for economic reasons. But why else do you think it matters?" I was inviting them both to reflect on the broader significance of nightlife. "I think the nighttime economy is important, and the particular kinds of venues that we are trying to save are important, because they build resilient communities," Lamé replies. "They create safe spaces. They are places where people can be themselves without question." Her passion for the role is obvious. "Even though we know that laws have changed, for example, to be more accepting of LGBT people, we're still facing discrimination. Hate crime is up. We saw a big spike in hate crime following the vote to leave the EU. These are all issues that are very much alive, and we need to make sure that we have spaces that exist in order for communities to thrive and survive."

I appreciate Lamé's last point, as it refutes another common narrative: societal acceptance has reached historically high levels, so we no longer need gay bars. She describes this as an "assimilationist mindset," what some academics call the post-gay thesis.[14] Lamé has noticed a pattern in who raises these arguments. "This is a question that is posed to me quite often"—do we need gay bars now that gay people can be gay anywhere?—"and it's pretty much nine and a half times out of ten coming from heterosexual White men . . . saying, 'Oh, but now you can get married, you don't need venues, you don't need your own spaces.'" Lamé urges caution. "Not everyone operates in this assimilationist model." Of course not, and this is precisely why LGBTQ+ people still need our own places—during the day as well as at night.

Peter, an activist fighting to ensure the survival of beloved bars like the Joiners Arms, adds a personal note to Lamé's official rebuttal of assimilation politics. "I'm married. I'm the least radical person out there. I'm a married, White, gay, middle-class man. I don't feel safe." Tell me more, I ask, without a specific prompt to see where Peter was going with this line of thinking. "There are situations where I don't hold my husband's hand, or I think twice about kissing him or expressing affection. That's in Hackney. The mayor is gay in Hackney! I still don't feel safe, fully safe, in every space." Compelled by his words, I share how I, too, sometimes feel unsafe holding hands in public or sharing a kiss with my partner. Peter puts his hand on his heart. "If I don't feel safe, then what on earth must it be like for a trans person, a person of color, do you know what I mean, like, all these people who are further down the pecking order of social acceptance? I just don't buy it." Peter dismisses unqualified arguments about acceptance as an explanation for why gay bars are closing. "Homophobic violence is on the rise," he says. "There have been really high-profile incidents of people being attacked for holding hands or kissing each other." Why then is assimilation such a popular perspective? "I think the word 'myth' is probably the most appropriate thing," Peter replies. "It's just not true."

In offering another argument, Dan Glass first reaches across the aisle. "I think the desire, or the need, or the belief to assimilate can come from very important places, because there's a genuine level of spiritual exhaustion from our community continuously having to fight, like every day is a battle, for a variety of reasons." I lean in closer to him. "I understand that people just want to put their feet up, and chill out, and be accepted, and just chill the fuck out. Trauma is at the root of it." Suddenly, I remember the anti-gay slurs I heard when I was in college; I felt outraged, and terrified, but underneath it all, I just felt drained. "But I think that simultaneously, that's quite naïve if we're looking at what is genuinely happening with the rise of the far right, who do not have our best interests at heart and do not want us to assimilate." If not assimilation, then what? "They want us dead."

City officials, activists, diplomats, DJs, and ordinary Londoners agree that how we come together at night presents a profound priority, like the breath of life. I read this in the mayor's report, I hear it echoed by the night czar and culture-at-risk officer, and I feel it from people like Peter and Dan. In all these moments, the closure epidemic seems so much bigger than a bunch of disembodied numbers. A sense of urgency grows in my mind and in my heart as I find myself wondering: how do cities communicate to citizens that nightlife is a priority? It's one thing for Khan to say so, but what strategies and policies signal their actual commitments?

Cultural Infrastructure

In 2019, the mayor's office published the *Cultural Infrastructure Plan*, a report that specifies how to preserve and promote London's cultural assets. Think for a moment about that phrase: cultural infrastructure. What an odd pair! The second word, infrastructure, points to the built foundations of cities. These are facilities or physical structures that support a place, which we can't buy or build on our own as individuals. Examples include buildings and bridges, roads, sewer and water systems, pipes, networks of cables, railways and subways, airports, and harbors. Some researchers think about infrastructure as a "connective tissue" that links people and places, while others offer metaphors like "the sinews of the city" which ensure smooth operations.[15] Now consider what happens when we attach the word culture to infrastructure. The resulting neologism foregrounds culture as the bedrock of a city.

In practice, cultural infrastructure is about the premises and places where cultural objects are produced (where culture is made, showcased, or exhibited) and consumed (where culture is experienced or sold). London boasts thousands of these places, which include museums, galleries, theaters, libraries, skate parks, community centers, performing arts spaces, legal street art walls, music recording studios, film and television studios, and now nightlife. A city's cultural infrastructure, places both old and new, tells the story of its heritage to its citizens and the wider world. "It gives London its character and authenticity," the report states. While cities routinely plan for their future when it comes to things like transportation, roads, hospitals, and schools, they seldom do so in a similarly systematic way for culture—and even less often for nightlife. To think about nightlife as part of its infrastructure is an example of a cultural policy and planning strategy that London is using to protect bars and nightclubs.

London is not alone in championing the premises and places where nightlife cultures are produced and consumed. In 2021, the German federal parliament, led by a housing and urban development committee, voted almost unanimously to reclassify its nighttime venues as cultural institutions rather than entertainment venues. The campaign began a year earlier and was spearheaded by the Berlin Club Commission (BCC), a group of venue owners and managers who protested in the streets by shouting "clubs are culture!" As with London, the economic rationale in Berlin was self-evident. When the BCC appeared in parliament before the decision was announced, they argued that nightlife venues comprise "the pulse of the city," drawing an estimated three million tourists who generate €1.5 billion (US$1.7 billion) for the local economy. Also similar to London, nearly one hundred clubs in Berlin have closed in the past decade, with an additional twenty-five under threat due to redevelopment. Locals describe the situation as "clubsterben" (translation: the club that dies or club dying). Some even say that the bars and nightclubs in Berlin will "forever be dying." The closure epidemic, the eternity of clubsterben—these phrases point to a serious international problem.[16]

The change in classification, from an *entertainment venue* to a *cultural institution*, is anything but small or subtle. As entertainment venues, nightclubs are compared with arcades, brothels, and casinos. The change to a cultural institution provides bars and clubs with the same legal status as museums and opera houses, protects them from displacement that can occur from redevelopment, and enables them to open in more parts of the city. Bureaucratic designations may seem like a banal detail, but they make a big difference! The change in the way nightlife is classified affirms the association of culture, creativity, and cities in the after-dark hours.

From jazz and blues clubs to gay bars, the message, as Pamela Schobeß of the BCC explains, is clear: "Music clubs are cultural institutions that shape the identity of city districts as an integral part of cultural and economic life. Now, an outdated law is to be adapted to reality. This helps keep cities and neighborhoods alive and livable and to protect cultural places from displacement." The change in legal status that Schobeß described had important material consequences. It prioritized the safeguarding of nightlife venues in order to protect them from redevelopment and further upheavals. The new classification also extended tax breaks to bars and clubs—a rate reduction for the amount of value added tax, or VAT—that they pay. Germany's financial courts ruled to lower the VAT paid by Berlin clubs, including places like Berghain, from 19 percent down to 7 percent.[17]

The unprecedented support for nightlife in Berlin prompted many observers in London to wonder about the situation closer to home. A headline in *Bloomberg* asked, "Berlin Protects Clubs and Nightlife—Why Doesn't London?" The writer, Sarah Wilson, speaks bluntly about why nightlife matters: "A city without clubs is a colorless place, and allowing them to disappear means marginalized communities vanish; young people flee the city, and arts and creativity suffer. With London fast becoming a playground for developers and a city that only the rich can afford, it would do well to replicate Berlin's example."[18] While London has yet to go as far as Berlin, creating an independent body like the Club Commission, the mayor has proposed recommendations to grow the capital's cultural assets. The *Cultural Infrastructure Plan* lists several priorities: we need to understand where a city's cultural infrastructure is located; create new places in the future; provide world-class opportunities; support culture at risk; increase investments in cultural assets; create policies that enable our creative industries to put down deeper roots; and provide guidance for how to stabilize cultural assets.

The report is "a planning tool," Bayes tells me as I read about cultural infrastructure with him. At first, I thought the prose sounded strangely familiar, saturated with a kind of palatable-to-the-most-people-possible blandness that typifies how politicians and bureaucrats often speak. Bayes probably sensed my skepticism. The plan for culture guides local authorities when they make decisions about the public applications they receive, he says in explaining its importance. The objective is "planning for culture in the same way that we do for housing or transport." His words start to feel more concrete, like the change in VAT in Berlin. Bayes offers an example: "If there are [developers] building new housing next to a vibrant LGBT venue or a vibrant grassroots music venue, how can those two uses coexist? And how can we use the planning system, rather than perhaps having some unintended consequences of people move in next door to a venue, then they complain, and the venue shuts down? How can we plan in a way that makes those two uses compatible?"[19]

Londoners agree that nightlife, as a cultural asset, should be protected from unregulated market forces. To make the case, Simon from Duckie begins with a quick review of London's economic history. Boris Johnson, who was the prime minister when I spoke with Simon, is a "conservative, pro-market force" who believes that we should "just let the market do what it does, and that's the best thing." Simon is skeptical. "That doesn't work for everything." Like what? I asked. "It doesn't work for fragile things, like culture, community." If we leave market forces unchecked and unregulated, then "culture suffers."

His remarks remind me of the cultural infrastructure plan, and we speak next about how to create vibrant scenes. "If you want good nightlife, good cultural life, good queer scenes, it needs to be a mixed economy." What does that mean? "A mixed economy is partly commercial—the busy hustle-bustle of the marketplace, bums on seats, and cash changing hands—and partly the intervention of the public sector to help creative, ambitious, cultural programming." As we endure a closure epidemic, we need to ensure that we rebuild nightlife in more sustainable ways. And for that to happen, market logics—competitiveness, pricing, offering an appealing product, and maintaining demand—require public support, like funding for the arts and culture, and municipal protections. Simon repeats the message: "For cultural life to be rich, we cannot leave it to the market alone."

In an interview with *The Guardian*, Lamé shared that the mayor has a keen interest in cultural infrastructure not just in broad terms but also its specific LGBTQ+ expressions. "Sadiq and I keep LGBT places close to our hearts and hold them in very high regard. And we've made it really clear that it's an integral part of our plan to grow London culture." She echoed the message to me in person at City Hall: "The mayor is very clear on this, that LGBT spaces are an important part of London. It's what makes London London."[20]

Folding gay bars into cultural infrastructure raises the provocative possibility of nightlife as resembling art worlds, like the offerings in museums such as the Tate Modern or the V&A. This is why Dan de la Motte, a performer and activist, applauds the effort: "This is a really strong signal from the mayor's office that he is on the side of nighttime spaces." Going another step further, Lamé, Bayes, and the mayor drafted a companion document called the *LGBTQ+ Venues Charter*. It provides a set of practical tools in the form of a "five-point pledge" that developers, property owners, and venue managers can take to support London's LGBTQ+ venues. "This LGBT venues charter is meant to be a way of identifying what an LGBT venue is in order to work with developers," Ben Campkin tells me. "And this is the first case where that's happening."

I've never seen anything like this, I say to Lamé and Bayes as I glance at the one-pager:

1. A visible rainbow flag should be displayed on the outside of the venue.
    a. The rainbow flag is a universal symbol of the LGBTQ+ community.
    b. The symbol could be displayed as an actual flag or alternatively a sign, sticker, or other physical signifier.
2. The venue should be marketed as an LGBTQ+ venue.
    a. This will be an integral part of the venue's business plan.

   b. Marketing needs to effectively reach the LGBTQ+ community, e.g., through social media, print and digital journals, blogs, and other relevant websites.
   c. Many LGBTQ+ venues display LGBTQ+ magazines/literature/posters in the venue itself.
   d. Venues will engage in community outreach, such as hosting events around significant dates like Pride.
3. The venue should provide a welcoming, accessible, and safe environment for all.
   a. The venue will welcome anyone regardless of background or identity, religion, race/ethnicity, gender identity or expression, disability, age, or sexual orientation.
   b. The venue will be accessible to disabled people.
   c. The management will consider adopting gender-neutral toilets.
4. Management and staff should be LGBTQ+ friendly.
   a. Door and bar staff will create a welcoming and safe environment.
   b. Door and bar staff will be LGBTQ+ friendly. There are LGBTQ+ friendly security firms in London who provide licensed security staff (many of whom are LGBTQ+ individuals themselves). There are also relevant training providers.
5. Programming should be LGBTQ+ focused.
   a. Where the venue programs regular entertainment, this should be principally LGBTQ+ focused.[21]

After I read it, twice for good measure, I ask if the charter has made a difference. Lamé replies that it "was written into what's called a Section 106 agreement, meaning that when a new development comes forward [at an existing gay bar], there will be a replacement venue in the new site." As a planning tool, the charter is flexible. It enables developers to build what they want while ensuring that they remain sensitive to the queer heritage of a given site. "The way that you can engineer a replacement LGBT venue," Lamé continues, "is that any operator that goes into that site has to sign onto this charter." The effects have been groundbreaking. "Section 106, that bit of legislation, had never been used before to re-provision for an LGBT space. We're used to our spaces being knocked down or turned into other things."

Replacement venues are one part of the mayor's plan, which also includes attempts to prevent closures in the first place. "Somebody has to stick their neck out and say we're going to put resources into trying to save these venues," Lamé emphasizes. Too often, LGBTQ+ issues are an afterthought. The mayor of London, similar to Berlin, wants to protect them. "That may not have happened if we didn't have a mayor who appointed a night czar and asked me specifically to deal with cases of LGBT spaces," Lamé continues. "It may not have happened if he didn't put the resources into appointing a culture-at-risk officer whose sole job it is to find venues that are at risk and to try and help them survive and thrive. How would that have happened if we didn't have a mayor that put resources into that?" For Lamé, the answer is clear: "There is no other city in the world that is doing this."

Successful cities do not grow from policies and planning procedures that emphasize exclusions rather than connections—like whether to invest in the culture *or* economy of a place—as if we lack the imagination to do both at once. After speaking so closely with city officials, however, I wanted to hear a little less about government interventions and a lot more about participation on the ground. How do Londoners make sense of the possibility of something like clubsterben? Ultimately, for culture to matter, it must be meaningful beyond the confines of the conference room.

Half Full

When I met Olimpia, who identifies as Italian and a queer lesbian, she was a twenty-three- year-old graduate student. As we chatted over a cup of coffee, I asked Olimpia if she had any advice for the night czar. "Nothing planned can create a queer space," she declared. I wasn't expecting such a strong stance, and it made me wonder whether queerness is compatible with something as legislated as infrastructure, cultural or otherwise. Why not? Olimpia answered with a metaphor. "You have a garden, and some people like to plant their seeds in a specific place, and make it look very pretty, and very sanitized, and very well thought out." This is what she has in mind for the work of the night czar. "The other approach would be to try and make your land as fertile and as iron-rich and vitamin-rich as possible, and then let it unfold, and see what happens." That plot would look different. "If the ground is fertile, then you will have all sorts of flowers growing on top of each other in no systematic way. And I think that is closer to queerness than the approaches Amy Lamé has taken."

I similarly wondered about the upbeat sounds coming out of City Hall. In our conversation, for example, I asked Lamé and Bayes if they knew about the DIY-styled pop-up parties that I had been discovering, not anchored to any specific venue or any one part of the city. "Yes," Lamé replied. I waited for her to say more, perhaps to share an example, but neither she nor Bayes added anything else. To help them, I described some parties, particularly those that cater to Black, Indigenous, and people of color communities. I talked about how their format is different from gay bars (episodic events, not established businesses), as is the language they use (club nights, not gay bars). As I described these differences, I wondered out loud whether club nights represent a different model of nightlife. They both nodded, but again had little to add. What do you think? I inquired directly. "I think it's brilliant," Lamé responded. "I think that for London, we're known for the diversity of our nightlife, and so the fact that these pop-up spaces exist is living proof that there really is something for everyone here at night in London. And I guess with our work in trying to preserve particular spaces, we want to make sure that the spaces for those pop-up events are able to survive and thrive as well."

The response was pretty neutral, although the choice of words was instructive. Lamé didn't mention any specific club nights, despite her long and close affiliation with Duckie, or whether the mayor was aware of their existence. The "as well" add-on, I think, separated club nights from the "particular spaces" on which the mayor's office focuses. I didn't intend my question as a quiz—Lamé and Bayes are area experts—but I noticed that they did not independently raise club nights, either as an expression of nightlife or when we were talking about the charter. Instead, they spoke in generalities. "While London is incredibly diverse and our LGBT community is incredibly diverse, we can be more diverse," Lamé said. "We *should* be more diverse. And there should be a better mix. Without a doubt. Because we are London." It's hard to argue the point. At least it projects an optimistic tone, although I find the language of "diversity" more unobjectionable than revolutionary.

Municipal perspectives are precisely packaged—surprise, surprise—though with some curious omissions and compelling additions. But what about everyday Londoners? How do they think? Othon and Gabriel, who organize a party called Papa Loco with themes of spirituality and other-worldliness, succinctly capture the entanglements between disruptions and new creations. "There is always an action and reaction." From one chat to the next, I learn that there are ways of embracing generative views about nightlife without denying the closure epidemic—or insisting on a one-to-one ratio of actions to reactions. Mark, a professor who studies drag, is direct, "It's not as if, well, one venue goes so we have to replace it with another." From where he sits and what he sees, "gay scenes are proliferating in different forms." What do you mean? "I think there's more dynamism within the gay scene." As I put together this puzzle, two ways of seeing kept coming up. The first is what I call spatial expansion, or thinking about nightlife beyond the gayborhood. And the second is what I term rescaling to the local, or evaluating nightlife not based on overall trends but on options closer to home. Londoners used some version of one or both of these discursive strategies to see the glass as half full, although within the inevitably varied messiness of their nightly routines.

Spatial Expansion

Imagine that you are looking down on London from a bird's eye view, pointing out LGBTQ+ nightlife places. What do you see? Soof, who is twenty-six and identifies as Pakistani British, queer, asexual, and gender nonconforming, provides a sensory reply: "I think it would be very tactile, like fuzzy, quite big. I think maybe it would be radiating, so it wouldn't necessarily be big in terms of the size or space it takes up but in terms of the shadow or the light it pulls out. Yeah, radiating,

I feel." I ask how the imagery of something radiating affects Soof's thoughts about nightlife. "I feel it's quite malleable," they reply, "like it grows and shrinks as new spaces pop up and close down, and there's space for more. I think it's constantly moving. I feel like it's changing and shifting." For Soof, there is little lament. Instead, they promote a perspective that emphasizes a productive pluralism—more change, not more contraction.

While Soof offers us poetry, others describe specific developments. Angel, the organizer of Gayzpacho, a party we will attend later, begins with broad strokes, "[C]ertain places might be closing because of gentrification and the price of property, but surprisingly, there's other places opening in other locations." Manuel also insists that what is consistent is change rather than closures: "The gay scene always reinvents itself." When I ask Soof, Angel, and Manuel where I can find these other places and radiating reinventions of nightlife, they each list three bars in East London: Dalston Superstore, the Glory, and Queen Adelaide.

East London supports a vibrant scene. "Part of East London emerging is a matter of Soho closing," Jonathan echoes. Cassie, a cabaret producer, similarly sees a relationship between closures in Central London, home to the most visible gayborhood, and the emergence of new scenes elsewhere: "I think that the mainstream culture of LGBT bars might be closing in terms of what you see in Soho, but at the same time, you've got everything new that's opening up everywhere else." When I ask where else, she replies, "Central London bars are closing down, but areas like Hackney [East London] or New Cross [South East London] where people have moved or migrated, a little bit further out, things are reopening." Elliott, a city planner who has lived in London for twenty-three years, says that movement of this sort is a perennial characteristic of neighborhoods and nightlife. "The scene has always moved," he tells me. "Before I came out, it was in Earl's Court in the west. Then it came to Soho. There's lots of things that have been in Soho a long time, but it's drifting on." The movement of places and parties can feel chaotic, sometimes scary, and absolutely like a municipal failure. But what these partygoers are telling us is that this movement ensures that nightlife remains vibrant and varietal. To appreciate what this means, we need to start using a wider-angle lens. "I think it's a good thing that places are spreading out and that we can be queer in larger parts of the territory," Angel says. "We don't have to concentrate just in Soho where we used to. My impression is that queer spaces are in key places around the city, rather than in the village."

Nightlife and neighborhoods are evolving in tandem. In decades past, the census shows that same-sex households concentrated in fewer places, like gay districts, and those areas gradually moved (from Earl's Court to Soho and East London, as Elliot said, or from Towertown to Boystown and Andersonville, as I found in Chicago). As the decades went by, we witnessed a unique geographic diffusion, or pluralism perhaps, that comes from an expanding residential imagination—more LGBTQ+ people feeling comfortable living in many more parts of the city. Nightlife is no different. If we live in more parts of the city, especially in a sprawling metropolis like London, then it makes sense that gay bars will pop up wherever people cluster. I like to use the general idea of spatial expansion to describe this pattern of living and socializing. Unlike images of a "perfect storm" from the mayor's office, "hands around necks," or "clubsterben" in Berlin, here we encounter something more life-affirming.[22]

Angel describes the emergence of new bars in East London as "a victory." Nearly everyone talks about this part of the city, "a glorious mixture of otherness," as Dan de la Motte calls it, that makes the area feel less like a gayborhood and more like a "queerborhood." Dan is well-known as a guide for "Queer Tours of London: A Mince Through Time." Founded in 2016, the tours celebrate London's queer geographic histories. "Against the backdrop of the mass closure of LGBTQ cultural spaces, Queer Tours of London are being developed to support London's queer activism, culture, and performance in all its glory," he tells me.

I ask Dan how he talks about bar closures in his tours. He begins by acknowledging the problem: "Spaces are under threat and at risk from a combination of draconian council legislation, draconian police attitudes, greedy landlords, and rising land prices." Just as his words start to resemble a familiar refrain of doom and gloom, Dan adopts another way of seeing. At the same time, he continues, "you're starting to see a renaissance of queer spaces." Renaissance. The word brings to mind a creative re-energizing of nightlife in the midst of ongoing disruptions. "You're seeing these really successful case studies," Dan continues, "such as the Glory in Haggerston, which is a queer pub and nighttime space on two floors which offers a diverse range of programming in terms of performance as well as a pub and a club atmosphere." Dan also mentions Dalston Superstore. "The first time I went to Dalston Superstore I thought, 'Oh my god, this is so incredible. This is such a great space.'" I hear a blend of resistance and renewal from Dan that comes from a position of geographic pluralism. I guess Soof was right: LGBTQ+ nightlife is definitely radiating.

Rescale to the Local

If there are more places to go—not just one gayborhood but queerborhoods across the city—how do people choose where to go out?[23] "I think that going out to a gay bar in Soho feels sort of like a cliché," Stefan says. He has his favorites, but the bars closer to home have more appeal (he lives in East London). "There's something nicer about having someplace more local that feels more relevant, even if just geographically." Stefan is thinking beyond the gayborhood, similar to our earlier discussion, but in doing so, he's also rescaling nightlife to a more immediate, local level. "People still want that coming together," Stefan explains, "but they want it locally. I don't want to take a train or a bus for thirty minutes." His desire for access refashions how he evaluates nightlife. "It's more the micro, smaller model of it, and the more viable way." Rescaling nightlife to local levels is the pragmatist's solution, as we will see, to London's many baked-in navigation challenges: vastness of size, radial public transportation networks, the expense of car ownership, and similar expenses associated with taxis and car shares.

For thirty-six-year-old Stuart, local areas are easier to access, despite abundant transportation options. "London and New York are bigger cities and are spread over a much bigger area," he explains. If you live in a place like that, "it's just such a huge distance to travel that you need to create those pockets nearer home, nearer where you live, because otherwise you're schlepping across tons of space." That's exactly why Ashley, age forty-six, and her friends "tend to like our local bars" and why they "go out mostly locally, in Stoke Newington." She describes the neighborhood as a hotbed for "entrepreneurial things," which makes her feel like "there's really good things happening around here." It helps that Stokie, as locals call it, is a lesbian enclave.[24] "Stoke Newington is like a mecca for lesbians," Rachel, age thirty, echoes. "There's a bar there, or there's a café there that's known to be a place that lesbians go to a lot." When I ask if she frequents those places, Rachel answers by confirming the importance of proximity. "I don't live near there, so I've never sought that space out, because it's just too much of a trek." As a validation check, I ask her to imagine what she would do if she did live closer. "If that existed in an area that I live in, that was my London, it would be different," she replies. "The gay spaces that I've been in have been created by a lot of gay people being there, rather than it being a gay space in general, if that makes sense." It does, I reply, as I repeat the words to myself. Rachel's emphasis on "being there" suggests the unique appeal of local access, rather than knowing that there may be a bunch of bars somewhere else farther away.

Unlike the pages of municipal reports, life on the ground is full of moving bodies. This, as Jonathan describes, creates challenges in getting around town: "It's a low-density city. The average building in London is probably three and a half stories high, which, if you try and fit millions of people into a city that's of such low density, you have to live in a sprawling place. It doesn't make it easy." Elliot the city planner adds public transportation into the mix. "The whole infrastructure has been built, and the road network has always been built, on a radial pattern." The cost of other forms of transportation also promotes thinking and acting locally. "Historically, the black cabs have been excellent in terms of navigating, but have been terribly expensive, and so they were a luxury for most people." Originally from Scotland, Kenny explains how all these things affect his night out. "It was much easier and almost more fun to go out in a local area where you could walk home, and not have any hassle, and where you'd probably see loads of people that you would see every week or every couple of weeks, so there was a bit of a familiarity to it." Makes sense,

I say, as I think about the hassle of hailing a taxi, or even calling an Uber, after a late night out.

While city officials are preoccupied with threats, the rest of us, regular people who want to go out after a long week of work, see other options. There is no simple or single truth in this story, although that useful complexity is masked by the pronouncements of academic theories, media headlines, and municipal reports. This is a consequence of what social scientists call "framing." Close your eyes and think about a window frame. Imagine that you are looking out of it. Now, go into another room, imagine a different window frame, and look out once again. What you see in front of you will change; it will depend on the frame you look through. To return to what Othon and Gabriel mentioned earlier, do you see an "action," like the closure epidemic, or a "reaction," like new bars and other nightlife scenes? As this thought experiment shows, reconciling people's lived experiences with official viewpoints, media reports, and academic theories is not an easy task!

Like me, Brooke also grapples with conflicting truths and multiple realities. "I see that death," they acknowledge, "but I also advocate for their existence." Brooke, an artist, was thirty when we met and identified as a queer lesbian, nonbinary, and Italian American. They deliberately slow down their speech and encourage me "not to lose heart because there are always other things that will emerge." I ask how I should think about the interplay between death and emergence—or negative capability, as Romantic poet John Keats puts it.[25] "The neighborhood you live in determines where you're willing to carve out a space," Brooke says, speaking as an artist and accenting the appeal of local opportunities for fellowship. Given the repetition of this theme, I'm puzzled that neither the night czar nor the culture-at-risk officer raised it. "On some level, it must be the case that people have always been making stuff in their neighborhoods," Brooke affirms, "and we just don't have the records because they're not recording their own history, and those buildings are gone, and we just don't know." Perhaps local spaces have a shorter lifetime, and perhaps things with shorter life spans have historical records that are harder for us to collect, let alone quantify. I can't be sure, but still, I thank Brooke for the pleasures of the provocation.

Beyond the Drama

You lose some—but you win some too. The people we met in this chapter showed us how to pivot from doom and gloom to an asset-based model of resilience and renewal. No one denies that gay bars are closing in alarming numbers, but those closures are not the end of our story. In government offices, appointing a night czar and culture-at-risk officer, publishing a report about cultural infrastructure, and drafting an LGBTQ+ venues charter all gesture toward the generative. Meanwhile, everyday people think outside the gayborhood box and maintain that there are vibrant options closer to home. These discursive strategies are linked, with the former (spatial expansion) enabling the latter (rescaling to the local).

In common, all these remarkable ways of seeing, from City Hall to the streets, show us the transformative power of a positive frame, a glass half full, rather than confounding our lives with dire representations of the social world. "It's lazy," Laurie immediately observed. Zax, a multiracial, Black and Hungarian artist, looks to the future by suturing it to the past: "It's never going to be over because we've always been there. You look back one hundred or two hundred years. There is still a queer London, even if we can't identify obvious queer spaces, or no one would have identified themselves as lesbian, gay, bisexual." We, and our places of fellowship, have always existed—and always will.

By considering a plethora of perspectives, we are finding ways to move beyond the drama of the closure epidemic. Recall when Olimpia remarked that "nothing planned can create a queer space." To my surprise, she adamantly objects to the charter. The basis of her resistance is the presumption that "the rainbow flag is a universal symbol of the LGBTQ+ community." Many queer-identified people reject that flag, as we will see later. They perceive it as inclusive only in theory, whereas in practice, the rainbow flag represents only some people, not everyone. Rather than something so stylized and overgeneralized, Olimpia wants to cultivate conditions for queerness to thrive. "I think that's what we should be telling policymakers is that there's only so much planning you can do around this stuff." Something like the charter is designed "with a space like Soho in mind," not the rest of the city.

This strikes me as a key point: if the mayor's office is evaluating nightlife by looking for rainbows, then other forms of nightlife become nearly impossible for us to see. It's no wonder that public narratives are consumed by the decline of gay bars, and people use rainbow flags as bandages. Despite their best intentions, these bandages have become blindfolds, making it harder for us to see the revolution in queer nightlife that is happening all around us.

Femmetopia

In a Basement

There are not many places where we can freely embrace and fully celebrate expressions of feminine genders, in all their glory and gorgeousness. Phoebe and Kat were chatting about this one day. "We were perpetual guests in others' environments," Kat told me. She wasn't alone in feeling like an outsider at gay bars, which often have masculine cultures and expectations. In 2018, *Dazed* magazine broke a story that woke many of us up: "Gay nightlife's violent femmephobia needs to end." Otamere, a self-described "flared, 70s-silhouetted, glittering, choker-wearing faggot," shared a heart-wrenching episode:

> I spent years avoiding clubs like XXL (a muscle-bound gay club near London Bridge) on the premise that it simply wasn't my vibe, sensing that its "One Club Fits All" slogan didn't quite ring true for my body. When my friends suggested going there a few weeks ago, I swallowed my discomfort, naively presuming that it would be short-lived. What I didn't know was that XXL's door policy explicitly refuses entry not only to women, but to anyone wearing what they described as "women's clothing"—heels, dresses, skirts—a laundry list that the bouncer reeled off to me when I arrived in my strappy corset top. I was told that I would be refused entry unless I changed or took it off.

I acquiesced, shrunk myself, and complied, in the knowledge that the humiliation would be over soon enough, and I would be with my friends who were already in the club ahead of me. As I walked in, the bouncer had one last sting. He let me know that, should I put the offending top back on while inside the club, I'd be thrown out. I wasn't the first person this had happened to at XXL, nor will I be the last. Door policies like these, and indeed the culture they represent, are all too familiar—not just in XXL, but in gay clubs and spaces all across the world.[1]

If not at a gay bar, then where else can we go to feel safe and seen as beautiful feminine beings? "We wanted to celebrate femininity, feminine energy, feminine power, feminine rage, feminine bodies," Kat asserted. This was the spark that set ablaze a feminine utopia—Femmetopia!—a club night that celebrates the expansiveness of gender, from faggotry through all varieties of femininities. Tonight, I was headed there, feeling fierce in my one-piece fishnet bodysuit.

Femmetopia occurred on the first and third Saturday of the month in 2018—for just that one sparkling year. Tickets were £5 (US$6) if you grabbed them super early, £7 (US$9) in advance, and £10 (US$12) at the door (although the bouncer said they don't turn anyone away for lack of funds). Following Kat on Instagram, I knew I had to make my way to VFD, a venue in Dalston that called itself "an originator and incubator of queer arts and entertainment." The East London hub hosts many parties, but with a consistent aim to nurture emerging queer talent. As I stepped inside, I saw a flyer for the event. "We have come to build a paradise in hell." The party's mantra was memorable, and it was plastered everywhere. Messages to "Dismantle the Patriarchy!" and "The Future Is Femme!" greeted me on a vibrant design of stars and painted faces. In the center of the flyer was the party's name, written in red with a soft cursive script.

I met up with Kat at the venue—"a dingy basement full of magic," as she affectionately called it. Lyall, the Maori-identifying owner, shared the sentiment, describing VFD on its website as "a basement of dreams." Kat and I walked down a flight of stairs and arrived in a concrete box below the street, a room without windows. Wearing

A flyer for Femmetopia focuses on making (and taking up) space for radical possibility. Photo credit: Kat Hudson.

go-go boots and a hand-painted cowboy hat, Kat at 5-foot-4 could reach up and touch the low ceiling.

The room itself was small, a cozy capacity of one hundred, and it was full of bodies of many shapes, sizes, colors, and sartorial styles. "Glorify all bodies for their individual beauty and power," I read on the VFD website and now could see in thigh-high stilettos and big black boots. Someone wore a thong with New Romantic–style makeup that made them look like an art portrait. I saw a queer Indian person in a sari and other partygoers in various states of undress. One person was in a dressing gown while another donned a homemade garment embedded with LED light panels. People presented with a nonconforming confidence I've never seen in a gay bar (I would never dream of wearing fishnets to a gay bar, but here, it felt easy-breezy). Phoebe and Kat created something unique and captured it in their "Femmifesto," a document that specified a strict no-tolerance policy for nonconsensual touching and sexual advances.

The music was loud, and our bodies, pressed together, were moving fluidly with it. After a few minutes, I noticed that the room looked like it was sweating; the intense body heat made the walls wet with

condensation. Drops of feminine magic showered us all night. As the moisture dripped onto my body, I closed my eyes and imagined being cleansed of patriarchal stains and scars.

In that moment, I also tuned into the sonic profile of the scene. "This. Is. My. Utopia. This-is, my-utopia!" I had never heard the song before, and I couldn't believe its synchronicity with the name of the party. Who is this? I asked. "Chicks on Speed," Kat replied with a smile. A female electroclash and punk band, its members used to earn extra cash at art galleries by hanging paintings to the walls. Someone said that they worked really fast, like "chicks on speed." The name stuck. With a heavy bass and distorted high-hat, the song was confrontational though uplifting. "Are you ready to shake up the world? Welcome to the revolution of love." The lyrics surfed across the sweat on the dance floor. We threw our hands up in the air and screamed. "Utopia is a mirror of multiple imagined worlds!"

In a matter of minutes, Chicks on Speed covered everything from feminism to gentrification. "Welcome to the rebellion, to our refusal as women to accept this new age of tyranny," I heard them say in one second, followed by resistance to urban redevelopment: "The cities are built. Constructed. And renovated—and goddammit, stop knocking down my neighborhood. This is my utopia. This is our utopia!"

I have spent a lot of time in gay bars around the world, surrounded by men wearing leather, hirsute bears drinking beers, and other masculine-presenting people. But I had never experienced a fantasy-come-true like this, a femme-led and femme-centered party that created another world of hopes and desires, mysteries and illusions, and an intoxicating feeling of freedom. That sweaty sanctuary of femininity celebrated a special collective consciousness, I thought as I left the party to go back home, my fishnets slightly torn, skin still sticky from dancing and kisses of condensation.

Back in my flat and flipping through my phone before falling asleep, I found my way to "Light After Dark," an exhibition Kat curated on the past, present, and future of queer nightlife. Accompanying the show was a collection of writings. One piece was penned by Angel, an artist who produced a work called "Serious Fun." In another offering, Rose writes, "The nightclub dance floor has the

◂ Phoebe, Kat, and Lyall: Welcome to Femmetopia at VFD. Photo credit: Nicol Parkinson.

capacity to connect us in ways that might seem unimaginable in the light of day, and these experiences stay with us—even after the party is over."

I closed my eyes and played back the night in my mind as I drifted off to sleep. It felt like I was in another world, in that beautiful basement full of magic and dreams.

2

Another World

The closure epidemic has undoubtedly disrupted nightlife. We can dwell on the causes of that disruption, as many do, but then we would be in the dark about its unexpected consequences, the remarkable ways that closures have urged new creative worlds. "If everything established is dispersed, and we can write our own rules, why would you use the same rule book?" The question is posed to me by Peter, the activist we met earlier. Peter is also involved with putting on a club night called Lèse Majesté, a "spectacular drag king and thing cabaret." When I listen to Peter, bar closures sound different, like getting a new lease on life after a near-death experience. We can get stuck in a fight-or-flight response after trauma and assume the worst. No wonder doom and gloom narratives about gay bars are so common. But after a disruption, it is also possible to do the opposite: to liberate ourselves from the rules and to reinvent them, usually in the direction of more joy.

For a moment, release the desire to pinpoint a precise relationship, whether causal or otherwise, between gay bars and other nightlife gatherings. Allow yourself to sit with the reality of multiple *nightlives*. The picture is now a little blurrier, isn't it? A mix of the familiar with something else that you cannot readily perceive, not yet. This approach might feel uneasy at first, but as we will see, it enables a better understanding of both gay bars and the big bang–like explosion of an underground scene of club nights.

This chapter provides an initial immersion into the world of these parties: how club nights are structured and put together, their many meanings and experiential qualities, and how they compare with gay bars. These parties pop up in all kinds of places, from dingy basements to dimly lit warehouses and world-class museums. It will be impossible for us to recognize them if we think about nightlife as synonymous with gay bars. Those bars are a part of nightlife—the most well-known part—but far from all of it. By expanding our vision to include club nights, we will grapple with the notion of nightlife as a field, as we called it earlier. And then, by traveling to these parties, we will recognize that the structure of that field is changing. Here's how: while nightlife was once *placed*–think: gay bars located in specific parts of the city—it is now increasingly *event-based*. "There is a much bigger emphasis on events," Ryan affirmed the next morning over a cup of coffee as we talked about Femmetopia. "These new spaces are more temporary than the older gay establishments," added Koen, a student of Ryan's who joined us. Gay bars are the tip of the iceberg; much more lies beneath the surface.

Nightclubs, Club Nights

Rather than going out to nightclubs, which are fixed establishments, many Londoners are now flocking to club nights, which are episodic events.[1] In the former, nightclub, the word "club" operates as a compound noun. When we hear or say the word, it produces an image in our mind of a particular kind of organizational form: a physical place where you and your friends can go night after night. Reversing the order and separating the words, club night, produces a different experience. The word "club" stands separately now as an adjective. The emphasis shifts onto the night, a fleeting moment in time, not a fixed place. The place itself, like VFD, is a descriptive modifier, a vessel for a set of experiences—a multisensory party that celebrates feminine energy, as we saw. The distinction between a nightclub and a club night, in other words, is at once observable and a play on words.

Brooke, the Italian American artist we met earlier, describes club nights as "the moveable model," while Stuart, a British magazine editor, calls them "moving nights." Two people from different backgrounds both drawing our attention to the same qualities: *spatial mobility* (club nights are often nomadic, while nightclubs and gay bars are fixed) and *temporality* (club nights are occasional events, while nightclubs and gay bars are more lasting establishments). These features of club nights create experiences that, for many people, feel freer. Consider Sink the Pink, a British bacchanal that occurred four times a year, sold 150,000 tickets, toured more than twenty countries, and lasted fourteen years (2008 to 2022). The club night was founded by lifelong friends Glyn Fussell and Amy Zing. In an interview with news network CNN, Zing explained their desire to be together without feeling restricted by the identities of specific places. "We would always go to clubs where we would be told, 'That's for straight people' and 'That's for gay people.' We thought, 'Can't we just party together, without being given this label?'"[2]

Can you sense the difference? Gay bars and nightclubs are established places that contain an experience which is difficult to replicate beyond that one place. The built structure, the four walls where you party, matters—and your experiences are enclosed within it. This is why, when a bar shuts down, it takes with it the experiences we created inside. No wonder we mourn! That place was "incomparable," we might say, "unlike any other," "irreplaceable," "the one and only," "no other place like it," and so on. Club nights revolutionize the format. They are episodic gatherings that are untethered to any one place. Instead, they prioritize people and experiences—races and ethnicities, genders and sexualities, art and artists, sounds and looks, performances and cabarets—and those qualities can thrive on their own, apart from any specific walls.

madison, like bell hooks, does not capitalize their name. They organize a techno fashion club night called Opulence, which centers the aesthetic practices of marginalized queer artists. "You can't be all things to everyone," they explain as they account for the shortcomings of gay bars and nightclubs around the world, noting how frequently one place feels indistinguishable from another. What's your vision? I ask. "I am drawn to the specific," they emphasize, "and like the specific." madison wants to create an event that "is not anyplace else. It's not pretending to be anything else."

Specificity here is a proxy for authenticity—places that breathe life into "a very specific world," madison continues. This is what club nights do best. "The club space is a way to create another world." The words stay with me—club nights create another world—and I repeat them out loud. madison nods, "I think that some of the most successful parties and club spaces are spaces that are worlds." The inverse contributes to the inadequacies of many gay bars and nightclubs. They are "quite generic and commercial, don't have an ethos." madison elaborates on this absence: "Gay clubs are not innovating. They're not pushing themselves." This is why those "spaces are just not compelling anymore." In short, "there's no there there." madison advocates for a worldmaking project. "I think that sense of being a world, or worldmaking, is really important." In conversations with madison and other people who produce club nights, I learned what worldmaking, a popular though abstract idea, actually looks like—and why it is that the cultural world of club nights feels like it has more space than built structures like bars.

I have attended many parties that represent this shimmering incarnation of nightlife. A few had only a dozen or so people. Others had thousands. That range in size was matched by their variety of experiences. Most occur outside the gayborhood in central London—thirty- or sixty-minute train rides and transfers are common. Club nights also have wonderful names, which signal the worlds that await you inside: Femmetopia, Femmi-Erect, Female Masculinity Appreciation Society, and Wotever World (people who identify with expansive gender expressions); Aphrodyki (lesbians); Transmission (trans+ individuals); INFERNO, Queer Direct, and Riposte (artists and performers); Buttmitzvah, Gayzpacho, and Hungama (ethnic celebrations); Lèse Majesté (drag kings); and BBZ, Cocoa Butter Club, and Pxssy Palace (QTBIPOC events).

Some nights feature specific sounds, like Anal House Meltdown (house); Chapter 10 and Opulence (techno); Horse Meat Disco and Disco Bloodbath (disco); Hard Cock Life (hip-hop) and Queer Bruk (Dancehall, Afrobeats, Soca). Others, like Misery, center sobriety and mental health, while still others, like Adonis, Duckie, and Little Gay

Brother, attract people who might also frequent gay bars. HOWL, which takes its name from the Beat generation queer Jewish writer Allen Ginsberg and his eponymous poem, brings together club night collectives from around the world, like Floorgasm (Berlin) and Possession (Paris), and enables each group to reach new audiences. The CAMPerVAN occurs in and around a mobile vehicle that the organizer drives across the city and the country. Sink the Pink attracted a breathtaking cross section of people in its fourteen-year tenure, while NYC Downlow, which still occurs for just five days a year in a small corner of the Glastonbury festival, replicates the seedy and sweaty New York bathhouse cum meatpacking warehouses as they looked and felt in the early 1980s.[3]

While distinct from gay bars, we know that club nights are not entirely new—nor are they unique to London. "The model has been used often," Peter affirms. Recall Miss Maud and the secret drags in DC in the 1880s, Bill and Bert going out for a rager in London in the 1920s, Ruth and Babe who threw blowout rent parties in postwar Detroit, and ballroom reclamations by Black and Latinx queens in Harlem in the 1960s. Club nights are part of this long lineage—and that by itself makes them valuable. "We have always been creative problem-solvers," Kat says. "Queer people have been finding ways of making these spaces for ourselves for generations."

Those gay bars that remain are open night after night in the same place; club nights, by comparison, are itinerant and irregular. They do not belong to one place (although some have residences), nor do they pay rent every week or month to a landlord. In fact, they operate on entirely different economic models, as we will see in the next chapter. Club nights are also reactionary. They stand on guard against all manner of injustices, from femmephobia and gentrification to the intersectional failures of gay bars. London-born Gideön is a DJ with thirty years of experience in the capital and in Berlin. The mastermind behind NYC Downlow, he sums up the pattern with a punch: "The more everything goes to shit, the more the underground bubbles up." Like every culture creative, Gideön emphasizes empowerment. "There's some really fucking amazing things going on," he declares, and "it's only going to get better, and more intense, and more radical the more everything fucks up politically." His advice? "Form as groups and create your own reality"—like Kat and Phoebe did underground in that dingy basement full of feminine magic.

That word, *underground*, points to crucial qualities of club nights, both material (as in subterranean, downstairs somewhere, off to the side in the spatial margins, or simply far from a cultural core) and metaphorical (as in experimental, non-normative, beyond the purview of the mainstream). Club nights are not exclusive, but they are not for everyone. Almost by definition, they are oriented to select audiences and are not always easy to see or find, "happening under the surface," as Ingo, the organizer of several parties, says. Ironically, these gatherings are going on all around us, yet most of the world is oblivious to them! Even the night czar lacked specific knowledge about them, suggesting that there are limits to government interventions in nightlife.

The clandestine characteristic of club nights, that they create worlds at once proximate and invisible, is a source of their appeal. They have an "excitement" that "a regular weekly thing doesn't have," Andy, who is fifty-two, shares with me. "Maybe it's because people are looking for surprising connections." I smile, as I like the idea of the underground as a place of surprises. Knowing that we will experience brief bursts of meaningful contact at a party that only happens a couple of times a year makes us anticipate it that much more. Club nights feel special, almost irresistible. What I experienced at Femmetopia stayed with me long after that night, like meeting someone on a vacation you instantly connect with and can't stop thinking about. We love moments in life, those encounters that are removed from the rhythms of the daily grind. They inspire us to keep reflecting, "Do you remember that time when . . . ?"

Moments are also empowering. By coming together at a club night, we are creating a gathering that flies under the radar, and thus is blissfully absent the power structures that shape so much of our life above ground. More often than not, club nights are "powered by a marginalized community," says Dan Beaumont. Eden, the founder of an event that mixes art worlds and rave-like scenes, thinks about club nights as a reaction against the normative tones of gay bars. Most of his friends stopped going to those bars a long time ago, he tells me, because "they were really mainstream, and it's not really a place where most of us felt comfortable." This motivated Eden to organize

Riposte (pronounced rip-PAST), a queer art techno party he started in Paris and imported to London. I ask Eden why he dislikes gay bars. "It's a mainstream community who listens to pop," he replies. The audience matters too. "I'm part of a rather special community who prefers the queer and techno scene, and artists, of London. All these people don't go to mainstream bars." Rejecting commercially produced pop music in favor of an "alternative scene," the people who go to Riposte are "radical in their position." The name of the night communicates its ethos. "It's like answering to something," Eden explains. "It's like, someone throws you a rock, and you throw another rock back." Riposte is a call-and-response—or a "protest against the system," Eden adds. "We have to create our own occasions."

While for Eden gay bars are limited by their politics and music, Gaby foregrounds gender. A French Arabic artist, they were twenty-five when we met. "Queer people did used to go to gay bars," they say. "It was 80 percent fun but never 100 percent fun." Why not? I ask. "Because it was always dominated by gay men. Forming subgroups and underground nights out was in response to what was happening in the mainstream." The repeated sense of these bars as "highly masculine and testosterone-fueled spaces" motivated Gaby to form Queer Direct. "If you're a gender nonconformist man who's more feminine, or someone who's wanting to transition but hasn't done so yet, I feel like those spaces [gay bars] can be really intimidating."

In these underground scenes, Dan, Ingo, Eden, Gaby, and other party producers celebrate queer cultures, from their experimental music to avant-garde fashion and progressive gender politics, from their artistic to sensual and sexual sensibilities—while, as Eden says, keeping it "all a big secret." You need the right networks to find out about the gatherings. "You have to know some people who will pull you into the scene"—or "ear to ear" as Eden calls it. Party producers are wary of people who come to consume the scene or simply to stare at it. What they want is to attract individuals who share the energy and ethos. "It's always an amazing feeling of alternative queerness and also radical queerness where we do what the fuck we want, and we don't really like conforming to society's standards."

It is perhaps no surprise, given the scene's delight in evading conformity and clarity, that the etymology of the term is similarly murky. Where or when did *club night* begin? Despite combing through academic literatures, and despite multiple conversations with nightlife historians and researchers, I have not been able to figure out exactly how old the term is or where it originated. I guess Eden was onto something when he called club nights a "big secret"! This also contributes to the phenomenon's relative invisibility. When I asked Londoners directly, they would reply much like Ben, who said, "Gosh, I have no idea. It just seems like one of those terms that has always been there." Even though I cannot precisely locate where the breadcrumbs begin, I still use "club nights" because it is the phrase that Londoners use; it has local appeal and emic resonance. No one I met thought of it as a term that carries potential for confusion or ambiguity. Nor do people express an attachment to it. During our chats, many casually replaced "club night" with "party," "pop-up," or even just an abbreviated "night." While club nights are parties, not all parties are club nights, implying social and cultural distinctions. The elixir of a club night exceeds the sum of its elements, a space with music where a bunch of bodies gather and dance.

As I reflected on the uncertainty over the name—or, rather, the variety of names—used for this particular kind of party and form of fellowship, I wondered if it was yet another indicator of its subversive power. If naming a thing establishes our power over that thing (to wit: colonialism), then not having a clear name or having multiple names—and keeping it all a big secret—does the opposite. It prevents one group from claiming ownership, and it prevents that thing from being co-opted. And I'm guessing it is also a way, whether subconsciously or very consciously, of giving the finger to the mainstream.[4]

Eyeline

From my first weeks in London, and each time I returned, I had this growing sense that there was a mismatch between the alarmist public narratives about nightlife and what I was seeing firsthand at club nights. Bar closures were obvious, but the underground scene was not. These two worlds are fundamentally connected, yet they reveal almost opposing visions of nightlife. When we talk about these things, most of us default to the discernible: famous nightclubs, like Studio 54, Limelight, Berghain, the Ministry of Sound, Fabric, and so on—or, quite simply, the watering hole down the street where everyone knows your name. Greggor Mattson, an American sociologist, proposes that gay bars are "iconic" precisely because of their visibility: "they are the most common and accessible LGBTQ+ places."[5] But if iconicity requires something to be identifiable, then it's no wonder that our compass doesn't point us to club nights! They are roaring underground, largely out of sight; they only happen from time to time; and many move around from place to place. Here is why first appearances can deceive. The dominant narrative—we are gripped by an epidemic of closures—will be riddled with blind spots if we fail to see the larger field, if we focus instead only on individual venues, and if we thus fail to flip the script from deficit to asset. Meanwhile, culture-makers are busy creating another world.

Our knowledge about how nightlife is changing is often based on widely circulating statistics, numbers like 58 percent and 37 percent, which describe closure rates in London and across the United States, respectively. To arrive at these figures that we have seen now a couple of times, researchers rely on bar listings in local newspapers and magazines, national travel guides, various websites, and community archives. This strategy of studying nightlife has been a methodological feature of the literature for decades and across countries.

No one has quantified an uptick in club nights. The reason? Those data do not exist—most party producers use social media rather than newspapers or travel guides—and thus it is impossible to produce comparable numbers that can support alternative arguments, let alone enable causal inferences. That club nights are episodic and often ephemeral, existing for a couple of months to one or more years, poses additional obstacles in assembling systematic figures. The fact that they are so often overlooked, without more concerted efforts like this one to give them voice and recognition, reveals additional layers of assumptions that we routinely make about who belongs in urban nightlife and who does not, where people go to find fellowship, and how researchers study these things. Because club nights are not visible in the same way as gay bars, and because they do not fit into our standard accounts about the closure epidemic, it is that much harder for us to see beyond those bars, trapping us in a style of circular reasoning. To get out, we must try to make the less visible more perceptible—and thus commit ourselves not so much to statistics but to prioritizing the feelings, meanings, and motivations of the people involved in the world of club nights.[6]

Ben, who I asked earlier about the origins of the term club night, also spoke with me about the prospects of building new forms of nightlife. He is a person of many talents, from writing for *The Guardian* to authoring a doctoral dissertation about gay bars in London. Ben described for me the challenges of breaking out of our cognitive molds. "Whether we're going to have the opportunity to build new institutions, whatever they look like—we can't imagine what they'll look like now—we have to be able to make those experiments and create new queer ways of being together that are valued, and celebrated, and cherished *because* they're different, not because they're acceptable. I think that's the fault line, and that's the challenge." It *is* hard to think counterfactually, I say softly under my breath, to imagine what something else might look like—and we absolutely *should* celebrate an experimental ethos. After all, creativity is the heart of both science and a great night out.

From one party producer to the next, each conversation made me more curious about understanding the relationship between club nights and gay bars—and also more aware of the complexities of that relationship. "A lot of these older places are dying, yes." Ben thinks this "should be fought, and is unjust, and is unacceptable." His words, tinged with sadness, remind me of those blinking lights we talked about earlier, the inevitability of change. Like others who adopt a mindset enriched by asset, Ben pivots. "But the real question is, what's going to be born, and who is going to fight to make that space?" Enter club nights, which provide "opportunities to imagine other ways of being." The cadence of Ben's speech starts to quicken. "There's a problem if those [gay bars] are disappearing and no other things to offer those platforms and those rehearsal spaces are emerging." We know, however, that other platforms *are* emerging.

The more people I met, the more I sensed a need to see closures as a crisis while holding space for creativity. Meet Michael, a public intellectual in London who is also the news editor at *Huck* magazine. Rather than causality, Michael and I talk about reframing the conversation—"not just being on the defensive," he says—to "setting an agenda." He invites me to see the world through his eyes: "We've always needed to be responsive because we've been oppressed. I'm interested in thinking about ways that we can set an agenda, and we can be active, and we can push forward." There are causal tones here—oppression requires an agentic response—but these exist between the lines. By flipping the story upside down, from being defensive to setting an agenda, Michael uses club nights to craft a more encompassing narrative. "There are these club nights that are popping up despite the problems that exist in nightlife," he says. The argument implies a relationship without specifying any one single form. "If we want to start building for the future, then we have to start thinking about how queer spaces exist in the long-term future. We can't just be firefighting." Of course not, I think to myself, since firefighting an epidemic is only part of the picture, only one story, only one way to express a relationship between the many moving parts of nightlife.

Pause for a moment on Michael's imagery of parties that are "popping up," what others, like Samuel, describe as "temporary nights." Now compare their words with how some researchers describe gay bars: as "anchor institutions," a phrase that draws attention to their relative permanence and persistence, at least as compared to a moment or an event.[7] These contrasting images—things popping up versus an anchor—couldn't be more dissimilar! Shay, the organizer of a popular party called Adonis, explains the difference: "There's a lot of maybe not permanent spaces but parties using other spaces. That seems to now be, over the last one and a half, two years, that seems to be escalating really rapidly." Club nights are episodic and roving. "The pop-up is the model," Alex says in more general terms. He organizes an alt-pop, indie-dance party called Knickerbocker. "Cheap to do, the venue's taking less of your money, in most cases, you can play to smaller audiences." The economic model makes intuitive sense, I reply. "Everyone's part of the gig economy," he adds.

What looks on the surface like decline, I think, is a more complicated reality for a couple of reasons. First, while club nights are organizationally distinct, they often depend on existing establishments, both LGBTQ+ and straight alike, to host their events.

Originally from Stockholm, fifty-six-year-old Ingo, who we briefly met earlier, is a lifeblood of parties "you've never heard about," including Bar Wotever, Nonbinary Cabaret, and Female Masculinity Appreciation Society, among others. They describe club nights as "takeovers," parties that appropriate a venue for a queer occasion, like a symbiosis between a regular place and a rotating event, each helping the other to survive. But as far as the event itself: "they are definitely not seven nights a week," Ingo observes. Glyn uses similar language. Club nights "take over spaces that you wouldn't normally be allowed in." That's how Sink the Pink started. "There's nothing more rebellious than being in a working men's club," he says about the party's origins at the Bethnal Green Working Men's Club. Over the years, that venue has hosted one-off nights and recurring parties (we'll attend one later). The wisdom of these observations is worth stating directly: different forms of nightlife interact with each other, rather than existing as mutually exclusive or oppositional expressions of bars versus events.[8]

Second, increasing numbers of bar closures are making club nights more visible, more diverse, and more differentiated, providing us with opportunities to have some fun and advance our knowledge about nightlife along the way. Changing how we perceive something can in fact alter how we experience the reality of that thing. This is called the Thomas theorem, and we can use it to expand our ways of seeing beyond the limited frame of an epidemic.[9] That deficit-enhanced frame conceals the abundance of creativity bubbling beneath the surface. "It doesn't all have to be negative because these spaces are closing," Laurie expresses. "We've lost some incredible spaces, but also, the future shows some incredible new spaces opening. I think you have to look at it with a more positive lens." Laurie leans into this generative complexity. "You have to look much deeper to see what's really happening in London right now." And what's that? I ask. "I don't think that queer nightlife is dying." If death is an inexact metaphor, what is more appropriate? "I think queer nightlife is thriving," Laurie replies—"but things are changing."

Laurie organizes The Chateau, the club night I described earlier as a church crypt with stained glass—or, as I think about it again, maybe a Madonna video from the '90s. "The Chateau seeks to change the narrative around LGBTQ+ venues," the social media account explains, "bringing positivity into the scene." Standing next to a bright yellow and cobalt-colored glass that depicts Adam and Eve arriving through an eye-shaped heavenly portal, Laurie articulates the message to me in person: "That's what I was trying to show with opening The Chateau, that the future is really bright," like the light emanating from behind him. Suddenly, Laurie becomes self-conscious—"I'm being so philosophical today"—but laughs it off and returns to the point. "I think that figure [58 percent closure rate], whilst super helpful and super relevant, it doesn't show the truth of what's happening in London now." He doesn't deny the numbers, but instead points out that they are only one side of the coin. "You have to look past it, and look much deeper into the way that queer people are operating now, which is outside of permanent venues."

From Buttmitzvah to Femmetopia, and quick peeks inside Sink the Pink and The Chateau, these are all occasional parties. You cannot attend night after night in the same place. "That doesn't have to be the way that queer spaces operate," Laurie says. "We are a temporary space; we're a pop-up." As more bars boarded up, people pursued other avenues for fellowship—and revolutionized what nightlife looks like, how it feels, and how people experience it. Regardless of what you call these events—itinerant gatherings or peripatetic parties, pop-ups or takeovers, traveling parties or one-offs, club nights or just nights—what we learn from them is unmistakable. The field of nightlife is becoming more diverse and differentiated, much more than what we have systematically observed before.

All the voices we have heard so far, incisive and insightful as they are, have come from people who produce parties. What about those of us who just attend, people who like to go out and have fun? Some months before we met, Stefan had immigrated to London from Canada. Our shared Canadian connection made us fast friends. I asked about his impressions of nightlife in London, especially in the context of so many closures. "There's a need to find a new model of bringing people together," he replied in a way that made it difficult to differentiate him as a reveler from a party producer. I asked Stefan to explain what he meant by a "new model." He said that he recently tapped into the underground scene. "Last Friday night, we went to this event. It's a one-night pop-up takeover. It gets people to come and meet each other in a more curated night out. Insanely popular. It's finding these new models of bringing people together." His emphasis on events that last for only one night, a pop-up party that takes over an existing venue, is something that many of us miss, even if they are hugely popular. "You lose the model of the bar, but keep the event." I like the phrase, I tell Stefan, for its simplicity and analytic elegance. It reminds me of words I heard from Lola, a bisexual-identifying African British cis woman, who echoed similar themes: "When you don't have those venues, you've got to find another avenue. You have to be creative." Notice the language, subtle though significant in what it can teach us: a venue versus another avenue. Lola could have said *another venue*, which would mean something quite different from another avenue.

More than just semantic, the perceptual pivots I was hearing from party producers and revelers alike capture a significant change in how nightlife is being organizationally restructured—from fixed places to events. Consider my conversation with Soof, who mused about these matters. "I think it's disappearing," they remark about nightlife in broad strokes. And then, a second later, they add, "but then I think that it's—it's not disappearing." I found Soof's hesitation instructive. "Maybe it's disappearing out of our eyeline or eyesight." I smile—*eyeline* is such a lovely word to think about the direction in which we are looking—and then I wondered out loud: why can't we see the change? "I think it's disappearing from visibility," Soof responds, "but I think, therefore, it's being compensated for in other areas."

Soof and I have a strong connection, maybe because we are both South Asian and queer. They sense that I want to hear more about these "other areas," a phrase which to my ear sounds similar to Stefan's "new model" and Lola's notion of "another avenue." We need to think about "nightlife beyond just a nightclub," Soof says without a specific prompt. The path to that conclusion was circuitous, I believe, because of the traps laid by *isomorphism*, a word that describes a pattern in how we often think about the forms of nightlife. Our instinct is to intervene by protecting existing bars or building more bars, as we saw at City Hall. The problem with isomorphic thinking, however, is that it conceals from our eyeline options other than the most immediate, the most familiar, and the most obvious. Yet people *are* awakening to new models and another avenue. Actually, I should qualify: lots of people have *long* been awakened to other ways of organizing nightlife, and the rest of us are starting to catch up. Several people I met hit the nail on its head with one-liners. "The broader gay scene is thriving even though individual bars are shutting," Liam told me, while Amelia shared that London is in the middle of a "shift" from bars to "parties or events that have a home that isn't permanent." The enthusiasm I heard was energizing—and yet, I became concerned in a new way. If club nights do not have a permanent home, nowhere to live night after night, then are their experiential qualities as fleeting as the night itself?

Ephemeral Forms, Enduring Effects

Even if something is impermanent, it can still leave a residue. This, Damien tells me, allows us to think about the effects of club nights in imaginative ways. "I like the transience of queer spaces because I see queerness as like a residue that moves and is always with you, and it occupies different spaces at different times. It comes to the surface like suds on a bath." Another lovely image, like eyeline. Damien is an education officer at the Houses of Parliament. He concludes with a counterintuitive but compelling argument: while club nights are ephemeral, their effects endure—again, like a residue or suds on a bath. "Queerness will go on forever, and it always will exist in different forms, in different places."

How is it possible for something fleeting to have everlasting effects? What I heard again and again, and what I felt each time I went to a club night, is that the worlds people create at these events live on for much longer than the event itself. In fact, for someone like Glyn from Sink the Pink, the event and the community are inextricable, although the latter endures beyond the former. "You build this community, and the event becomes the pinnacle." The connections run deep and outlast the party. "That's been part of Sink the Pink's success, I think, is that your friendships become bigger than just from one club night."

Club nights foster a deep sense of belonging. Rosie, the filmmaker we met earlier, remarks, "If you go to any of these club nights, it feels like they're actually a really closely-knit group of friends." I sensed this too, whether I was surrounded by mostly men at Adonis, drag queens at Sink the Pink, or femme-inistas at Femmetopia—color and glitter, skin and sweaty bodies beyond the binaries. Everyone couldn't possibly know each other, I thought each time as I took in the scene, yet there we were, all of us together. "They are places where community is formed," Rosie affirms after I share my reflections. And then came the key assessment: "Even though it lasts for a short amount of time, I think the bonds that are created are actually quite strong," like those near-instant friendships at a summer camp for kids or a retreat for adults. I absolutely felt the spirit of that community in my fieldwork. The interviews and nights out were tiny slivers of time, far removed from my daily life at a computer, in a classroom, or on the other side of the ocean, yet they birthed strong friendships that I still gladly maintain. The intensity of our experiences, that they are beyond the bounds of our normal life, make small bits of time meaningful in supersized ways.

There is nothing to suggest that bonds like these have not always been shaped by brief moments on the dance floor. But these days, our technology-bloated moment means that it is even easier to keep up those connections. "Some of them [club nights] will have private messaging groups and private social media groups," Rosie adds, "and so they're creating these queer networks, basically, which is quite amazing considering that it might just be once every three months or something." Not all our connections have to be reinforced daily to have meaningful effects. Weak ties can also have strong effects, as the BBC reported about a classic study in sociology: "close friendships are important, but research shows that building networks of casual acquaintances can boost happiness, knowledge, and a sense of belonging." Think about the small talk you had the last time you were on a dance floor, or at a house party, a conference, or a group chat on Zoom. Those varieties of conversations, even if quick and casual, teach us all sorts of things, like how to cope with life in lockdown, how to dress for an upcoming event, or how to take advantage of a job opportunity.[10]

Organizers anticipate these outcomes. "You're always wary as a promoter," Alex from Knickerbocker begins, "because people come up to you and say, 'Oh my god, your night's great, your night's so different, I feel so safe here, I just love it, everyone's really nice." Alex does not discount the compliments—"it's great to hear all that," he admits—"but I am also aware that that is what you say to the people that run the night." While some people may be self-interested, a sense of belonging still emerges at the party, for both regulars and newcomers. "It was that sense of community and the sense of an audience" that Alex found so moving. "It was probably the third or the fourth party . . . where we were like, 'who are these people that are here? We don't know who they are. Why have they come here?'" At first, Alex expected that only his friends would attend the party. "That's always a really exciting feeling when you're like, 'Oh, this is a different crowd tonight. We've not seen these people before.' But we also have our regulars, obviously, who we know, and have indeed made really good friends just by putting the night on." That sense of belonging stays with him. "Being all misty-eyed, that's one of the really nice things about the night, making a whole new trench of friends."

Belonging is easier to feel but harder to define. "I think with Chapter 10, there's definitely a collective experience there that I can't quite define, but it's very recognizable, and it's to do with all those people in one room," Dan, the party's founder, tells me. After I ask if we can think it through, Dan points to another way in which club nights have enduring effects: the pursuit of a common goal. "I think everyone who's there, we're all looking for the same thing, basically," he says. "I think that's what brings them together. And I think that's true for whoever's DJ-ing, and the people on the dance floor, and me, and everyone who's involved with the party. We're all looking for the same thing. I think that's the collective mission of all of us. I don't think we've found it, but we're all at least looking together."

Dan's idea of "the same thing" and "the collective mission" hints at something profound. A cynical reading would be that yes, everyone loves club nights because they are fun, and the common goal is to drink and dance. But Dan's follow-up remark—"I don't think we've found it, but we're all at least looking together"—suggests something aspirational, something that I think gets at why these nights are so evocative and why we keep going back for more. The feeling of belonging that we experience at these events enables us to imagine another world. When we do this together, we have the potential to remake what we perceive is real, and thus what becomes real. Some of us go out to escape the burdens of life. Some go out to drink, do drugs, or hook up for the night. But I believe, like Dan, that we also go in the hopes of finding that something else, even if it is more nebulous. Sometimes that hope is actualized, sometimes just anticipated and not fully realized. Either way, the value of the quest remains, and it is strong.

Even if it is challenging to define or explain in advance the things we seek on a night out, the opposite is true about what we do after the party. We talk about it. We post photos. We remake the night into a narrative, and then we re-live it each time we tell the story. Larger than us, the stories we tell about a club night are cultural objects, and they, too, endure beyond any single event. “I love stories,” Glyn says with an infectious smile. “I love storytelling. I love hearing other people tell stories.” What is it about stories and storytelling that is so powerful for you? “I think that you can only really continue with our culture, our clubbing culture, if you move past the actual night, and you start allowing people in, and telling stories, and inspiring people.” Like the oral traditions of cultures around the world and across millennia, the narratives we weave about nightlife stitch together our legacies and mobilize us to act in the service of a different, if not better, world. In fact, telling stories about your night out can cement a sense of belonging—to a specific event and what it represents, to the time in your life when you are having these experiences, and to the collective identity of a group of people.[11]

Telling stories, especially after the party, outside the bar or nightclub, ensures that the power of that moment will live on. But there is also a practical reason for club night storytelling—the hope of more nights, more options, and an invitation that can inspire more people to create them. One of the most consequential ways in which Glyn told stories about Sink the Pink was at a talk he gave in April 2018 at the Victoria & Albert Museum, an art and design institution that holds a permanent collection of more than 2.8 million cultural objects, books, and archives spanning five thousand years of human creativity. I met Glynn that night. He was part of "a panel of nightlife legends," as I read on the website, curated by the museum and called "Club Nights and the Queer Revolution."[12] When we connected again a month later, I asked what he hoped to accomplish on that panel. "I'm at a point now where it's very important for me to talk to people," he says, alluding to a storytelling sensibility. "I'm always trying to push our community forward." You never know who will be in the audience, Glyn says, a researcher like me or perhaps someone who dreams of starting a night of their own. "By sharing other people's stories and doing things outside the club—there might be someone in that crowd that's wanted to start a club night that then had the courage to do it. That's the only way that we're going to continue to do this." Glyn is realistic, and he recognizes that there is a limited window in his life when he will want to be a party producer. "I'm not going to be running clubs forever," he realizes. "Someone needs to take the baton. And I think that by doing things like that, I would hope that it inspires somebody else. That's why I do it."

Glyn's interest in pushing the community forward is something that many culture creatives share in common. Consider that nearly ten years have lapsed since the UCL report initially documented declines in gay bars. The world has changed since then, and we must move with it. "What's more important is the way queer culture is changing," Samuel from The CAMPerVan emphasizes. That story of change, the survival of nightlife in dire circumstances, is of course our primary concern. "There's a need to have to transform to stay alive," he adds. "The most interesting thing" that's happening in nightlife right now, Samuel remarks, is "these different types of emerging spaces." To him, this suggests that we need to think outside our silos. The loss of gay bars is real and important—"people literally died to create these spaces and to have a space where they felt safe," Amir, a Swedish and German Egyptian policy worker, remarks—but what we are seeing today is diversification, not uniform decline. "Whilst it's a shame that a lot of these nights aren't in permanent queer venues," Samuel continues, "the fact that they exist, the fact that there's so many new nights, is something to be celebrated."

I'm not convinced that lacking a permanent home is necessarily a shame. There is something magical about collecting moments in your life by going to different places, and so impermanence may confer its own benefits. And, as we will see when we talk next about the economics of these parties, lacking a permanent venue can be a great boon to their financial feasibility. What's more important, I think, is Samuel's final point: the abundance of these nights is something we should applaud. By telling stories about them, we commemorate them, we celebrate them, and we ensure that they will survive in our hearts and minds, like that glorious New Year's Eve drag show almost a century and a half ago in Washington, DC, Ruth and Babe's off-the-hook house parties in postwar Detroit, and the Adelphi Rooms in London where I can picture Bill and Bert joyfully dancing the night away back in 1927.

Global—But Covert

Club nights happen around the world. Amir, who knows I live in Canada, enjoys speaking with me about developments closer to my home. "To bring this back to the context of Canada for yourself, Amin, there's a really good example of a queer pop-up, and it started out of Toronto." While I live in Vancouver, more than two thousand miles from Toronto, I still smile at the effort. "It's called Jerk. It's organized by this DJ named Bambi, and she created the event as a response to the need for a queer party in Toronto. There was not enough going on." The void was a function of the same closure epidemic in Canada that is affecting other countries. Rather than opening new bars, or only opening new bars, Bambi, like club night organizers in London, reimagined what was possible in the larger field. "So, she formed this queer pop-up called Jerk, as in jerk chicken, which was only once or twice a year." What started out small eventually exploded. "The party's gained so much success that she's been able to go on tour, so she's been to Halifax, Nova Scotia. She went to other cities in the US." Amir sees this as "a really good example" of how club nights "operate under these circumstances of not having a fixed venue, but just pop up in a city once every few months," usually in "underground spaces or in warehouses." This makes it harder to see them and measure them. "They're just not in the mainstream consciousness." But that does not deny their existence or their extraordinary success.

Matt from Buttmitzvah moved to London from Boston, where there has also been an "interesting and valiant effort to try to revive the gay night, the gay experience." This brings Matt to a more general reflection about temporary events: "Nights have existed everywhere," he says. Bar closures in London have simply made them a bit easier to see. "I think they just took off in London as people saw them [gay bars] dwindling." The phrase Matt uses, took off, is a useful way to access the subtler, not-quite-causal relationship between closures and club nights. What I hear is not that gay bars closing meant more club nights opening but, instead, the closure epidemic meant that the importance of club nights increased. Rishi Madlani, a Labor Councilor with an Asian-Gujarati background, offers another comparison. "I used to live in Frankfurt," he says. "There are very few LGBT venues left in Frankfurt, but they have a lot of LGBT nights that people come together for." Sound familiar? The councilor's words resemble the "other areas" Soof told us about, the "new models" Stefan saw when he moved to London, and the subtle notion of "another avenue" that Lola raised.

Party-hopping from Buttmitzvah to Femmetopia, and with so many others still to come, we have seen how club nights create another world. Their covert characteristics—"a big secret," as Eden said—makes them quintessentially queer. The tendency to appear and then vanish, in underground places at that, has "everything to do with the fact that leaving too much of a trace has often meant that the queer subject has left herself open for attack." Penned by José Esteban Muñoz, I extend the theory to club nights to emphasize that the experiential is essential. "Instead of being clearly available as visible evidence, queerness has existed as innuendo, gossip, fleeting moments, and performances that are meant to be interacted with by those within its epistemological sphere—while evaporating at the touch of those who would eliminate queer possibility." Words lush with sensory details, Muñoz has a way of slowing down the water that slips too fast through our fingers. This "invisible evidence" of queerness takes the form of "ephemera" for Muñoz, while for us it was the moments and memories that linger long after the last call. Club nights do not exist as visible evidence in the built environment, like gay bars and nightclubs, whose trends we can track and quantify into tidy statistics. We already navigated our way through the challenges this poses, but now, with Muñoz's guidance, we might ask with more defiance: so what? Queerness delights in being messier, which is simply to say that club nights, and the worlds they create, "stand as evidence of queer lives, powers, and possibilities."[13]

The CAMPerVAN

Behind Railway Arches

Spring and summertime in London are so great. After months of hibernating under grey skies, these days full of light release pent-up party energy. This afternoon, I was on my way to The CAMPerVAN, an event that had something to do with a caravan in a parking lot somewhere far away from my flat. What was this, I wondered: a performance space by day, club night by night, outside—and free?

I was scrolling through my phone, trying to find the directions on Facebook (back then, the go-to app for information). The event seemed to be around a brewery that opened in a former garage space, near a grocery store, hidden behind converted Victorian brick railway arches in East London. It was like a big secret, stuffed into the crevices of a gentrifying neighborhood. The Deviant and Dandy, a brewery with a fabulously queer name, was somehow standing down the street from a Burberry outlet.

The day party started around 2pm, and I arrived to find a sun-soaked scene: a crowd of maybe fifty people, laughing, sipping beers and lemonade, and eating burgers from a bright yellow food truck tucked into a back corner. It looked like a barbeque in an alley, as the space was long, narrow, and enclosed on three sides by the backs of buildings. The center of the action, however, was a caravan—what people in the United States call a camper—a 1990s-esque Esprit mobile vehicle painted midnight blue. The camper was parked against the far wall of the alley, and it sat by itself on the concrete. Walking through the crowd—T-shirts and shorts, hand-rolled cigarettes—it was clear to me that the trailer had seen better days, with its scrapes and slightly faded paint, but these imperfections added to its charm. A rectangular hole was cut out of the side and the extracted piece mounted on hinges to forge a makeshift stage. The platform, which I assumed was for performances, was about a meter deep and slightly wider—big enough for a drag queen death drop but not much else. Around the platform's perimeter were lights that reminded me of Broadway in New York or the West End in London, although in this case, with a distinct mix of glamor and DIY subversion. Behind, a white curtain concealed whatever was inside the caravan.

A beautiful dark-skinned man in an all-white outfit sat atop the stage, reading a series of short poems about the passage of moments in time. The verses were haunting, the voice a near whisper, and the crowd was hushed, faces locked on the speaker and slowly nodding, as if connecting with a common nostalgia or reflection. The scene looked like a literary gathering, albeit one in an alley or parking lot, not a club night.

The reading ended, the audience erupted in applause, and I took a loop around to see if I could find Samuel, the founder of The CAMPerVAN. My search was sound-tracked by the vocals of the next performer, who was singing. Weaving in and out of the swaying crowd, I chatted briefly with someone who loved this particular party. This was not just any campervan, Imani told me about that blue beauty on wheels, but *The* CAMPerVAN. The wordplay, I thought, was genius. These vehicles—whether you call them caravans, trailers, or campers—are sometimes considered in Britain as working class, associated with crime, drug abuse, and benefit scrounging. There is no

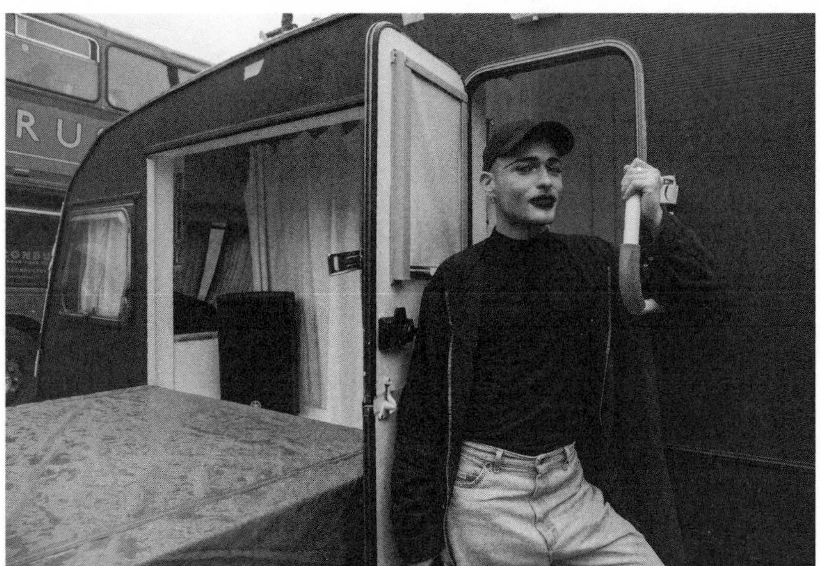

Meet Samuel, the creative founder of The CAMPerVAN.
Photo credit: CAMPerVAN Image Archive, courtesy of Samuel Douek.

hipster celebration of glamping here. "Obviously, these are just smear tactics to demonize the working class," Imani told me. As a name for a party, The CAMPerVAN fused working-class and queer cultures, proudly reclaiming both.

Samuel created the mobile performance and party space in 2016 to protest gentrification and to provide a platform for queer artists. From drag acts to live music, poetry readings to dance, rap battles to panel discussions and film screenings, this portable structure exploited capitalist spaces. The van could insert itself into small areas, like a parking lot, where it thrived in momentary bursts. In its earlier days, Samuel created a gold awning from emergency blankets which he used to partition off a space and show films using the white stage curtains as a projector screen. It looked nothing like Buttmitzvah at the cavernous Troxy, and it was so different from the basement of Femmetopia. But its oddity, like the oddity of each club night, was part of the point; these parties felt connected because of their other-worldly creativity.

I eventually found Samuel, and we swapped stories about nightlife scenes in the city. The CAMPerVAN, he said, was "a transportable

A performance space and portable club night, The CAMPerVAN is always ready for pop-up joy.
Photo credit: CAMPerVAN Image Archive, courtesy of Samuel Douek.

queer performance and community event space that can be deployed anywhere in the world"—a traveling, self-funded party, basically, within the vicinity of a caravan that would set up shop anywhere they could hitch for the day. "The desire to build my own queer space was a response to the ominous discourse that London was, and still is, experiencing an epidemic of closures when it comes to nightlife venues," Samuel continued. His voice got a little louder as the crowd got more boisterous. If you could, how would you rewrite that discourse? He smiled at my question. "I think that the biggest thing to come out of the wave of closures was the emergence of nights, temporary nights. It's very impressive to see the resilience of the queer community and its ingenuity and adaptability." Part of what made The CAMPerVAN feel so special, I reflected back to him, was that it was *not* at night, that it was happening in the afternoon. Samuel nodded. "For me, it was important to create a space where this could happen during the day, outside of drinking and drug consumption"—although I would later find out that there was a nighttime act too.

Samuel sounded smart, strategic, and full of feelings. At some point, all the gay bars that were closing became less a disembodied discourse and much more personal for him. "The feeling of loss

▸ Vogue battles, always a ferocious, fabulous fight.
Photo credit: CAMPerVAN Image Archive, courtesy of Samuel Douek.

among my friends was palpable," Samuel says. "The venues where I had grown to become who I am today were vanishing." Rather than just lament the loss, Samuel wanted to do something about it. "I didn't set out to resolve the disappearance of queer spaces." Nor was he in it for the money (he's happy to break even). "I wanted to determine what makes a space queer and whether I could recreate these characteristics." Listening to him, this young culture creative who had just abandoned years of architecture training to pursue a career in filmmaking, I remembered a conversation I once had with Peter. If the system starts to break down, and we can claim an opportunity to rewrite the rules, why use the same playbook?

The CAMPerVAN had just completed a two-week tour of seven European cities, where Samuel took over parking lots, gallery exteriors, the smoking area at the back of clubs, and other under-used spaces. He described the program as a loosely coordinated series of protests through performance, designed to bring together diverse audiences in a makeshift place for both day and nighttime events. The CAMPerVAN was a long way from the blacked-out windows of bygone gay bars, or even some of the cookie cutter bars in Soho today. At a later point, Zöe and Fiontán joined us. They were a trio of friends who performed, ran the backstage, maintained the vehicle, and planned all the events. I could see that The CAMPerVAN brought them joy. They expressed gratitude for the community it built, both in London and across Europe, not to mention in farther reaches of the world. (The Facebook page had members from many countries.)

The soft vocals that provided a soothing background to our conversation eventually ended, and then, suddenly, a high-energy vogue battle began. The crowd, once gently swaying, was now screaming. The four of us clapped and finger-snapped the spins and dips. The voguing soon segued into a DJ set as an evening breeze drifted past us. Those who were there for the day party looked like they left on a high, while some of the others who remained began to disrobe, revealing outfits destined for a fantastic party. Samuel told me that he had the space until only 11pm, although there was some plan in the works about an after-hours somewhere. For now, for me, this moment in a random parking lot was all I needed. It was time to dance.

3

When Capitalism Crushes

By now, it should be clear that demand, or lack thereof, is not the problem. Recall Richard's market analogy about looking for Russian eggs in a big city, or the culture-at-risk officer's confidence that "the demand is there." Soaring land values and redevelopment are the culprits that matter most. I can still hear Ben in my ear describing the pitfalls of a gay bar trying to stay in business amidst speculative real estate practices: "It's not a question of whether it's *commercially viable*; it's a question of whether it's *maximally profitable*."

Increases in business rates (a term for taxes) and sky-high rents are challenging bars to remain economically viable. High operating costs and escalating land values interact to price many renters out and motivate landlords to maximize profitability by changing the use of a building from commercial to housing. All this has devastating consequences for the nighttime economy in terms of the scale and scope of places to go out. A couple of days after his parking lot party, I was discussing these matters with Samuel. He paused for a moment, took a deep breath, exhaled with equal intention, and concluded, "The traditional business model of a queer club is not really sustainable."

We have already seen how club nights experiment with nightlife, especially its organizational structures and worldmaking qualities.

But club nights are also an experiment in economics. Consider the operating costs. Renting a space can require anywhere from £500 to £20,000 (US$630–$25,250), and these fees are signed in a lease (under the table is rare, too risky for people with day jobs). Organizers do not have to pay for security, liquor licenses, or cleanup, as these costs are typically covered by the venue. Partnering with a production company can add £500–£1,000 (US$630–$1,260) to the tab. Then you have the performers, who receive a minimum of £50 (US$60) but upwards of £200 (US$250) or more. And don't forget the light crew, technicians, insurance, props like projectors and disco balls, promotional materials, and of course the DJ—those costs range from £200 (US$250) to £4,000 (US$5,050).

To put it together and into perspective: organizers face upfront costs from £1,000 (US$1,260) at a minimum to £30,000 (US$38,000) for a flashier occasion, although most accumulate between £3,000–£5,000 (US$3,800–$6,300) in total expenses. Tickets cost £5–£40 (US$6–$50). If a rented venue has a capacity of 500, and if the night sells out, that generates somewhere between £2,500 and £20,000 (US$3,000–$25,000) in proceeds [£5,000–£10,000 (US$6,300–$12,625) are the numbers I heard most often]. But if capacity is 3,500—like at Troxy, where we partied in the preface—then a club night where everyone pays £20 (US$25) at the door would bring in £70,000 (US$87,500). I don't know exactly how much it cost to produce that event, but even if we estimate the upper end of expenses (£30,000 or US$37,890), that can still produce a decent profit.

Three qualifications are worth noting before you rush out to create your own party. First, if we discount the hours organizers invest (10–12 per week on average), the profit total drops. Second, your friends will want to be on a guest list, and that will affect your proceeds from ticket sales. And third, some venues require a deposit, usually £1,000–£2,000 (US$1,260–$2,525), in exchange for a spending cap. If the venue makes a certain amount at the bar—£5,000–£10,000 (US$6,300–$12,625), for example—you as the organizer will receive your deposit back and keep the full earnings from ticket sales. However, if the venue does not make the cap—because young people are drinking less these days, for instance—then you will lose the deposit (but still keep the ticket sales). Not all venues require deposits—in some cases, just a flat fee to reserve the space—but they might keep all the bar earnings. Although successful club nights manage to negotiate a cut, the stress is not trivial.[1]

The episodic form does afford some financial freedoms, however. Absent the hassle of taxes, hefty rents [business rental costs in Soho, where space is a premium, range from £37 (US$47) to £410 (US$518) per square foot per day, with an average of £150 (US$190)], staff paychecks, overhead costs, and the daily expenditures associated with running a business, it seems clear that club nights use a different economic model than gay bars and nightclubs. Still, for most producers, putting on a night is not a way to pay their rent or mortgage; occasional parties provide an unreliable and unsteady source of income. It is possible to make a profit from time to time, although how much can vary tremendously and nothing is guaranteed. What makes club nights interesting, then, is not that they are money-making machines—in the eyes of an economist, they might actually look like a failure—but how these freelancers manage to prioritize creativity over the crushing forces of capitalism.[2]

This chapter is not an exercise in accounting for the pounds and pence of nightlife but, rather, an inquiry into some of the clever economic initiatives of club nights. If running a gay bar presents a less sustainable model, as Samuel said, then how are party producers ensuring that they have a better chance of survival? What specific strategies are they using? The closure epidemic unexpectedly, perhaps even counterintuitively, encouraged more growth in nightlife. How did that happen?

Crack Capitalism

Club nights are adaptive. They are "essentially just temporary," Laurie from The Chateau reminds us, "a temporary space of some sort." That the format has become popular—"Lots of people do pop-up shops"—suggests to Laurie, as it did to Samuel, that "the way people market their business and operate it has completely changed." The words they each offer are slightly different, but the underlying idea is consistent. Stefan, the Canadian who recently moved to London, articulates the change in a memorable way: "You lose the model of the bar, but you keep that special event draw." This alternative model appeals to many people. "How would you like to make some money by having what is a fun, gritty, slightly pushing-the-boundaries party in an alternative venue?" Jonathan asks, as if inviting me to plan a party. I was tempted—but how does anybody even do it in exceedingly expensive cities like London?

Making money by organizing a single-night, avant-garde party is a "different way of operating a business," Stefan counsels, and it involves a "different financial model." I have seldom read this insight in media or academic coverage about nightlife, nor did I hear it from the night czar, who had more to say about gay bars than club nights anyway. Here, lessons from the retail world are instructive. A lot of people today, Laurie continues, "can't afford to do an actual shop because the overhead is so high, so they do a pop-up shop for a week, two weeks, a month." The temporary form, whether for retail or nightlife, is "a more fluid way of operating, which is really beneficial, and I think feels very practical considering the issues that come with running businesses." What makes it practical? I ask. "You can try something in one location, try another location. You can collaborate with people."

In *Crack Capitalism*, John Holloway writes about how people look for opportunities when the walls of the capitalist world feel like they are closing in. "The method of the crack is the method of crisis," he says in an effort to redefine what opportunities look like. Holloway is interested in how labor activists refuse to think about capitalism as a form of domination and instead exploit its structural weaknesses, hence "the crack" as a method of power reversals and economic survival—or, as he says, "we wish to understand the wall not from its solidity but from its cracks." By speaking with club night organizers, I discovered an application in nightlife: creativity can survive in a closure epidemic, even when capitalism crushes with the encroachments of privatization, escalating land values, and housing insecurities. Said differently: crack capitalism emerges as an attractive option in disruptive moments as we look for new openings in unexpected places.[3]

This is how Laurie found a space: "Before we came here, this was an ex–religious-themed cocktail bar. It's a twenty-acre hotel called the Church Street Hotel, and they created this bar, this religious-themed hotel bar in 2014. It closed in 2016, and then it just sat empty, completely unused, for two years, just gathering dust until we found it." The provisional use of vacant or abandoned spaces illustrates a creative intervention in the capitalist city, an "experimental utopia," Henry Lefebvre might say, using a phrase that bridges our prior explorations into the underground worlds of club nights with our focus now on their economic profiles—but this is happening in actual, existing spaces, rather than those we simply imagine (which is Lefebvre's focus).[4] Eden, the founder of Riposte, describes the process as "organizing in alternative spaces," like an unused hotel bar. Laurie and Eden are both working in the cracks; their practices defy traditional notions of how to run a business. The event "can be whatever you want," Eden explains.

Crack capitalism, the underground, temporary gatherings—these are all compatible images. I see them as part of a broader conversation among researchers who write about cities under conditions of austerity. Sociologist Fran Tonkiss describes interventions in difficult moments, places where possibilities can live in secret, as marginal urbanisms, interstitial actions, edgework, and experimenting in tight spaces. Borrowing ideas from researchers like Holloway, Lefebvre, and Tonkiss can point us to smaller places that many people do not see yet where some of the most exciting developments in nightlife are occurring today.[5]

"We might be here for a long time. We might be here for only another couple of months. Who knows?" Laurie is not worried about it. He finds pleasure in exploiting cracks in the capitalist city. "I love repurposing space into more beneficial uses for the community and for society," he beams. "There's way, way, way, way, *way* too much empty, unused space in London that sits there because property developers—it's cheaper for them to sit on the building than to actually do anything with it." This glut of unused space does nothing for anyone except a handful of developers who are calculating their profits. But putting these spaces to creative use, Laurie argues, is good for everyone: good for the city, and especially good for LGBTQ+ communities. "Finding these pockets, putting ourselves into them, and making something that feels necessary, important, and needed for the community is so exciting." In urban areas that bear "physical scars of disinvestment, disuse, and decline," to borrow again from Tonkiss—that is where queer cultures spring to life.[6]

Looking for openings, crevices of creativity, can give party producers "more control" over their events, as Shay, the organizer of Adonis, tells me. "It's your thing that you can move around. You can find the right space. You can be successful and move to a bigger venue, or you can certainly move it to a smaller venue." More control, sure, but what about money? The pop-up structure "gives me loads of flexibility," Laurie echoes, "because if we suddenly start to lose money, I can say, 'Okay, that's it. We're done. See you later.' And I can go and do something different. It's a really nice, flexible way of operating a business. It's a great model. It allows us to be way more daring than I think venues that have permanent leases." This is why "pop-ups are all the rage in London," he concludes. "It's the thing."

It seems wise to look for cracks—it's the thing—but where are they? madison and I chat for a bit about gayborhoods, which, having written a book about them, is one of my favorite topics of conversation. But speaking with them took a surprise twist. They describe a bookstore that doubles as a gay bar. "I talked to the owners about how they work it," madison says, "and they said that they don't make any money off of book sales." Bookstores based in gay districts often struggle to survive due to the high rents. How is this one getting by? "They have a little bit of an endowment from donors, who want it to stay in this gayborhood. They told me that the rent is like $17,000 a month to be in this gayborhood where they're not making any money, basically."

For madison, the example raises questions about the constraints and possibilities of place, or the location where you base your creative initiatives. "I'm not a business person, but it just doesn't seem to make sense to pay so much money only to be in a gayborhood—and you're not making money. You're going to be closed in ten, five years." Seems likely, I nod (especially if you don't have an endowment!)—and then madison lands an argument about relocating to a less expensive area and repurposing the extra revenues to creating unique experiences. "Imagine if you could give up on the gayborhood and move to a new place where you might pay $4,000 a month in rent. If your budget was $17,000, imagine that you cut it down to $10,000, and you paid $4,000 for rent. Then you have $6,000 a month to invest in experiences: bring artists in, have DJ nights, make it a destination." Although the bookstore was already operating as a bar, it did not offer a memorable experience. madison, however, feels that it has the potential to go beyond being just another bar to becoming something spectacular, if only the money wasn't tied up in steep rents. "You're spending money literally just to be on this particular street," they repeat. "It's something that really stuck out to me, and I thought, maybe it's time to move—or not invest so much in the street but in what you're offering people." This is exactly how crack capitalism works: where you are affects what you can offer. It's also why many club nights occur outside central London, where organizers locate vacant, empty, disused, or underused spaces and "invest in experiences," as madison says, in the service of creating another world.

The imagery of cracks also applies to time, or the number of days you operate your venture. Matt from Buttmitzvah breaks it down: "From an economic standpoint, you should try and make money by capitalizing on people's one night out, that they're going to go out on a Saturday, rather than just spreading that over time." He is influenced by the same financial pressures that capitalism exerts on all businesses—"real estate has gone up, rent has increased"—but the situation has unique effects in nightlife. "If you charge the same amount for a beer, you won't be able to make your rent back. Won't work." What *does* work? Matt compares club nights with themed "gay nights" that some straight bars host: "You can think about some of these bars who said, 'You know what we should do? We should probably have a gay night to encourage people to come.' Charge people to come, which is awesome. But then, they don't end up coming the rest of your nights." Just when I thought Matt's argument was about the lack of demand, he pivots toward incentives that come from the strategic use of time. "But you see, from this single night, I made a lot of money. This is all economics." The straight bar that hosts gay nights shares with club nights an ability to sustain a long-term venture with a smaller number of events. Time is thus another crack. "Why keep the bar open if most of the money that you make is on one or two nights? Why spend all this time and energy when it's not actually giving anything back?"

The temporary form can present a more sustainable model in the context of gentrification, certainly, but also in an era where sexuality is becoming a less central way in which some of us define ourselves. "We don't live in an age where it's like, 'Oh, we need that space for community,'" Matt continues. "You don't need that space for community. You want a few spaces, and you want them to exist. People will go to them." Matt references gay bars in Boston, where he lived before London. "That's why Boston has four, because people still go to those. You want to go to a gay bar, and so those will still exist." Decline in numbers, in other words, does not mean the decimation of nightlife. The same insight applies in London. "You'll go to the ones in Soho, the gay bars, and hang out on the street corner." His experiences in both cities suggest a lesson about the regularity of offerings. "There will be gay bars. All of them will not close, because people will want to go to a gay bar. But you don't need a million, because people don't go to a million regular pubs. But they *will* go to different nights."

Matt is not in it for the money, but for those who are, the world-making qualities of club nights we considered before can also provide an alternate business model. "It's an economic opportunity to capitalize on experiences, because people want experiences." Matt and I talk at length about this idea—the "experience element," as he calls it, echoing madison's emphasis on "investing in experiences." By operating as a collection of moments, rather than fixed establishments, club nights are thriving even as gay bars close—"because people want experiences," Matt affirms. "People end up feeling more connected with somebody when there's something else grounding them, rather than just being in a bar." Operating in the cracks of places and times, club nights cultivate that something else as a unique set of experiences—and "people are willing to pay" for it.

Community Enterprises

The financial pressures that party producers face motivate them to rethink and rework the relationship between the accumulation of profits and a focus on their target communities. "Gay bars are far more business orientated, and they are far more about generating capital, and less about forging real community and supporting each other," Tia tells me. Twenty-five years old when we met, Tia identifies as Black British and a queer woman. She is part of a collective that organizes BBZ (pronounced "Babes," an acronym for Bold Brazen Zamis). "I would say that's one of the biggest differences," she says. The statement, while previewing a crucial contrast, still lands harshly. I suspect that some gay bar owners would strenuously disagree, particularly those who owned their establishments thirty or forty years ago, when, as we have seen, they were community anchors. Perhaps gay bars from those decades had a similar ethos as club nights today—other worlds where more of us felt like we belonged. But as bars became mainstream, some people began to perceive them as more capitalist than communitarian. Dan, who you might recall is a bar owner and a club night organizer, remarks on how nightlife has changed: "People are disrupting normal mechanisms for gay spaces because, in London for the last twenty years, the gay scene is largely a commercially driven enterprise, rather than any kind of specifically socially led organization." The greater visibility of club nights has brought with it innovative ways of thinking about the economics of nightlife—the possibility of partying without prioritizing profits.

We met Michael, the public intellectual, earlier. He comments on a greater awareness of, and preference for, communities over capitalism. "If we want venues to survive, then we need to build communities around them." But how? I ask. "You embed them in a community, rather than just seeing them as a profit-making vehicle." Michael compares gay bars in Soho with those in East London, places like the Glory and Dalston Superstore, who make material investments. These bars "are actively run by people who are part of this community and are fostering activities, whether it be letting their spaces be used in the daytime for community groups, whether it be putting on events, or queer history events, or film screenings, or talks, or competitions, pub quizzes, whatever it might be."

Many organizers see their parties as *community enterprises*. Angelica, the founder of Choose Your Own Adventure, a sober dance party, prefers club nights to gay bars because they are "community-owned and "community-run," whereas bars are perceived as more corporate and commercial. Party producers do "need to cover some costs," as we know, "and so they generally charge, but as little as they reasonably can do to make it as accessible as possible." Some events, like The CAMPerVAN, are free. This raises a question about ticketing policies, which provide an example of how club nights serve the role of a community enterprise. In our chat, Michael drops what he calls a "small" point but which I receive with immense implications: "A small thing, but if you can't pay the entry fee, but you want to come, and you can't afford it, then you're allowed in." While free entry is not a standard expectation for all parties, the allowance, when it does occur, positions organizers as people who "build communities around them in the area, looking to have regulars, rather than just being places people flock to at night for an event."

As Michael says this, I think about Pxssy Palace, "an arts platform rooted in intentional nightlife," as they define themselves. The event, organized by a collective of activists, artists, and partystarters in London, celebrates "Black, Indigenous and people of color who are women, queer, intersex, trans, or nonbinary. We provide space to dance, connect and engage, whilst encouraging . . . expression and exploration of our authentic selves." The collective uses a ticketing policy that aptly illustrates Michael's point about access and inclusion: "We have a number of free or discounted tickets for QTBIPOC (queer and trans Black, Indigenous and people of color) guests in our community who cannot afford to pay full price," they state on their website. Brooke, the queer lesbian we met earlier, articulates the experiment that parties like Pxssy Palace are exploring: "I think there's a real commitment in these new or emerging spaces that we take very seriously unwaged people. Everyone is welcome, and you don't have to have money to come." Consider another example, again from Pxssy Palace: at one of their parties, they offered "Pay It Forward" tickets. By purchasing it, a reveler contributes to a slush fund that the organizers use "to offer free and discounted tickets to lower income QTBIPOC."[7]

As of February 1, 2022, Pxssy Palace implemented a tiered ticketing policy that prioritizes their intended demographic. Straight White cis men who wish to attend pay £112 (US$140) at the door, while Black and ethnic minority individuals who also identify as queer, nonbinary, or trans pay £16.80 (US$21.20). White partygoers who are trans or nonwhite straight women pay a mid-range price of £24.64 (US$33.63). Organizers initiated the new policy as their events became more popular, attracting upwards of seven hundred people every month, many of whom did not represent their intended audience. "Our party is for Black, Indigenous, people of color who are women, trans and nonbinary," Nadine Noor, a member of the collective, said to *Resident Advisor*. "We can center them by offering them cheaper tickets, and people outside of those groups can understand their privilege." Noor recognizes that there are people within LGBTQ+ communities that also have economic privileges. "Of course, there's plenty of people within our community that earn a lot of money or come from generational wealth. So, no matter who you are, you should pay with your heart and your wallet."[8]

The optics of these policies position parties like Pxssy Palace as a community enterprise, rather than a for-profit venture. *The Advocate* spoke with the collective and confirmed that "the pricing scale would benefit poorer individuals who could attend." The group elaborated their position in another interview with *Dazed*: "The idea behind the tiers is to respond to the unfair economic imbalance that exists within our society. The gender pay gap between women and men is just the first of many disparities within the trans, nonbinary, Black, Indigenous, and people of color community." Pxssy Palace describes their tiers as akin to "the concession model" where students or pensioners are offered "concession tickets to widen accessibilities." Their intention is to prioritize those too long left out. "There aren't a lot of places that BIPOC queer women, trans, and nonbinary people can go to and feel welcomed, never mind a place where they are actually embraced and supported." Rosie sees their approach as a defining feature of club nights. "That's a kind of thinking that I like about these new queer spaces," she says. "They're thinking in this very lateral, horizontal way."[9]

Yet another instance of using proceeds from a ticketing policy to help underserved or at-risk community members comes in the form of a "taxi fund." The Pxssy Palace collective explains the basis of this simple yet ingenious venture: "Our Taxi Fund is set up to contribute to BIPOC trans and disabled guests' travel expenses to get home safely from our events. We collect donations for the Taxi Fund on the door, throughout the night, and on our PayPal, which is linked on our Instagram and website." This initiative, like their ticket tiers, also attracted considerable media attention. *Dazed* writes, "This club night is making sure trans people of color get home safely." We know that trans people of color are systematically targeted for hate crimes, and as co-organizer Nadine Artois says, "Trans femmes of color are the most at risk of these forms of abuse." They continue, "Now that we have substantial, regular guests and followers, we are in a position to offer our most vulnerable guests a safer way to travel home." Also interviewed in the story is Travis Alabanza, an acclaimed performer and writer. Alabanza praised the taxi fund: "Myself and a group of trans friends read the message last night and let out a sigh of relief and a smile. In a climate that often erases our struggle, it felt important to be recognized and heard."[10]

In my conversation with Erkan, a Middle Eastern British activist, I hear a personal perspective about why these kinds of initiatives matter. "I know that, for example, as a genderqueer person of color, my aesthetic when I go out in the evenings has put me in a place of discomfort many times in public," they share. "I can be seen as quite provocative. But my aesthetic is nothing compared to others, for example, trans women of color who are trans every day. They don't just put on this as aesthetic or gender performance just for the evening, or just for the show. They do it on a daily basis." Tiered ticketing policies and taxi funds invest in community in ways that commercial logics miss or simply ignore. It would be remarkable for a business to make any kind of concession to its customers, after all.

One final example of club nights as community enterprises comes from programming strategies: some nights, when organizers make money, help pay for other nights, when they may lose it. Laurie and I talk about the crowd that comes to The Chateau. "It varies night to night," he replies. "Most of the time, we're not nearly as diverse as I would like to be, but it's about where our heart and where our ethos lies." And where is that? I nudge. His reply reveals an inventive initiative. "Some nights, we are full of White gay bears dancing to Madonna," Laurie admits. "And that's fine, it's great." Then comes the revelation: "Also, the White gay bears generally have money. So, on a very basic, commercial level—it's not always the case, but if I'm generalizing—some portions of our community are more able to prop this bar up financially than others." Repurpose the revenues, basically. Parties that attract more privileged LGBTQ+ people keep the night afloat, which then can expand opportunities for other groups. "Hopefully, we break even," he says. That add-on statement—"hopefully, we break even"—is important. It suggests a cultural designation of club nights as for people and for communities, not for profit. Laurie continues, "On Saturdays, we generally throw a bigger party, a more typical gay party that we play party tunes, and people can dance. People end up drinking lots on the bar. That pays for all the other stuff that we want to do that doesn't generate any income."

The economic approaches that The Chateau and Pxssy Palace use remind me of an idea called *progressive redistribution* or repurposing.[11] Boosting opportunities for groups who are actively struggling, like QTBIPOC individuals, requires organizers to engage creatively with other members of the community who have more financial resources, like White gay men. An agenda based on shifting resources in progressive ways, from one group to another, expands access, representation, and feelings of belonging, which is a redistributive effect. Revelers like Brooke recognize these efforts. "I think that this is something organizers think about," she says. "You think about what you are making money to do. Who are you creating the space for? You could use one to cover the costs or the lack of profit from the other." For Brooke, the movable model of club nights describes the physical circumstances of the party and their economic experiments: redistribute funds that you receive from one group in order to support other individuals who have less financial means.

Dan, who told us earlier how nightlife has changed in London over the past twenty years, brings these ideas into a framework that articulates the main theme of this section. Many club nights are "community enterprises," he says, or "social enterprises," by which he means "a community interest company or some other mechanism that isn't profit-driven in the way that a limited company would be." A community enterprise or community interest company is a non-charitable business structure whose objectives are social and philanthropic—helping other people or existing for the benefit of the community—rather than maximizing profits for shareholders and owners, which is what a limited company like a bar would do. To meet these social objectives, a person with a registered community enterprise is expected to reinvest their profits back into the business, or to members of the community that the business serves.[12]

A DJ, party producer, radio host, and venue owner, Dan occupies a unique position in the field of nightlife. He owns Dalston Superstore in East London, and he also organizes club nights like Chapter 10 and Disco Bloodbath, both of which have acquired "legendary" and "bacchanalian" status.[13] We compare these different forms of nightlife. Gay bars operate "in the context of capitalist economics," Dan tells me. "The need for financial exploitation is the priority" because "opening a venue is expensive." The large numbers of bar closures created an opportunity to experiment "with spaces operating along different economic lines." How so? I ask. "The response equals spaces governed along different models that are not necessarily commercial," he replies. In other words, the closure epidemic changed the "traditional business model of a queer club," to bring us back to what Samuel said at the start.

To make more concrete Dan's notion of a community enterprise that uses a nontraditional economic model, let's consider a specific case: The Joiners Arms, or Joiners for short. That pub was legendary, counting among its regulars Alexander McQueen, Rufus Wainwright, and Sir Ian McKellen. David Pollard opened the bar on 116–118 Hackney Road shortly after Tony Blair's landslide election victory in May 1997, and it quickly became an institution in East London. Pollard was dedicated to the fair treatment of his staff, and the Joiners was among the first pubs in the country to pay its employees a living wage. The place had an "eclectic" and "dicey" vibe, as geographer Johan Andersson describes it, which was enhanced by its "edgy location" in a part of London that once had a reputation for "urban disorder." These qualities contributed to its popularity. An "unassuming 'spit-and-sawdust' pub," the Joiners embodied a long-standing East London tradition—the working-class pub. Its culture was the opposite of Soho's sanitized gay aesthetics, something its patrons welcomed. These factors created a feeling that the Joiners was an authentic, if hedonistic, queer space. That the bar often ignored licensing hours and remained open when other places had shut down for the night only furthered its countercultural charm.[14]

The Joiners closed on January 15, 2015, long before I arrived in London, when the property was purchased by a developer called Regal Homes who was looking to build luxury flats on the site. The pub was part of a geographic triangle of LGBTQ+ venues, including the Nelson's Head nearby and George and Dragon. All three closed in close succession. A number of other gay bars closed around that time as well, including Candy Bar and Madame Jojo's in Soho, the Black Cap in Camden, and City of Quebec in Marylebone. Awareness was spreading that these closures were not isolated incidences but a systemic threat. This consciousness sparked a protest campaign called the Friends of the Joiners Arms (FOTJA), which emerged in 2014 as rumors spread about the bar's impending closure.

Soon after the Joiners closed, FOTJA secured an "Asset of Community Value" listing. The designation gave them priority to purchase the building and determine its future use. From this victory came a creative vision—to reopen the space as London's first community-run queer pub. "The Joiners is now forever lost because no one can recreate it, and we are not the people who ran it," Amy Roberts says in an interview with Power to Change, a group that works with community businesses to address their needs. In 2022, Amy, who identifies as Welsh and a queer lesbian, was the chair of FOTJA. "This is true when any venue or space is closed," she adds. "It is lost. However, our campaign was born out of that energy." In these words, I recognize an example of a community enterprise. "What we aim to create," Amy says, "is a not-for-profit, truly accessible space that centers the needs of the most marginalized within the LGBTQ+ communities. We want to reimagine what a queer space can be by reinvesting profits back into the services and events we can offer."

Two years after the Joiners closed and in response to activist pressure, the Tower Hamlets council told the developers that their vision for offices and luxury flats on the former site of the Joiners will receive planning permission only if they include a pub that will "remain a lesbian, gay, bisexual and transgender-focused venue for a minimum of twelve years." The council later increased the requirement from twelve to twenty-five years. *And* they extended a crucial late license to the pub, the same one it had before it closed (a late license enables longer opening hours beyond the standard municipal curfew, 11pm on weeknights and midnight on weekends, for the sale of alcohol, an extension to 2am on Sunday through Wednesday, 3am on Thursday and Friday, and 4am on Saturday). *And* the council mandated that the developers must pay the first year's rent for the new Joiners. *And* they had to contribute to the fit-out costs of the new venue. These were unprecedented victories. "It's about changing the conversation at the highest level," Ed Bayes, the culture-at-risk officer, explains. "These things don't happen without a really strong campaign. When a successful campaign works is when they get the people with the decision-making power to get on board with them. A loud, passionate, grassroots campaign was really key." The Tower Hamlets council, who have decision-making power, were compelled by the campaign. "I am pleased that following consultation with the developers, the GLA and the Friends of the Joiners Arms, the development committee has granted planning permission for an LGBTQ+ venue at the site of the Joiners Arms," John Biggs, the mayor of the borough, told the press. "Tower Hamlets is leading the way in reversing the decline in LGBTQ+ venues which we have seen across London."[15]

FOTJA established themselves in March 2018 as a community benefit society (CBS). A more formalized way of talking about community enterprises, a CBS is a legally recognized group whose objectives are to benefit the local community, in contrast to a cooperative society, which benefits its members.[16] The CBS is led by a management committee, and one of the things the group can do, as FOTJA explain on their website, is "issue community shares: a withdrawable, non-transferrable equity investment into our CBS. It's withdrawable because, under certain conditions, you can take your money out of the organization. It's non-transferable because you cannot transfer or sell your shares. And it's an equity investment because you buy shares in the organization." Eight years after Regal London purchased the land and subsequently closed the Joiners, this is exactly what FOTJA did: they launched a £100,000 (US$126,250) fundraising drive to open what they hope will become the UK's first community-run LGBTQ+ venue. "When you buy shares, you help us raise funds to cover the starting up costs of our community-run business. But you also become a member of our CBS: as a shareholder you get one vote (independent of the number of shares you buy). This means you get to vote on how the community-run business evolves and elect the Management Committee," a process which happens every year at their annual general meeting.[17]

Using crowdfunding to motivate the construction of a democratic queer pub is an extraordinary economic innovation. The campaign is still selling shares, and I purchased one in solidarity. Contributions start at £25 (US$32), and the campaign welcomes it as a "fightback" against the closure epidemic. "We're asking people to invest just £25," Amy said to *The Guardian*. Like Pxssy Palace's door policies, FOTJA also issued a pay it forward option. "For those that can't afford it, we're offering a 'pay it forward' scheme too, to make sure that as many people as possible have a say in how this new queer space will be run." For the same amount, the pay it forward option enables people to purchase shares for others. FOTJA then assigns those shares to people who would like to become members but cannot afford it. Amy Roberts describes the joy the campaigners feel: "I'm so proud to share the work we've done to turn this utopian idea into a real space, one that can survive as a viable business, will create opportunities for queer people to work, perform, create, socialize and just 'be' on their own terms." On August 16, 2022, after seventy days of campaigning, the group accomplished their objective—exceeded it, in fact, when 2,260 investors raised £127,735 (US$161,250). Their plan is to continue fundraising while the campaign works with the city to secure a site.[18]

The Power of the Permanent

Experimenting with economic models frees club nights from some constraints that burden bars, but this doesn't mean that organizers never desire something more permanent, as we see in the case of the Joiners. But why would they, you might wonder, given the many advantages of the temporary form? Lest we overstate the appeal of events that operate in the cracks of the capitalist city, let's consider another point of view presented by people who desire longer lasting institutional structures.

Stefan thinks the idea of transience is "exciting and of the moment, merry London, to have your finger on the pulse of what is going on," but this is not always a good thing. Permanent spaces can outlive trends, Lyall tells me. A London-based fashion designer who has worked with Beyoncé, Boy George, Lady Gaga, and Madonna, Lyall is a "style soothsayer"—and the owner of VFD, the basement of dreams in East London where we went for Femmetopia. I ask Lyall about the differences between permanent places and club nights. "The main thing is that we are here all the time," Lyall replies. "It works sometimes in our favor, and sometimes against us, because those ephemeral pop-ups become these incredible, like, 'oh wow, look, it's happening, and we've all got to go.' A lot of focus can happen on those." When VFD opened, "everybody did their one-off parties here." But they would move on to another place. "Then what happens is another venue or another space opens up, and everybody goes somewhere else."[19]

Some club nights aspire to what Lyall has achieved. "I would love to," declares Lewis, who we met in the introduction. "So many of my other friends would love to, but the financial backing is not there. Or if it is there, I have no idea how to go about it, because it's not really accessible to people like us." Money matters, as we have seen several times, but especially for certain people. I realize this once I ask Lewis what they mean by "people like us." They reply, "A lot of queer people I know are either from working-class or middle-class backgrounds, and they don't have hundreds of thousands of pounds sitting there to be able to rent out or buy a venue and make this a queer space." Lewis organizes INFERNO, a club night that celebrates broad definitions of beauty (we'll hop over to that party later). The class-inflected aspects of queerness made an impression on Lewis. "If we had a permanent venue, it would be great," but then they pause and repeat: "It's just not accessible to people like us." Lewis raises a painful observation that research supports. One study found that, despite being perceived as less risky overall, queer people are 73 percent more likely to be denied a bank loan compared to heterosexuals. And even when they are approved, they face higher interest rates and fees.[20]

Even if Lewis could purchase a permanent establishment, they still would not replicate traditional business models of nightlife. They prefer a hybrid approach that blends commercial and community enterprises with day and nighttime offerings. "We could have a coffee shop space for the day, and then on Thursday, Friday, Saturdays, we'd have more of a functioning nightclub space." Financial restrictions pose challenges for queer people who have dreams like these. "All the people that I know who run parties are mainly working class," they reflect. "Nobody I know here identified as queer is upper class." Lewis finds this quite remarkable. "I was thinking about this on the way here. Isn't that fascinating that I can't really name one of my friends who are very wealthy who identify as queer?" The question lingers in the air. "I know a few gay men who are filthy rich, but they identify as gay men. And I'm like, isn't this interesting?"[21]

Kat from Femmetopia shares the sentiment. "I meet so many people whose dream is to open up their own space," she tells me. "Everyone wants to open up their own space, or their own queer restaurant, or their own queer bistro, or club, or whatever it is. And it's just the reality of how much money any of us actually have." Kat shifts from abstractions to a time when she was looking for a place to live. "I was talking to a few of my friends, and I was just like, 'Look, I work in nightlife. I also work at a bar, I make art, and I'm broke.'" Reminding me of Lewis, Kat zooms out from her personal situation to identify a pattern. "There's less money in our community." And this affects how nightlife is structured. "I think that that certainly has a part to play in how we construct our spaces." Across the board, the real culprit is cash. "I don't think the idea of having a permanent venue is outdated, because everyone still wants one. But I just don't know how feasible it is with the current economic climate, in London anyway."

The tension in these voices is unmistakable. Club nights have qualities that vaccinate them from the closure epidemic, yet permanent places still appeal to many people. Peter, the activist we met earlier, sidesteps the contradiction by describing club nights and pubs as servicing harder and softer needs, respectively. "There are other needs that aren't taken care of" by one-off parties, he says. Such as? "Going for a pint, or stopping off somewhere on your way home from work or going for a date." Peter describes these as "softer needs" in contrast to the "harder needs of like, I want to stay up really late," or "I want to listen to some really loud music." Dan Glass, another activist, reframes the distinction that Peter makes between temporary and permanent spaces as representing resilience and humanity, respectively: "We should celebrate temporary spaces because it really brings truth to the fact that we are resilient, but permanence is what we need in terms of our full humanity." Twenty-six-year-old Joe agrees. Club nights are a "problem," he says defiantly. I'm startled, since few people have ever described a club night in this way. When I ask why, Joe talks about time. "It's the fact that it's only one night of the month." Joe wants to feel like he belongs more steadily. "It's like, where the fuck are you going to go for the rest of the time? You need a permanent place. It's good for people. It's a hub for them to go. That's what people want: they want a place they can go to all the time." Variety may be the spice of life, but roots—a place we can go all the time—can bring distinct comforts.

Regardless of whether they praise pop-ups or desire something more persistent, organizers are always experimenting with economic models. Someone like Nadine from Pxssy Palace is acutely aware that "our community doesn't have very much money." Still, they want "a place of our own where we can set our own rules," including instituting "anti-caps business measures." What are some examples? I ask, intrigued by the phrase to describe anti-capitalist approaches to nightlife. "I'd like to make everything as cheap and free as possible." While Nadine opposes the brutal logics of capitalism, they recognize that "it's very, very, very complicated," since "I still need to eat, and pay rent, and live here. It's not something I can put in place now. But it's something that I want to be able to put in place in the future if we were to have our own venue."

Meanwhile Use

Amy and I chatted in 2018 and then again in 2022, years after FOTJA secured planning protections from the council. Efforts to reopen the Joiners have been slow and mired in red tape. "Five years since we initially secured those planning protections, the development has yet to go ahead—and the Joiners sits empty." Speaking on behalf of the group, she expresses mixed emotions about the outcome. "As much as we are happy that the property developers have not been able to go ahead with their plans at the site—and I hope we have shown the power of community organizing in the face of power and money—it does show the limitations of protecting queer spaces through planning protections."

A protracted fight for a permanent venue was unsustainable without some occasions for fellowship. Activists like Amy and others in the campaign wanted to create moments to sustain the spirit of the iconic pub and the energy that fueled the fight. And so, on November 16, 2018, they hosted the first of what would become a bimonthly cabaret club night called Lèse Majesté. Peter, who is also a campaigner for FOTJA, explains their many motivations, each with air quotes: "I think the idea of running parties or nights evolved from the initial idea of 'keeping the spirit of the Joiners alive,' when we thought we might actually be able to just reopen the original venue, to 'keeping our name out there' and 'making space for us and people like us,' into something more consciously like, 'What can we do that other people are not doing, that we need or want to see?'" Amy links the club night to the joy the group felt from securing planning protections: "After winning these protections, we got even more organized. We actively engaged with the broader LGBTQI+ community to recruit more volunteers. We incorporated as a Community Benefit Society, and we started running regular queer nights. This was a really exciting time for the campaign. We were creating nights and testing ideas rather than fighting back against something. Collective queer joy is far more exciting than planning documents!" We laugh while recognizing the power of the words. Those phrases—"testing ideas rather than fighting back" and "collective queer joy"—I find quite striking. So much scholarship focuses on the fighting back part. It's easy to forget, though we shouldn't, that finding moments of joy are just as important for our survival.

Lèse Majesté is an expression of queer joy. The name signals its "political messaging," Amy tells me. Lèse Majesté means the insulting of a ruler—"fighting back against property developers," she explains, "and showing that the value of our spaces cannot be quantified."

(Again, I hear in my mind the distinction between commercial viability and maximum profitability.) In their business plan, the group describes their intentions to re-center who feels like they belong in nightlife scenes: "These nights celebrate and center queer women, trans, nonbinary people, and platform Black and POC queer/trans performers and DJs. Lèse Majesté nights have been instrumental in creating much-needed inclusive nights for marginalized members of the LGBTQI+ community." FOTJA did not want the club night to become a group of "Joiners nostalgists," Peter says. "There was a whole world of drag kings and female and nonbinary DJs who just did not get platformed at all."

The campaign is still waiting to reopen the bar, but tickets for Lèse Majesté sell out. Although the party has become popular, the group desires something permanent, as we heard from other people as well. "Our goal has always been about securing a permanent space," Amy says. Why is that? I ask. Amy draws my attention to questions of scale and identity. "As much as we have our not-for-profit model in use throughout the production of Lèse Majesté from the tickets alone, like reinvesting revenues into creating more paid roles or increasing performer fees, we will be able to do this on a far broader scale with our own space, from hosting more nights and also having income from a profit-making bar." While this first point is connected with capitalist logics, Amy is intentional about ways of using permanent venues that are not shackled by those logics.

Regarding the second point, identity, Amy tells me that a party can be temporary, but queerness cannot. "At the moment, we have virtual or temporary spaces, but it's really difficult to wait and only be queer on the last Tuesday of the month." Peter expresses the same message. "What has been torn down are those permanent physical structures that we can exist in twenty-four seven. They form and hold us together as a community, and they've been ripped away from us. So, it's really important that we're fighting for something permanent."[22]

To accommodate insatiable demand, to make their events even more accessible, and to feel like they can exist in a more permanent way, the group is trying out something new: transfer their programming into a hybrid organizational form that is both temporary and permanent. In the prior section, we assumed that nightlife expresses itself in two general ways: more permanent places, like bars and nightclubs, and those which by comparison are temporary, like club nights. Yet there are numerous ways for nightlife to emerge! In London, another way, called *meanwhile use*, is an organizational form that lies somewhere in between the bar and a club night in terms of its temporality and spatial fixity. Returning to the Joiners, again as a case study, can teach us about this innovation.[23]

The model of a "temp-perm space," as FOTJA describes it in their business plan, converts what one think tank calls "forgotten spaces"—vacant buildings in the cracks of capitalism that are currently unoccupied and unused though awaiting redevelopment—into socioeconomic value for the local community. Meanwhile use is a loose designation for activities that can occupy an empty space during a window of opportunity while it waits to be developed for another purpose. The possible "before uses" (before a site is redeveloped) are expansive, from retail shops to bars, street food, skate parks, art galleries, and artist studios. In a policy report, Nicolas Bosetti and Tom Colthorpe explain how the model works, and why it works so well: "Meanwhile uses are usually defined by their short time frame, which makes them relatively affordable. Most landowners charge low or no rents for meanwhile spaces." The combined strategic and economic advantages of this model are the ability to execute an idea, or enact a project, on the cheap.[24]

The idea of exploring a meanwhile use space to throw a club night "will allow us to test our ideas and business model," FOTJA says, "as well as generate a surplus to fund our long-term aim to move into a permanent space." Peter tells me more about the economics: "The general vibe was, we cannot wait for the developers to get their act together, demolish the building, build a new one, go through a competitive process to win the lease, and then set up and open a space, particularly considering that by 2020, we had already been waiting and fighting for over five years. I think the pandemic had something to do with it too, as there was more of a feeling of trying to set up something quick and agile." Amy adds that meanwhile use models provide opportunities to learn. "Ultimately, we will be in the strongest position possible to secure a long-term lease after running a meanwhile use space," she says. In the interim, "having a venue, rather than temporary nights, will allow us so much more freedom in what we can create and facilitate others to create."

The viability of a meanwhile use space makes Amy rethink what it means to call something permanent. "It's interesting to think about quote 'permanence' here," she begins with air quotes. "Although the Joiners was a pub since the mid-nineteenth century, it was an LGBTQI+ pub from 1997 to 2015. As we have seen from the closures of LGBTQI+ spaces across London, there is no guarantee to a permanent venue." The model they are pursuing now lies on a continuum between an event that happens only once and lasts a couple of hours to a pub that has been around for centuries. "The meanwhile use space model is typically on the scale of years, as opposed to a pop-up, which is weeks or months," she explains, differentiating club nights from meanwhile uses. "I see this far more in-line with and offering some of the same benefits as a permanent space." The goal is to find a suitable site, agree on lease terms, redevelop and fit-out the space, seek planning conditions to change the use class, and obtain a license, if necessary (it will depend on the planning conditions that are granted to the space). Their plan strives to "generate surplus revenue from a viable business model."[25]

Meanwhile use spaces present an alternative to permanent venues when those are not available, are too expensive, or when a group desires something more regular and stable than an occasional club night without a residence. Peter says, "The idea of a meanwhile use space came from asking ourselves, 'How can we bridge the gap between putting on one night every two months, and opening a long-term space?'" Even though they seek to transition from less to more permanent, the club night component will remain consistent. "Our Lèse Majesté are run by FOTJA and will definitely be a regular feature in the new home," Amy reassures me. But they also want to support new initiatives, like Laurie and Lyall. "We are passionate about others being able to host nights in an accessible queer venue." A permanent place will give FOTJA more security, which in turn will enable them to redistribute their financial successes to supporting other groups. "We want to break down barriers to who is able to host nights, and we want to make more people feel they have a space where they are included and celebrated."

As a case, the Joiners moves our thinking outside a binary framework of bars or nights. Amy explains, "Though our transition will be somewhat linear from temporary nights to a meanwhile use space to, hopefully, a more permanent home, I certainly see a meanwhile use space as a massive step away from temporary nights." The point is not to ask which is best; they all have trade-offs. "Running a permanent venue is a huge undertaking," Peter admits, "and as a group of people working in full-time jobs with little experience of actually running a venue, it would have been taking on a lot."

Club nights, on the other hand, enable all kinds of experiments. "The advantages of temporary nights are you can concentrate all the stress and hard-work into a short period of utter terror," Peter says playfully. "To put it in project-speak, it's using agile methodology instead of the old orthodoxy of project management." Not knowing this language, I ask him what it means. "We'd book a date, arrange the lineup, get the artwork designed, then put the tickets up for sale, and then panic about how few we were selling, and how much it was all going to cost us, all in a six- to eight-week window." Sounds like a whirlwind! "It's developed into a really successful night," he reflects back in soothing tones, "which makes some money for the campaign but also generates income for performers, DJs, and the freelance staff we hire to help out. I like to hope it will continue to evolve and will be one of the big nights that we do when we open a space."

The emphasis on evolution is important. A half century ago, the mere fact that there was a building that was identifiably gay was a huge achievement. Many maintained blacked-out windows for privacy and safety, if not intentional anonymity. The relative permanence and institutionalized presence of the gay bar was a victory—political, social, and economic all captured inside the built structure. It's no surprise that we mourn the passing of these places, these embodiments of our history and civil rights. And yet, that permanence may no longer be exclusively essential. What matters now is for us to recognize a plenitude of possibilities for structuring nightlife, each with economic trade-offs. We can assemble these options on a continuum from less permanent (club nights) to semi-permanent (meanwhile use) to more permanent organizational forms (bars).

Club Night Economics

When I began writing this book, I knew that economics would matter to the story I would eventually tell, but I limited my thinking to land values, redevelopment, and gentrification—recurring ideas in the UCL study, mayoral reports, and research in my home discipline of sociology. These concepts wrapped my imagination in frameworks of loss and deficit, and they directed me to think in isomorphic ways about gay bars, focusing on why they are closing without seeing much else in the field of nightlife. The Londoners I met, however, took me to new places that prioritize creativity and community over capitalism.

Each person I spoke with helped to refine how I thought about the economic foundations of nightlife. "There's a certain poverty to the debate already," Zax pronounces with authority. "We're only talking about venues that extract money from us." For Zax, conversations about bar closures are located in narrower habits of mind. "We're framing this debate in very capitalist terms because we think those are the only community spaces that we have left. But within my lifetime and beyond my lifetime as a queer, and then as an actual living being, there have been so many other kinds of spaces that are about more interesting things." Club nights provide an example of these "more interesting" things—and they are thriving beyond impoverished public and academic forums that focus on the loss of gay bars. That these occasional gatherings are succeeding suggests to Zax, as it did to Samuel and as it does to me, that "the economic model has shifted massively" and that "there are different ways of organizing." The structure of club nights, and their economics, are each enormous topics on their own, yet the more we explore, the more these ideas fit together.

Here, we considered the many bold (and necessary!) economic principles that culture creatives are exploring to ensure that queer nightlife survives beyond the current spate of closures. Crack capitalism, community enterprises, redistributive efforts, and meanwhile use models all promise emancipatory possibilities. After critiquing the "traditional business model" of a bar in our conversation, Samuel concludes with a revision, what he calls a "social democratic business model" that encompasses many of these initiatives. This is a more sustainable approach, he argues, because it redefines success away from an exclusive focus on profit margins. As a "micro business," a phrase Dan uses, club nights are freer from traditional capitalist pressures, including escalating rents, responsibilities of staff, and other costs that come with owning a venue. Parties provide a creative outlet not just for partygoers but also for the organizers, who are quickly learning how to create new worlds—even when capitalism crushes.

The Cocoa Butter Club

Underbelly

The buzz was infectious on the Southbank. People were chatting about which artists they had seen before, while first timers were intoxicated by the suspense. "Spaces like these are so important," someone behind me said while I waited for my Pimms at the atmospheric outdoor bar. I'm at Underbelly. The pop-up entertainment festival, which takes place inside a 400-seat spiegeltent, features all kinds of live acts, from stand-up comedy to circus and cabaret. That Saturday night, I paid £20 (US$25) to see The Cocoa Butter Club, an award-winning performance company that showcases Black, Asian, and racially othered performers. Founded in 2016 by Sadie Sinner—the UK's sixth most influential cabaret star—the company calls itself "a creative clap back to cultural appropriation, lack of representation and imitation, such as black-facing." Their stage celebrates artists with intersectional lives—people who appear as afterthoughts, if at all, in mainstream creative industries, people whose work has been a main influence but never the main event.

Shortly after I was seated inside the tent, the show started with a recitation over the loud speaker of what sounded like a manifesto: "Performers of color are under-booked and under-represented but through no fault of our own." Everyone stopped shuffling and listened. "The people who write the screenplays and stage plays did not grow up seeing bodies like mine in a positive light. We are often pigeonholed into playing the sassy best friends, the felon, or the cook. Now, don't get me wrong—we *can* cook, but we can do so much more!" The audience laughed. "So, ladies, gentlemen, and those who transcend the gender binary, please disregard the archetypes, throw away the tropes, and let's celebrate the melanated!" The deafening applause suggested the deep resonance of the words to an audience filled with faces that looked like mine.

Standing 5 feet 9 inches in flats—6'1" in heels—creative director "Sadie Sinner the Songbird" stepped onto the stage to introduce the program. Her dark skin and cheek piercings glistened under the theater lights. Sadie serenaded us with a songbook that visited Black vocalists, highlighting tracks by Beverly Knight and songs of revolution by Andra Day. Tonight, Cleopantha—ranked third in the World Burlesque Top 50—kicked off the show. A fierce performer who blended political commentaries about the global Black Lives Matter movement with Janet Jackson tracks from *Rhythm Nation*, Cleopantha was already well known in the city as a superstar who combines hip-hop with striptease. Wearing a silver two-piece and black knee pads, she had us screaming with her sexy moves, especially when she removed her bra to reveal fist-shaped pasties!

From vocals to burlesque, politics were front and center. The night gifted me drag kings like Mr. Wesley Dykes who, wearing a black harness under a red fur coat, delivered spoken word poetry, artists like Demi Noire who danced with fire, aerial performances, ensemble dance routines, and lots of big, shiny rhinestone costumes.

Near the end of the program, Sadie welcomed to the stage Zaki Musa, "the flying pole king of queers." Zaki appeared with an LED mask, a leopard print leotard covered in rhinestones, and 6-inch black

The always-smooth Cocoa Butter Club flanks Sadie. Photo credit: Aimee Mcghee.

heels. He sauntered down the stage, accompanied by the sultry sounds of R&B. Zaki slowly took in the sight of all of us in the audience as a flying pole was lowered to him. The beat dropped, Zaki gripped the pole as it was lifted into the air, and he started to spin. He lifted his feet over his head and back again, pulling off tricks I couldn't believe were possible while suspended in the air. The audience held its breath as Zaki looked down on us from the top of the circus tent.

Soon enough, we were all on our feet, singing again with Sadie as she belted out "Show Me Love," a beloved house track from the 1990s by Robin S. We danced and hugged as the cast left the stage. And then, just as we thought the night was over, crew members appeared out of nowhere, quickly removed the seats from the tent, the DJ hit play—and a dance party began!

Wearing a knee-length sparkly red dress, Cassie, who is the producer of the show, joined me on the makeshift dance floor. "What did you think?" she asked as we jumped up and down together. "I loved it," I beamed. Smiling as she listened, Cassie explained that the motivation of The Cocoa Butter Club was to correct underrepresentation "with every cabaret performer we can find." How do you do that? "We want to see Black aerialists. We want to celebrate Southeast Asian drag kings and South Asian burlesque performers. We want to encourage Middle Eastern pole dancers and Pacific Island poets."

And that they did—flamboyantly and sensually. In that sweet moment together, we seized the joy of being melanated, something that, as I walked across Waterloo bridge back home and then down memory lane later that night, I realized has not always served me so well.

4

A Core of Whiteness

The words still make me cringe.

I had spent the day working on my dissertation—I was a grad student in the mid-2000s—when a friend called, convincing me to take a break and meet him at Roscoe's, a gay bar. There was so much we loved about the place on a Sunday afternoon in Chicago: singing to retro '80s and '90s music, cheap pitchers of Long Island ice tea, free popcorn, billiard games inside and summer sun outside on the patio where we wound down the weekend arm in arm.

My vocal chords, tingling a bit after I had belted out my best Whitney, demanded a drink—and so I walked to the bar to order a pitcher. The place was buzzing, as always. A twenty-something White guy walked up next to me as I was waiting for the bartender. He didn't say hello, just tap-tap-tap on my shoulder and then, "Where are you from?" I turned and looked at him. "I'm from here." "No—where are you *really* from?" he insisted, with a grin. I was trying to be polite; that's what my parents taught me to do when my Brown skin drew attention. I explained that my parents were born in India, but I grew up in the suburbs. "I've never been with an Indian guy before," he said as he traced his index finger along my forearm.

I froze.

Was I embarrassed? Angry? I couldn't tell in the moment—but I had the sense of feeling small, like someone tried to steal my joy. I pulled my arm away. "I'm not your ethnosexual adventure."

It sounded better in my head.

Earlier that morning, I was reading Joanne Nagel's *Race, Ethnicity, and Sexuality*, which provided me the language. But the words, and the triumph they were supposed to create, got lost in translation somewhere between his flirtation and my fury—and a futile attempt to manage my feelings by retreating into my mind. He shrugged his shoulders and walked away to rejoin his friends. I tried not to watch them, but I still saw. They huddled together, looking first at him, then at me. And then they laughed.[1]

I'm of Indian descent, although I was born in Karachi after partition forced my parents, then kids, and their parents to move to Pakistan. Some part of me, on my mom's side, is Persian. But I grew up in the Midwestern United States, although I also lived for a long time in the South and the Northeast. Now, I call the west coast of Canada home. I have dark skin and big brown eyes. After going to gay bars for the better part of my adult life, I have noticed that some people, like that guy in Chicago, seem intrigued when they see me; others, as best as I can tell, don't even notice that I exist. Both types of moments can make me feel diminished, an experience shared by many people of color, like we don't belong in those places. "When someone asks you where you're from, and they're like, 'Oh, what did you say?' We all know what that means because we've all experienced it." Soof's words in London reminded me of that moment in Chicago. "We all know how loaded something like that question can be."

Always Under Attack

Although I love gay bars, I have been hurt many times by racially charged interactions in places I thought were supposed to provide a refuge. As an academic, I have also witnessed, in countless pages of scholarship, how assumptions about race color the arguments that researchers make about gender and sexuality, neighborhoods and nightlife. All this made me curious about the concerns of the people

I partied with in London. What would they identify on their own, without any prompt from me?

I was surprised by how specific their focus was—race was by far the primary problem people returned to again and again. Its centrality comes from the places on which public discussions about nightlife focus, and the experiences, especially in gay bars, that people are primed to think about as a result. Ben Campkin, who, recall, is the lead author of the UCL study, remarks, "The media discussions that have been dominating this debate have largely been about White gay men's spaces because the vast majority of licensed premises are owned and run by White, gay, cisgender men." madison, the founder of Opulence, offers a companion argument about why we need to broaden the conversation beyond the bars: because of "racism in the gay community," they say unflinchingly, which is "the reason that a lot of these parties exist." If our response to the disruption caused by bar closures is to champion them, and *only* champion them without offering careful critiques or support for other opportunities, we might miss what madison is drawing our attention to: there are problems, like racism, associated with gay bars—and new worlds are forming in an effort to reorient nightlife, to create new centers, for people who have felt excluded in those bars.[2]

It's not just the party producers who say these things. Racism "definitely exists" in LGBTQ+ communities, as Matthew, who identifies as Black, emphasizes. "There is a difference of how you're treated depending on your race—or your experiences will be different." In one study, 80 percent of queer Black respondents, 79 percent of queer Asian respondents, and 75 percent of queer South Asian respondents reported racial bias from *within* the LGBTQ+ community.[3] This pain provides the raw material for creativity. "Marginalized people stride through their annihilation, turning pain and struggle into opulence," madison adds, leaving goose bumps on my skin. Gay bars were, and in many places around the world still are, a radical invention, because they create a place where many LGBTQ+ people feel like they belong. No matter how much better things have become, no matter that sex is decriminalized and our relationships legally recognized, knowing that there is a door you can walk through, a room in which you can feel utterly yourself, is a source of unending power. That power, historically, derived from experiencing the gay bar as a refuge from the wider homophobic world.

But today, there are groups of LGBTQ+ people who sometimes need a refuge *from that refuge*. Naeem, who helps to run BBZ, explains how these underground parties confer feelings of safety and belonging that are not possible for everyone to enjoy at the bars: "It's important for people who experience a lot of fuckery in their day-to-day lives, as there are very few spaces where no self-surveillance is happening, where marginalized people feel prioritized and where they are in communion."[4]

Even if an individual at a gay bar is not being actively hostile, queer people of color still anticipate mistreatments. Why? you might wonder. For the simple reason that a minority sexuality does not vaccinate people from racism. Jonathan, who identifies as Mixed race, tells me that he had to unlearn the assumption that gay people could not be racist because they, too, were oppressed. "I remember when I was a lot younger and going out into Soho and going to gay spaces, this naïve thinking that because everyone in the room had understood oppression or prejudice in some way that they couldn't be racist." That perspective changed as he synched his experiences inside gay bars with his daytime life. "It was a rapid education of 'that's not the case.' It mirrors the rest of my experiences engaging in society. Certainly, I have experienced racism in gay spaces." It's unavoidable, Jonathan says with a slightly anxious laugh, "because there are White people everywhere." He has become accustomed to questions like "But where are you *really* from"—as I have—or telling people at gay bars, "Don't touch my hair, or whatever it might be, whatever the specific experience."

Matthew shares another example that will be familiar to many readers. He is most aware of being racialized in a gay bar "when you're told that you're good-looking—*for a Black guy*." That, "or when people actively look for a Black guy. It's difficult for me." Matthew had to learn that gay men, by virtue of possessing a sexuality that is still sometimes stigmatized and often discriminated against, are not exempt from harboring racist sensibilities. When someone decides they want to have sex with you because you're Black, like what happened to Matthew, or because you're Indian, like what happened to me, those moments of being objectified, reduced to less than a whole person, are painful. And so, despite the gay bar's fantastic importance, it is not always a place where everyone feels like they belong.

Whether a graduate student in Chicago or a researcher in London, race frequently rises to the surface of my interactions, as it did for many of the people I met. But *how* it does is not always the same—and that difference matters. As do the power dynamics of the places where our interactions occur, the forms of belonging and nonbelonging they fashion *within* LGBTQ+ circles—those things absolutely matter. madison poses a question that, with its haunting prose, can point us to the insights these differences hold: "What does it mean for queer people of color to embrace the body, a body that they're told to hate, a body that they're told they shouldn't have, a body that is always under attack?"

Bigotry Without Bigots

Following the killing of George Floyd, the networks PBS and NPR jointly conducted a poll about whether people—Americans, in this case—recognize racial disparities in their daily life. Thirty-two percent of those who responded to the poll in 2021 said that the police treat people of color more harshly. This number is up seven percentage points from a similar poll conducted six years earlier. There are significant racial disparities in these perceptions: 25 percent of White respondents said that people of color are treated more harshly, whereas 61 percent of Black respondents felt the same. These differences persist when pollsters ask questions about race relations and racial progress more generally. In 2019, the Pew Research Center asked, "Are race relations in the US generally bad?" About six in ten Americans (58%) said race relations in the country are, in fact, bad. And here's what the numbers look like when we break them down: 56 percent of White respondents agree, compared to 71 percent of Black respondents. Eddie S. Glaude, Jr., a professor of African American studies, offers a pithy explanation: "White America just doesn't see the state of race in the same way." We can never fully understand how another person perceives the world, of course, but we know, almost by default, that all of us have some biases and blind spots. And yet, it seems clear that there are stark differences in how different groups of people think about race.[5]

Everyone we are meeting in this book lives in London, not the United States, but British commentators arrive at the same conclusion. *Al Jazeera* reports, "Britain has faced an uncomfortable reckoning with race since the death of George Floyd, a Black American, at the knee of a US policeman in May 2020 sparked anti-racism protests around the world."[6] To take the pulse of local attitudes, the European Social Survey asked a representative sample of Britons about "biological racism," or whether people believe there are innate differences between racial and ethnic groups. This was the question: "Do you agree that some races or ethnic groups are born less intelligent than others?" Those who would answer yes are seen to espouse attitudes about racial superiority, a core component of racism. Here are the results: 19 percent of the British public agreed with the question, a substantial minority (about one in five). Those who subscribed to notions of racial superiority were more likely to oppose immigration and to express "nativist" views, such as the importance of English ancestry to identify as truly British.[7]

Discriminatory behaviors can accompany attitudes like these. In one study, a group of researchers changed names on a job application to reflect typical Black or Muslim backgrounds. For every ten positive replies that a British applicant (e.g., James or Emily) received, a person with a recognizably African (e.g., Akintunde or Adeola) or Pakistani name (e.g., Tariq or Yasmin) received only six. *The Guardian* replicated the study by sending expressions of interest from "Muhammad" and "David" to a thousand online advertisements for rental rooms across the country. For every ten positive replies that David received, Muhammad received only eight. These findings provide evidence of persistent racial basis and discrimination in Britain, like in the United States. Aware of these studies, Aisha, a party organizer, concludes that there is a "core of whiteness to every experience in the UK."[8]

The numbers aren't far off. In 2019, 85 percent of people in Britain identified as White, 8 percent as Asian, 3.5 percent as Black, 1.8 percent as Mixed, and 1.9 percent as "other."[9] Lola, who is African British, lives with someone who travels to other countries to get away from that core of whiteness. "My housemate, an Asian gay guy, goes to the States every so often just so he can not feel invisible somewhere for a while, you know—because you just don't exist." Lola slowly shakes her head. "A lot of people are really tired of very White spaces."

It's a curious and confusing sensation, being a visible minority yet feeling invisible as a whole person. Consider that guy who insisted on knowing where I was really from. For me, the answer was obvious: I'm from Chicago. But that response did not look logical to him—Chicago equated with White, but my face was not. Did that assumption make him racist? Many White people, researchers find, will tell you that they are well-intentioned, color-blind even; they "don't see any color, just people."[10] Still, that man at Roscoe's enforced an outsider status for me with his insistent question. Sometimes, people like him are "even trying to be culturally sensitive," Sapna Cheryan and Benoît Monin argue in their work on identity denials. "When people compliment an established Chinese American legal scholar on the quality of his English after he gives an elaborate talk, they are trying to be nice. And when strangers ask Asian Americans where they are really from, it is often in an effort to show cultural awareness and to respect regional differences rather than lumping all Asian Americans into one amorphous identity." That may be the case, but when you hear questions like it regularly, "it serves as an oppressive reminder that they are not perceived as American"[11]—or British. Being well-intentioned does not negate or excuse racist behaviors.

From pollsters to people going about their daily lives, what we have seen and heard already—and we're just getting started—is reminiscent of what Eduardo Bonilla-Silva calls "racism without racists." I would guess that many White gay men would object to the idea that they are racist—or sexist, or transphobic, or biased against any specific segment of LGBTQ+ people. I guess it's possible that guy in Chicago had no idea he was being racist with his words or the nonconsensual way he traced his finger along my forearm; he probably was trying out a line. Maybe he thought he was being flattering, in much the same way that I have seen men at straight bars saying awful things to women without understanding why their approach, or what they say, comes across as cringe-worthy. Many of our biases are baked in. And so, here we find ourselves in a core of whiteness and white ignorance, subjected to interactions where queer people of color, out to enjoy themselves, experience bigotry without obvious bigots. To understand the revolutionary power of club nights, places that provide a refuge from the refuge gay bars once provided, we need to examine the serious problems with the current White, gay, male-dominant discourses of LGBTQ+ culture.[12]

A *Good* Gay Venue

If an entire country can feel for some people like it has a core of whiteness, then it should come as no surprise that smaller pockets, places like gayborhoods and gay bars, will present in similar ways. "It certainly is predominately White in Soho," Sam, who is Mixed race, says. Many find this feature of the gay district jarring, since London is the most ethnically diverse region in the country. In fact—and quite unlike the demographics of the country as a whole that we saw earlier—the capital has the *smallest* percentage of people in the region who identify as White British (36.8%) and the *most* who identify as Asian, Black, Mixed, or coming from other ethnic groups (46.2%).[13] Elliot, an urban planner, picks up on this disparity between the city, which is racially diverse, and Soho, which presents as White. "The gay scene is very White compared to London's overall demographic makeup," he remarks. "You expect it to be more diverse." Whiteness affects how his friends experience gay bars. "I know from my Asian friends, just their experience, that the gay scene can be quite racist. It can be quite exclusionary to people who basically aren't White." Michael, who identifies as Jewish, sees it too—and it influences where he and his friends go out. "There are gay bars, but they don't really cater to a wider variety of people than gay middle-class White men. I don't really see that as a place that most of us would frequent on a regular basis."

This portrait of a blanketing and stultifying whiteness might feel a little extreme to you. After all, what about all those rainbow crosswalks? And Pride stickers in storefronts? Advertisements on bus stops? Katayoun, a twenty-two-year-old genderqueer Iranian, responds to the objection: "I feel like a lot of LGBT ideas have been so whitewashed and capitalized on, like the whole thing of 'some people are gay, get over it,' or 'love is love.' Yeah, but so what? What are you actually achieving by saying that?" It's a great question, and I also explore it with Erkan, who talks about the operations of power. "Queerness is cool," they say about the sea of rainbow crosswalks, stickers, and ads. "It's a currency. It's something which you can weaponize." Symbols as weapons is a strong though apt analogy, something we have seen at other times in history. It can help us think through the conundrum of being marked yet still feeling invisible in gay neighborhoods and at gay bars. "The narrative," Erkan explains about the symbols of sexuality in Soho, "is a way to co-opt a space without having to hold yourself accountable for the racial aspects." Flying the flag, in other words, provides the optics of diversity and difference while remaining silent specifically about race and racial representation.[14]

One of the most common ways of ignoring racial accountability is by denying others the right to define who they are and, especially, where they are from. Chris and I swapped stories about our experiences in gay bars. "Even though people say, 'Where are you from?,' I always say 'British,' and then they imply like, 'Where are you *actually* from?'" These are the moments when he wonders, as I did in Chicago, why people push. It's because "I'm darker or got dark features," he speculates, and because he is multiracial. Chris tries to "downplay it," telling people who ask that "my mum's half Mexican. That's just what I say. That's where I get my color from, is how I word it."

After we banter for a bit, Chris tells me that "I see myself as kind of White," although he quickly corrects himself: "Well, no, I wouldn't say White. That was the wrong word. I see myself as British." He acknowledges that "I have a weird relationship with my ethnicity because, I don't know, I just see myself as British." Perhaps it's his multiracial background. "When the forms come on, I never know what to put on them. Is it Mixed British? Is it Mixed Other? So, I just put British." As I hear the words, I wonder if our need to belong is so deep and so fundamental that it can motivate some who are multiracial to identify as White. "I don't ever see myself as different," Chris says, even though he is visibly not White. Aisha was right to assert that there is a "core of whiteness to every experience," although we hear from Chris how people internalize this atmospheric quality of race and race relations.

Like others, Dwayne, who identifies as Black British, is also fatigued by the implied assumption (or at times the overt demand) that everyone should try to fit in or be passively inclusive. "I think it's no longer acceptable to say we're inclusive. You have to prove it, and you have to mean it." While Dwayne enjoys spending time in Soho, he thinks the amount of attention gay bars pay to race is inadequate. "If you do a head count on a Friday, Saturday night, there won't be many people of color in Soho." This is an easy enough observation to make on any weekend night on Old Compton Street. "As wonderful and as iconic as Soho is, it was led by White European-origin men. And so, it's no surprise that that's how it looks now. They've catered for it. That's how it's shaped, and that's how it's become." Gay bars, while vital, can reflect a legacy of whiteness.

Fixing the problem needs to go beyond putting up rainbows. "You can't just stick a rainbow flag up," Dwayne continues. Actions speak louder than symbols. "It's no longer just enough to be a gay venue. You have to be a *good* gay venue." Dwayne uses this provocative idea as an act of protest against rainbow-washing or other gestures that passively declare "everyone is welcome here because we're all gay." That kind of messaging glosses over real differences between people. "There was a time when we just needed a gay place, somewhere to feel safe and comfortable," Dwayne adds to extend his argument. "It's not enough anymore." What then do we do? "Everyone needs to be involved in the conversation," he replies, gesturing as a metaphor to empty seats at the table where we were seated. "If I was young and coming out again as a Black person in London, it's important for me to see somebody who looks like me." While Dwayne cannot say for certain "whether it's a conscious thing or not," the way gay bar owners manage the identities of their patrons, he can see that "it's happening," the use of rainbow flags without addressing other ways in which we are different, like race. "There's nothing in Soho for me," he concludes.

I love Dwayne's clarity, a blunt assessment of progress and our shortcomings. A couple of generations ago, the opening of a gay bar was a radical act. We now require more from these venues than for them to just exist. Consider an example about a staple at many gay bars: drag shows. "Do you watch *RuPaul's Drag Race*?" I nod and say yes to Lola. "Last season, Charlie Hides [a White British American drag queen] had a blackface character called Laquisha Jonz at the RVT [the Royal Vauxhall Tavern, a gay bar]. Someone got in touch with the RVT and said—didn't go to him [Hide], just went to the RVT—and said, 'He has loads of characters. Can we just not have this [one] character? It's not cool.'" How did the RVT respond? I ask. "RVT ignored it," she reports. Lola tells me that the person who made the complaint, Chardine Taylor-Stone, created a petition—and a thousand people signed it. I was able to find the complaint. In it, Taylor-Stone writes, "Laquisha Jonz is a racist act based on misogynist stereotypes of Black working-class women. It is outdated, offensive, shameful and has no place in the LGBT community. The LGBT community is more than just White gay men, and we all should be able to feel that we are safe and respected when attending places that are meant to be for ALL of us."[15] Imagine how you would feel if you were a queer person of color and suddenly found yourself watching blackface in a gay bar. madison answers how you would experience the place: "it's not really for you."

The blackface controversy by a fifty-two-year-old drag artist from Boston made international headlines. Hides "has come under fire for portraying offensive black characters," *The Guardian* notes, and they were "not removed or edited out of the show." The controversy acquired enough momentum to force Hides to cancel additional performances in London. James Lindsay, chief executive of the RVT, released the following statement: "RVT has been monitoring the ongoing situation with regard to complaints about the act Laquisha Jonz. Our venue is steeped in rich LGBTQ history, and we pride ourselves on supporting the community as a whole. It is for this reason that the character of Laquisha Jonz will in the immediate term not perform at RVT." Lola says that Taylor-Stone, the person who set up the petition, continues to receive "harassment" for the situation "from his fans, who are like, 'What's the problem? Leave it alone. Why are you so pressed about this?'" Hides and his fans "live in this bubble," Lola says, where racism is not real. "How have you missed that blackface is not a thing anymore?"[16]

What makes a gay venue a *good* gay venue will vary from person to person and place to place, but our individual definitions and institutional actions reveal what we have (or have not) endured in our own lives. The distinctions we make in these moments matter. For example, to say that gay bars are safe places or that they challenge social norms about sexuality requires us to assume a heterosexual audience. On its own, this is too simplistic a view because it leaves race unarticulated and thus unaddressed. But now look what happens when we allow a self-reflexive assessment among LGBTQ+ people—they as their own audience creating distinctions between "gay venues" and "good gay venues": the core of whiteness becomes impossible to ignore. Gay bars might feel like safe places vis-à-vis heteronormative expectations, but they can still feel like unsafe places, against a White background, for people of color.

Intersectional Failures

If whiteness functions at once as "nothing (invisible) and everything (normal)," to borrow from English professor Tammie M. Kennedy, then how can people stir it to the surface? The Hides/Jonz controversy shows that exclusions can have multiple, interlocking parts—"a racist act based on misogynist stereotypes of Black working-class women," as we heard earlier. Consider another example. Nadine from Pxssy Palace tells me why they seldom go to gay bars: "I never feel comfortable at these places, especially because it's run by White gay men, and they've got the exact same problems as White straight men. I don't see a lot of differences between them, apart from who you choose to sleep with." For Nadine, whiteness is not exclusively about racism; broader power dynamics are also at play. Nadine draws our attention to a gap between the people in LGBTQ+ communities who have power, often expressed as White *and* male, and everyone else. In doing so, they expose the intersectional failures of gay bars. Proposed by Kimberlé Crenshaw, a pioneering scholar of civil rights and critical race theory, the idea of intersectional failures highlights situations where one form of inequality, like sexuality, can override others, like race, gender, and class.[17]

Tia and I also talk about these ideas. Recall that she is part of a collective of Black queer artists who produce BBZ. The club night is an arts-inspired, curatorial party designed to uplift queer women, trans and nonbinary individuals, and people of color in nightlife. As someone who does this work, Tia is tuned into identity politics. "Bars in Soho are very, very, very heteronormative, and very focused on gay men," she stresses. "Those spaces are also very White." To describe a bar as focused on White gay men *and* to call that place heteronormative might seem like a contradiction. A shorthand for such a place is to call it "homonormative," a word that describes the tendency among some LGBTQ+ people and places to leave uncontested the norms and values of heterosexuality.[18] The refusal to critically interrogate one category, like sexuality, makes it easier for others, like race (whiteness) and gender (maleness), to slip unnoticed through the gates of power and privilege. This is why, Tia says, "nightlife doesn't allow for people like myself, or people of color in general, to be able to just exist."

The association between gayness and whiteness is so entrenched that places which historically have been gay *and* Black are not remembered as such, or are seen *only* as Black but not gay, falsely implying the impossibility of Black gay existence. Em, a thirty-two-year-old White lesbian, speaks with me about Brixton, an area of the city that has a multiethnic population with a well-known Afro-Caribbean, Jamaican, and West Indian heritage. (She knows the place well because she teaches about it.) Historically, Brixton was a gayborhood—"but only if you understand that a gayborhood can simultaneously be a Black cultural area," Em explains. Most Londoners grow up learning that Brixton is "a Black neighborhood, and that it's rough, and it's where there were riots." That creates perceptual blocks to see it as also gay. "People can't imagine it as a gayborhood." I ask about its history. "It was a gayborhood," Em replies, "but it wasn't exclusively a gayborhood because it was a site of general left activism in the '70s and '80s and '90s. Now, it's got a high residential population, but there's not much queer culture. The bars have all closed. It meets some of the criteria of a gayborhood and not others." The nuance that Em offers to what a gayborhood means, distinguishing commercial, cultural, and residential components and then assessing how those meanings reflect racial and class experiences, is seldom expressed in the literature on gayborhood studies.[19]

In our conversation, Em describes Brixton's emerging identity: "Black people are seeing it as a gayborhood." In fact, some people of color "favor queer events in Brixton because they are less likely to be racist than White queer events [in Brixton] or queer events elsewhere that target particular populations." Katayoun sees land mines like these all across London. "I think a lot of bars are really into the idea of making sure they have more diverse events going on, so there's a lot of opportunities out there for anyone who's doing POC nights or a trans-specific event." Racial bias often halts the possibilities. "It's really hard to actually feel encouraged, because all the bar managers are people that don't even want to talk to you because you're not a White gay man. They can be very unapproachable." Profit takes precedence over political progress in these instances, which is how racial capitalism operates. "We need to encourage more people," Katayoun says, "because that's the only way we can change. I don't believe in begging White men or White people for giving us spaces."[20]

Intersectionality is a popular idea in policymaking, the sciences and social sciences, in public health, in activist circles, and among older and younger generations. Its favorable reception and recognition do not make the concept easy to understand, however. In order to grapple with multiple identities, some people engage in a thought experiment where they explore how experiences that are unique to one group might apply to another group. Consider a conversation I had with Julia. She discusses how race and gender jointly imprint onto the body: "I think how a White gay man walks through the city is different to a Black gay man," she says. That difference comes down to "racism," she adds, with gender privilege operating in the background as an assumption of being able to confidently occupy public spaces. Julia thinks "a lot of the city is geared towards a very White male thing. That's largely because, I think—let's say the Black community, or an Asian community, or any minority community struggles to find their own space." The many reasons for this struggle have a feature in common: "That has to be because you experience things differently. There must be something in that."[21]

Julia's experiences are informed by her identities—a thirty-something who identifies as Mixed race and a cis lesbian. Making gender explicit now, moving it from the background to the center, Julia allows herself to become vulnerable for a moment, sharing what it's like to take public transportation as a woman. "I was on the tube, and there was no one else on it." Immediately, I sense her anxiety. "It was quite late. And this guy in front of me goes like this to adjust his belt [she motions with her hands]. In that second, I thought he was going to take his trousers off and show me his penis." Moving through the city as a woman has primed Julia for encounters like these. "And that is because I have been shown a penis in the city four times. It's a pretty normal thing that any girl gets used to, is to go, 'Right, okay, this guy's about to show me his penis.'" The defensive position creates a feeling of difference—and danger. "What am I going to do? How am I going to play this? Am I going to bury my head in the sand and pretend to not see? It turns out he wasn't actually doing that at all. He was literally just adjusting his belt." Still, the experience left her shaken. "As a woman, you, from a very young age, have had to figure out and navigate that you are not as strong, and more likely to get raped, and so on. That means when a man adjusts his belt, I'm prepping myself for something that no man, I don't think, has ever experienced. I don't think any man would have ever, if they were sat in front of another man going like that with his belt, would ever think, 'Fuck, what am I going to do now?'"

Julia imagines that these "belt buckle moments," as she calls them, also affect people of color. "That's me from a female perspective. I think if you are Black, you might have those moments. I don't know what it is, because I'm not Black, but you will have your belt buckle moment where you go, 'This could go awfully bad for me. What am I going do to protect myself?'" I nod my head, as memories awaken. If someone calls me a "fag" while I'm walking down the street, which has happened more times than I care to count, it affects how I occupy space in the city, how I move along the streets. I become similarly alert when someone screams a racial epithet, leaving me to wonder whether the words will escalate. Homophobia and racism have presented as my personal belt buckle moments, sometimes separately, other times together. In saying this, I by no means intend to compare homophobia and racism, even though I experience both, but like Julia, to see if I can leverage an experience that I have had in one context as a way to better understand another set of circumstances. "How you experience the world is different," Julia says. I couldn't agree more—but the question for us right now is whether this kind of emotional work, the cultivation of empathy, accompanies the thought experiment. Julia doesn't think so. After all, few men sitting on a train, across from another who adjusts his belt, would freeze up and think themselves the target of sexual assault. "I tried to explain that to my very White male friends," the belt buckle moment she shared with me, "who are very smart, and sometimes I think, 'You just don't get it. You don't get it, and you don't see it.'"

The wider the gap between cognition, what we understand intellectually, and compassion, what we relate to emotionally, the harder it becomes to challenge the intersectional failures of gay bars. Meet James, a thirty-year-old gay man who identifies as White Irish. "I think gay bars are a great place," he says enthusiastically, "and it's a safe space. It's a great social environment, and you can hang out with friends. I think it's a good way of connecting with the wider society." Safety is a relational quality; it looks and feels different depending on who you are and with whom you are interacting. And so, I ask James who he has in mind. "A safe space for LGBT people," he replies. For *all* LGBTQ+ people? I wanted to follow up, although delicately, just to make sure. "Yeah. I think so. Definitely." After mulling it over a moment longer, James realizes his blind spots. "Obviously, I'm a White gay man," he says without any additional prompts. "I'm very privileged within the community." Although he recognizes his race and gender as sources of privilege, James thinks about his sexuality as locating him in the minority. "But I think definitely for gay men, they are a safe space." He does not intend to be exclusive—"I'd like to think that L, B, and T could feel safe and comfortable in those spaces"—but his positionality makes it difficult for him to appreciate the experiences of people who may not feel like they belong in those same places where James feels safe.[22]

James nervously asks "if that makes sense," and I nod without saying anything else. Still, he cannot shake his discomfort. "That makes me really sad," James says. Why are you sad? I ask. He tries to imagine what it might be like for someone else, maybe someone who looks like me, the person sitting across from him. "I think somebody else not being able to have that safe space is really tragic." I ask if his friends and he ever talk about race. "Uh . . . ," he hesitates. "I don't know if we do," he admits. "I don't think so. Not really." James describes himself as "the classic English person" who plays in a "gay rugby club" and socializes with friends at gay bars in Soho. They are "not a hugely diverse group of friends," he acknowledges. "I grew up in Henley, which is, I don't know if you know, it's a little town, but it was almost exclusively White. So, I think I've sort of fallen into that." I hear no malice in his voice or in his words, and he takes no pride in his very White world. What James now seems to be seeing is just how much he does *not* see. If a gay bar is full of other people like James, then how will that place feel for someone who is marginalized by more than just their sexuality?

Sometimes, White gay men can see their privilege, even if it might be difficult to talk about it. "It's the . . ." twenty-nine-year-old Sam trails off without finishing the thought. "Yeah, I'm gonna say it, why not—White gays are some of the most privileged people I've ever met, even more so than straight White men sometimes." Curious about the comparison, I invite Sam to say more. "Because they feel that their battle has been fought and won," he replies, alluding to the contentious debates about whether we have entered into a post-gay society. "They think they can go to any bar and enjoy anything that's going on, and acceptance, and they're not gonna be beaten up by it."[23]

This is a fallacy. By the end of the 2010s, one in four LGBTQ+ people still reported experiencing discrimination in everything from employment to housing. Among these individuals, 68 percent and 44 percent, respectively, said that it negatively affected their psychological and physical well-being. Rather than liberalizing attitudes that affect all LGBTQ+ people, these studies identify ongoing challenges with inclusion and belonging. Sam is familiar with some of these studies. "Hate crimes for LGBT people is on the rise," he echoes. However, White gay men sometimes don't see the bigger picture. "They don't want to have anyone tell them they're different anymore."[24]

What Sam describes does not make all White gay men racist all the time, but it does suggest the intersectional failures of gay bars as institutional expressions of LGBTQ+ communities and cultures. "Historically, White men were able to get into a position of power, so it makes sense that they own all of these spaces and these venues," Tia explains. Dwayne adds that being in a position of power, whether by race or gender or both, affects your consciousness. "As a society, we have these conversations about women and the need to empower women because the social hierarchy is dominated by men. But when we say that about people of color, or people who identify as gay, everyone runs away, or society says, 'No, no, it doesn't matter.' Of course, it matters." How? I ask. "I'm not saying that because of the hierarchy that White gay men who are leading our scene are racist," he clarifies. Dwayne draws an analogy with Fortune 500 companies to distinguish systemic racism from racist individuals. "When you talk about systemic racism, it doesn't mean that all CEOs of the top 500 companies are racist. It means that those at the top identify as men, usually straight and White. It doesn't mean the company is racist. It's just behavior." Dwayne circles back to how your background affects what you think is real and how you act. "You behave, and you lead, and you create policies by your own experience." Much of the power that White gay men hold is the result of their structural position, their privilege in the LGBTQ+ world relative to others. This opens the possibility that some of these individuals are unconsciously perpetuating problems because they are in a silo of their own experiences, unable to see or appreciate other points of view.

More than just a color or racial category, *whiteness* is a capacious ideology of power. When people talk about not being seen or not feeling welcomed in gay bars, they often use the word to reflect on the intersectional shortcomings of those places. These experiences within LGBTQ+ communities are as common as they are fraught. Anecdote after anecdote, sometimes it seems like White gay men are the new White straight men—the ones with power, the face of public places. Some of us may want to believe that their minority sexuality will make them uniformly progressive, or at least more compassionate, exempting them from the biases of their heterosexual counterparts. While this is sometimes true, racism does not discriminate by sexual orientation. Hence, the irony and tragedy of White gay men: they struggled for generations to cultivate a place of belonging in a bigoted world and to create communities that could be out and proud—yet now they are at risk of recreating similar circumstances that they spent decades trying to overcome.

An Intravention

If you go out to a gay bar in Soho, the most visible faces you see will appear White—and this will affect how you feel in that place. "Growing up, I just never thought it was something for me," Katayoun says about being queer. They describe images of White gay people, mostly men, that they saw around them. "Until I was maybe fourteen, I was like, Elton John and George Michael are the only gay people in the world!" They don't mean this literally—"like, not just them"—but what they represented, "what they stand for, like the White gay man." This they found suffocating. "I just couldn't imagine men of color being gay." Aisha, who described the "core of whiteness" in Britain, recounts how in high school, they too thought that being queer and racialized was impossible: "That's just something [White] men do." Later in life, Aisha met people who identified as queer *and* who looked like them. "When I met people that looked like me who said they were queer, I realized that's what I was—then I felt at home." Everything changed after that. "Queerness was this amazing new thing, like looking into a fresh future." How would you describe that future? I ask. Aisha replies that it's like "looking into something that basically represents the complete other side of the spectrum, and complete other reality of everything I ever learned."

This is exactly what it feels like at a club night—a "complete other reality" where White plus gay plus male is neither the assumed nor the default setting. Equally important are Aisha's words of "everything I ever learned" because they hint at how club nights can counter the assumptions that a person had once made, the things they thought they knew or were true. The power of these parties is their ability to alter the understandings we inherit, to flip them over, to create and experience other worlds.

For these reasons, I think about club nights as an *intravention* that can heal scars of exclusion and estrangement by scrambling and subverting the power dynamics of nightlife. Marlon Bailey defines that word as a practice that comes from within minority communities. He studies HIV/AIDS prevention strategies in Detroit, where public health interventions were designed to contain the infection among Black queer people and to keep the so-called general population safe. The problem with models that are imposed from outside the group, like government officials, is that they define particular bodies and communities using a set of biased assumptions—hence categories like "at risk" or "communities of risk," both of which stigmatize Black queer people. Based on his study of ballroom scenes, Bailey calls for a shift from *inter*vention to *intra*vention as a way to capture how groups who are marginalized by multiple vectors of power draw on "their own knowledge and ingenuity"—often exploring strategies like performance and dance in nightlife scenes—to construct a "community of support." Participants at the ball articulated a "counterdiscourse," Bailey argues, and they built a "site of refuge," relying on each other, rather than the government, for support during the AIDS crisis.[25]

I think we need an intravention to the intersectional failures of gay bars. More and more, we are understanding why, as madison says, people "take it to their own to start a night and create the world that they want to see." Like balls, club nights also articulate a counterdiscourse, other ways of being and other worlds of belonging. Unlike balls, however, club nights are not just responding to a hostile heteronormative world (e.g., racism from government interventions) but also exclusions from within LGBTQ+ communities (e.g., racism in gay bars). Club nights are thus a *refuge from the refuge*, places that provide relief from the soul-crushing, deeply disappointing, and awfully inevitable-seeming experiences that queer people of color can have at gay bars. "I was tired of going to parties where I felt ostracized for being queer," madison adds, "parties that didn't have a lot of people of color in them, parties that had DJs that were basically White men with the occasional White woman." The disillusionment could have been devastating, but madison prioritized creativity over exclusions. "I wanted to do something about that."

Club nights are a contemporary iteration of a rich legacy of creative destruction, reinvention, and cultural revolutions in nightlife. The closure epidemic has made these places more essential today, amplifying their unique forms and evolving significance in the field of nightlife. Erkan provides a powerful perspective about this outcome: "What needs to be commended in this situation is the fact that loads of queer people of color have developed the organizational capacity to be able to approach institutions and venues and organize outstanding events. Regardless of the lack of access which their identities may give, they still fight against all the obstacles and create these spaces." Club nights represent an intentional and radically inclusive vision for nightlife, one that addresses queerness at the intersection of multiple identities. They are places where people turn their pain into opulence.

Hungama

In a Converted Warehouse

One day at a midweek pub gathering after work, a new friend turned to me, somewhat out of the blue, and excitedly asked, "You're South Asian *and* queer?"

"Yes," I stammered in reply, startled by the sudden question.

And then, with even more thrill, they added, "What are you doing Saturday night?" I didn't know it then, in that frenzied moment, but the invitation would change how I experienced and thought about nightlife.

Saturday night came quickly. We took the train east from Covent Garden to Hackney Wick, nearly an hour's ride with transfers, and then walked for another while longer by a row of dimly lit, almost derelict looking structures. My friend pointed ahead to a door that looked to me like every other door we had just passed, leading into a building that again looked to my naïve eyes like every other building. "This is crack capitalism," I thought as we finally arrived and walked inside The Yard Theater, a late-night music venue in a converted warehouse that provides space for new ideas and new stories.

The room was large, but still, I felt immediately embraced by it. In front of the DJ booth, projected on a bare white wall, were clips of classic Bollywood videos. I recognized them instantly—*Devdas*, *Kuch Kuch Hota Hai*, *Khabhi Kushi Kabhie Gham*—and my heart tugged with

Scenes from Hungama, where "fierce" is always fashion-forward.
Image courtesy of Hungama (@hungama_ldn).

the sweetest nostalgia at the sight and sounds. The film projections, animated by a choreography of lasers, illuminated a full dance floor. But even that dance floor was unlike any other I had been on before. There were turbans and spangled saris. And bindis. So many sequined bindis!

This was Hungama. An Urdu word, it loosely translates to a celebratory chaos or commotion, a jubilant disturbance or disruption. The club night centered South Asian cultures—and honestly, it blew my mind. I didn't know any gay bars that did this or sounded like this, nor did I realize how good it would feel to be in a place that did, to

▸ Meet Ryan, multicultural maven and Hungama founder.
Image courtesy of Hungama (@hungama_ldn).

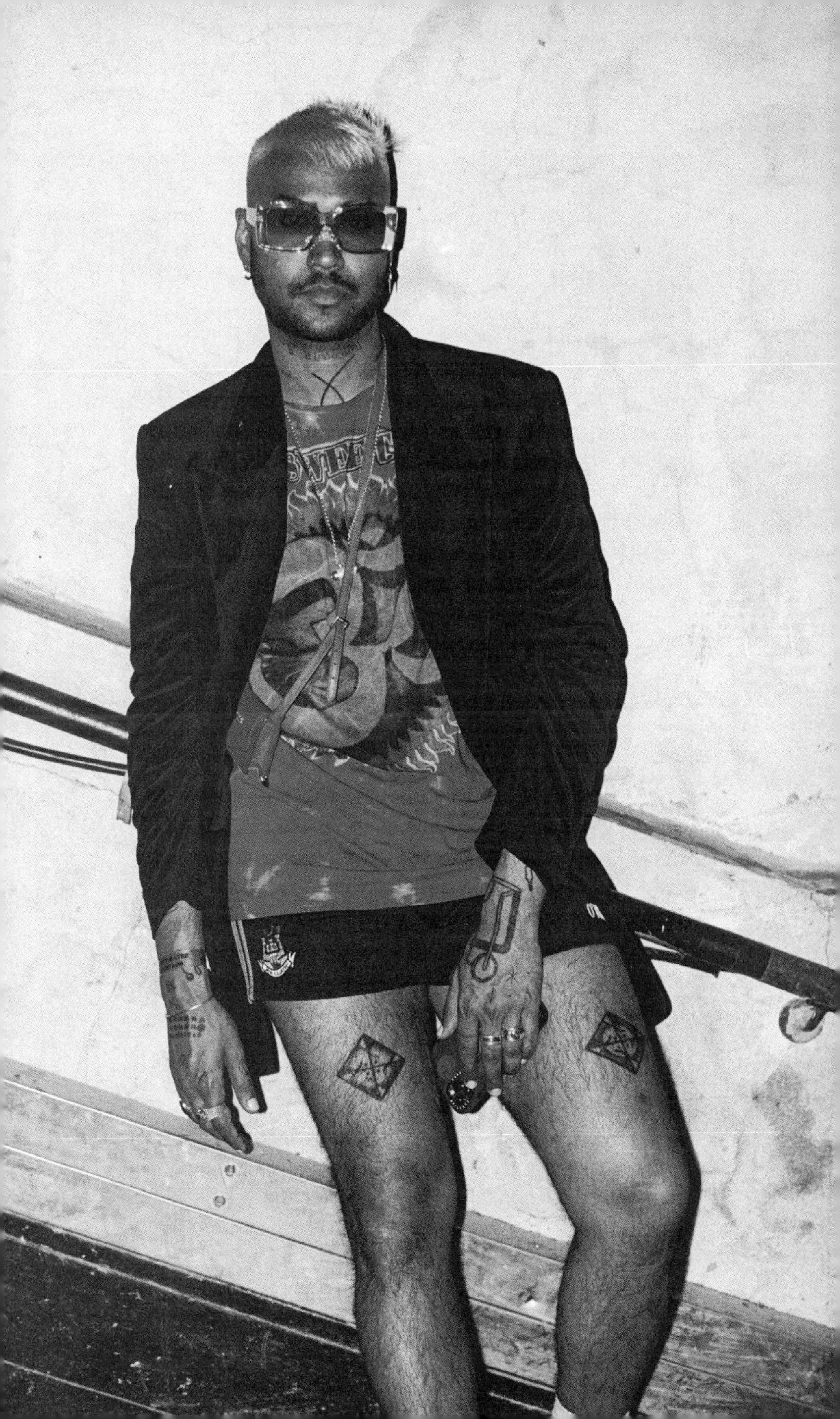

"My eyes are up here!" A visionary look at Hungama.
Image courtesy of Hungama (@hungama_ldn).

sing songs in Hindi on a queer dance floor. For the next four or five hours, nobody asked me where I was *really* from.

Ryan Lanji is the creative genius behind Hungama, and a DJ at the party. Two hours into his set, as I was reliving my childhood in an adult body that knew how to move better, Ryan took a break and joined me. I expressed wonder at what I was seeing and hearing, especially given

Emancipatory revelry at Hungama.
Image courtesy of Hungama (@hungama_ldn).

statistics about bar closures and the alleged demise of nightlife that everyone was talking about. "I don't think nightlife's in decline," Ryan objected. Placing his hands on my shoulders, one after the other and then slowly rotating my body in a circle, Ryan invited me to take in the scene. This didn't look anything like a place in Soho, I said. "Exactly," he replied. "Queer culture is evolving."

As we danced, I took note of how seamlessly Ryan switched between singing Bollywood hits and debating theories of diaspora. The South Asian experience is like "mercury," he reflected. "We're shape shifters, and so at moments we can become quite Black-oriented, or we can become quite queer, or we can become quite straight, or we can become quite White." I looked around to see if I could observe this mercurial character. When my eyes returned, Ryan told me that at Hungama, people could "embrace their chameleon." The audience is like a "color wheel," he noted. Ryan was right—and there we were, spinning together.

Hungama is part of "an explosive underground scene," *Vogue India* writes in its coverage of this Bollywood banger. Organizers like Ryan are "toppling the very structures that had so far alienated them from mainstream clubs," and they are creating "a nightlife movement that [QTBIPOC individuals] can claim as their own."[1] In the inimitable mix of sights and sounds at Hungama, I finally discovered a world that welcomed me, a cultural center where I belonged.

◂ Scenes from Hungama, where bindis beckon you back home. Image courtesy of Hungama (@hungama_ldn).

5

Reorientations

Hopefully, I am convincing you that club nights are a significant, and significantly different, alternative to the more common and visible forms of nightlife. We have seen, behind the scenes, the many experimental qualities of club nights and why they craft another world. They speak truth to power. "I think that's been a really empowering experience for a lot of people that I know," Rosie remarks. "It's given people so much confidence, because these are the people who are normally completely excluded from the mainstream party circuit." I want to push us even further now—beyond a plethora of points of view, creative organizational forms, and capitalist pressures—while recognizing that all these things are always at play. Club nights, I believe, are nothing less than a revolutionary shift in urban nightlife. The reason is simple though certain: the foundational ethos of club nights is radically inclusive—and intentionally so.

That night at Hungama, I understood what it means to reclaim nightlife so that Black and Brown people can occupy its center. Years later, in 2023, I receive a DM on Instagram about an upcoming party: "This Friday: Where You Really From?" A sudden surge of longing fills my heart as I read from Vancouver about this event in London that will feature DJs from Hungama. The digital flyer reads, "If you can understand the emotions that arise by the sentiment of this statement, then you'll know exactly why it's important for us to come together and create a new explosive vibration." A collection of memories, from being bullied as an immigrant kid at school to feeling fetishized at that gay bar in Chicago because of my darker skin, rise to the surface of my awareness, booming like a bhangra beat. I relive these times as I read the words, but something about the notion of an "explosive vibration" makes me feel freer. "Let's celebrate a night where we can be who we are and galvanized by where we are really from without hesitation and limitation, a new migration."

An ocean away, I wasn't able to attend the party, billed as "a celebration of queer euphoria and joy," but I had heard similar ideas many times before. "There's a real effort to make space for marginalized groups who aren't often in the conversation, to produce space," Zax told me. Tia similarly said, "I think that marginalized people, people who are of color, femme-presenting, queer—we have such a sense of community because we have to." That's why a party named "Where you really from?" is transparent about its goals: "We prioritize and center QTBIPOC in the space." What I *saw*, what I *heard*, and what I *felt* at events like Hungama—and there were others, so many others—forever changed me. There I was at the center of a dance floor that centered me in return.

In club nights, the subaltern speaks—and we dance with joy, like I did at Hungama and The Cocoa Butter Club—but is that to say that the parties *re-center* nightlife? The word came to my mind on those dance floors, and I heard it repeatedly from others, but it seems an impossible argument to make. It's like saying that nightlife has a whole new center, or that club nights are now the center of nightlife as a whole. I cannot substantiate either claim, as I would have to demonstrate that there is, in fact, some kind of a center. But more important, how much do the organizers of club nights actually care about *the* center of nightlife, of occupying it or becoming it? Club nights are powerful *because* they proudly claim the margins, *because* they find freedom underground. Those places, more marginal or peripheral than central, feel more experimental and revolutionary than anything we would call a center, or find in it. The center is the *opposite*. And so, it seems imprecise to say that club nights are re-centering nightlife, that their objective is to position themselves in the mainstream. This is not a story about assimilation![1]

Reorientation strikes me as a more apt image and analytical device, as it involves an active search to determine where we are located in relationship to a changing environment—without a presumption that any center is the most desirable place. As we will see, many club nights (although not all) enable QTBIPOC folks to emerge from their experiences of exclusion to find a place not at *the* center—but *their* center, places of their own choosing and creating. Nightlife is a cultural field, and as such, I think it can have multiple centers, each with dominant and dissenting players. Many club night organizers go to gay bars, after all, and bar goers enjoy club nights too. We also know that some bar owners, like Dan, produce their own club nights. There is not just one world, but a slew of social worlds with fuzzy and overlapping boundaries. In this field, this multicentered geography of nightlife, things are not mutually exclusive or singular, where one winner takes all, even though power dynamics are absolutely and always at play—within each center and across all the centers.[2]

In response to repeated instances of bias and bigotry, QTBIPOC folks are claiming places for themselves, and once inside, they are creating alternative scenes. The key is that these gatherings are happening in spatial and symbolic undergrounds, places where people flip all kinds of power scripts. Club nights are thus reorientations, opportunities to experience nightlife in other ways, to reacquaint ourselves with its many possibilities, to determine, and then determine again and again, where we are located and what is our purpose in relationship to a constantly changing environment. The results, as Nadine tells me, are euphoric: "It almost feels like the beginning of an orgasm to be around people that are a reflection of yourself."

Self-Care as Warfare

Every night out is not ecstatic, and nothing ruins a good night like prejudice. The more people I spoke with, and the more stories they told me about gay bars, the more I heard about bias bubbling up. One encounter flared a few years ago at a Black and Brown-person pop-up party hosted inside a gay bar. The organizers "were selling zines called Black Fly zine," says Nadine, who identifies as Scottish Pakistani. "The zine is about sexual freedom between POC people."

At one point during the night, "this White girl had a problem with it, and she started getting angry about it." The organizers kept their cool, indicating that "this is a positive magazine," and said, "Here, you can buy it." The creator of the zine intended to celebrate people of color. "There were no White people in the zine," Nadine tells me—and that's why the woman was bitter. Party organizers told her to "remember what night you're at"—and then the conflict escalated. "The White girl got so angry, even though they [the organizers] weren't being angry with her." Then, "she threatened to call the police, even though nothing was going on." Why did she do that? I ask. "For doing absolutely nothing apart from selling a zine." Eventually, the bar owners got involved. The venue promoted itself as "inclusive," Nadine says with an eye roll, "but because it's White-owned, they sided with the White girl. This is the kind of thing that goes on."

I felt frustrated and fatigued all over again. By now, I had lost count of the number of people who had told me stories about biases endemic within LGBTQ+ cultures and contexts. Belt buckle moments, blackface, where are you really from, and a body that's always under attack—these moments of intersectional failure kept occurring, over and over. A major problem in London is the lack of fixed venues that are owned by people of color. Lyall, who owns VFD, makes this point: "Weirdly, in the whole of London, I'm the only person of color who's queer, who owns their own venue, and runs it—in the whole of London. Apparently. That's according to the mayor's office." This is hard to believe, both for me and for Lyall—"to think that I'm the only one seems to me utterly ludicrous." Yes, but in Lyall's case, it motivates him to help others. "That also makes me even more alert to the need for these sorts of spaces." He allows access to VFD for culture creatives with ideas for a club night. "In the last couple years, I've been working with more people of color and QTBIPOC people and groups."

Assessing problems is just the first step. Nadine, for instance, did not want to waste their time complaining about racism. Instead, they wanted to shift the paradigm. "There's not enough Black- and Brown-owned spaces in London that cater to us, that are *for* us," Nadine emphasizes. "That's why I think it's important to have it centered." As we talk about racism, Nadine says that we need a response from within QTBIPOC communities—an intravention, as I called it earlier. "It's so important to have something that's Black- and

Brown-owned." This motivated them to form a collective with three other friends (Munroe, Skye, and Kasang) and use an approach they call "self-care as warfare."

Taking care of yourself is a radical act, but we have to do it, even if it involves a fight. Small house parties grew to 250 people, which propelled the trio down a path toward forming a club night, which they called Pxssy Palace. The party, as they say on their website, is "rooted in intentional nightlife." Munroe describes it as "a space where queer people of color can go and just express themselves and not be judged." Pxssy Palace was "born out of frustration," Nadine tells me. "It wasn't like we decided, 'Okay, well, let's do a club night. Let's do this.'" The other "gay places"—their words—"were all controlled by either White men or gay White men. We got really frustrated, we were fed up with it, but we didn't know how fed up with it we were." Their party is about "celebrating Black, Indigenous, and people of color who are women, queer, intersex, trans, or nonbinary. We provide space to dance, connect, and engage, whilst encouraging consent, sexual freedom, pleasure, expression, and exploration of our authentic selves." Pxssy Palace uses an intentional politics of intersectionality to reorient nightlife away from gay bars.

As I spoke with more culture creatives, a pattern formed in my mind: people who started their own night weren't in it to become rich, or because they were bored. More often than not, they were fed up with the status quo and wanted to do something about it. "Club nights will prioritize people of color," Rosie says. The goal of representation is part of a holistic effort that includes progressive redistribution initiatives, like the ticketing policies and taxi fund we considered earlier. "It's not just in the space that you're being prioritized," Rosie explains. "You may be a trans woman of color, but it's really the whole experience of getting to the venue. How do you get in? What happens when you're in there? How do you get home? How you're treated on social media?" This attention to detail is seldom seen in a regular bar. Club nights thus present a fundamental challenge to how nightlife organizations are structured, and what they are expected to provide. The practices that Rosie mentions, which we also heard from others, provide evidence that club nights are a completely different entity in the field.

Repeated confrontations in bars, like what Nadine described about the zine or the blackface moment at the RVT, motivate culture creatives to reorient nightlife in ways that allow QTBIPOC folks to feel recognized and respected. Let me introduce you again to Sadie. Identifying as Black British and Zambian, recall that she is the creative director of The Cocoa Butter Club. Sadie, who has had more than her share of similar infuriating experiences as Nadine, describes for a reporter from *BuzzFeed* why she founded a club night: "The Cocoa Butter Club was born from a frustration of seeing people who blackface," she says. "I was just sick and tired of it—that Black *bodies* aren't getting booked, but bodies that can do things which have strong connotations to Black culture *are* getting booked," even if they perform racist acts.[3]

Amidst this aggravating set of circumstances, the closure epidemic has offered some consolation and comeuppance. Sadie tells me, "I think there's a small joke when all of these places are being closed down, which is: How many people of color were their clientele? How many versions of not-a-cis-White-gay-man were these venues catering to? Perhaps those are the venues that are closing down, and the venues that are thriving or starting are ones which are founded by people of color." No one I had spoken with had been quite so blunt about bar closures. "What we need is more representation," Sadie offers as a proposal—and "culture pride." She has worked hard to "unlearn that my Blackness makes me undesirable." That had to go "out the window," Sadie confidently remarks. "I lost my Blackness because these places do not center our Blackness."

The Coca Butter Club is an award-winning company that showcases queer performers of color, as we saw at Underbelly. I wanted to hear from Sadie how she imagines the relationship between her night and other cabaret offerings. "One of the things I make clear about The Cocoa Butter Club is it centers Black bodies, but everybody is welcome," Sadie shares. "I have to make that clear, because there are always going to be the people who—I mean, it happened, you know, 'I can't believe she started an all-Black cabaret. How dare she?'" How do you respond to people who say things like that? "I was like, 'Actually, it's not an all-Black cabaret. It's a non-White cabaret. That's very different.'"

The distinction draws attention to the many centers of nightlife. If you go to The Cocoa Butter Club, then Sadie assumes that you understand what the place means, its impulse and inspirations. The audience members "all have in common that they value bodies of color, the art that they create, and they believe that they deserve a space." Sadie wants to catalyze conversations about recognition. "I want people to talk about it," she asserts. "Don't leave here saying, 'Oh, it didn't matter that they were Black, it didn't matter that person was Indian, it didn't matter that person was Chinese.' No, it did. It mattered that these people all had to start a night themselves, all had to get together and do this in one place. It *does* matter."

Cassie, who we also met, is involved with producing the show. "People of color need to see themselves on stage," she tells me—and in ways that push past "the trivialization of our culture," Sadie adds. She has in mind the mass-market versions of Black culture as fun, something White people can copy to feel cool. "Doing the walk, who's going to be the queen—the pattern is actually quite vapid," Sadie says.

Black people, like all people of color, have become wearily accustomed to seeing caricatures, or stereotypes, or trivialized versions of ourselves on stages, screens, and dance floors. That affects how we see ourselves—or, to put it more directly and to make it more personal: it can limit how you see yourself, how you imagine who you are, and what you think you can do. "That's ultimately why The Coca Butter Club exists," Cassie explains. She and Sadie share the vision, which is "always about centering bodies of color." Do you ever invite White performers? I ask Cassie. "No," she answers, "because White performers can go anywhere." There are not enough QTBIPOC places in London. "If there's no other space for performers of color, then ours should be special, and it should be sacred to that instead of being something that everybody can join all the time." Just as nightlife can have many centers, so too can inclusive spaces coexist with those that celebrate QTBIPOC individuals. "There should be some spaces where people of color can use the stage, and it centers them only, because that doesn't happen anywhere else."

A baseline of dealing with bias, along with the need to see yourself reflected in the places you go out, motivates culture creatives like

Nadine, Sadie, and Cassie to create new *nightlives*, plural, and prioritize themselves at one or more of its many centers. This is what I mean by reorientations—and it differentiates a queer space, like a club night, from a gay bar. "To me," Michael explains, "a queer space is different in that it's not defined by White gay men. And what it does, doesn't necessarily fit into the norms of what White gay men would want to do in a space." Consider as well my conversation with madison. I asked about Opulence, the name of their party. "With names," they reply, "describing something that resonates" matters, and it has to be "part of your vocabulary." This is where celebratory racial politics come into play. "There's a scene from *Paris Is Burning* that is showing, at a Vogue ball, one of the announcers talking to one of the contestants who's voguing." I love the film and know the reference. "And he says—he spells out the word opulence. He says, 'O-P-U-L-E-N-C-E. Opulence. You own everything. Everything is yours.'" That iconic scene, featuring the artistry of Junior LaBeija, captures a moment, a cultural moment, of reorienting the world with Black and Brown people at its center.

Lucia is committed to the same practice. "Racial diversity is definitely something that we hold important to us, and something that we're continuing to work on, because we need to welcome POC trans people back into the queer community," she says. "I feel like they just feel alienated from the whole community." A twenty-two-year-old trans woman, Lucia organizes Transmissions, a club night that champions trans+ people of color (the term trans+ includes all individuals with gender expressions beyond traditional norms, including transgender, genderqueer, agender, and nonbinary). "The whole queer scene, I would say, is very whitewashed, and isn't welcoming enough to POC people." In an interview with *Dazed*, Lucia explains the effects of club nights in the context of whitewashed scenes in nightlife: "I want them to leave [the party] knowing they're part of a fierce community that loves and cherishes them for who they are, and they don't exist just to entertain or to be fetishized, erased or abused. I wanted them to take a piece of our power with them and to be inspired to exist relentlessly."[4] In the pursuit of self-care, parties like Hungama, Pxssy Palace, The Cocoa Butter Club, Opulence, and Transmissions center the other, relentlessly—no matter how fierce the fight.

Expansive Gender Expressions

Inside Riposte, I see taped to the wall a "safer space statement" that reads:

> Riposte is a queer party organized by gender non-conforming people for the LGBTQIA+ community. Allies are welcome if they are respectful and aware that this is a queer space.
>
> Respect people's pronouns and personal space. We will not shy away from removing anyone who does not share our ethos or breaks our rules.
>
> We all take up space—some more than others. Your space is valid. But be mindful of the space you take and be generous when sharing it.

Like race, gender is also accented in the intersectional ethos of club nights, although, as the flyer shows, the discussion happens in particular ways. Lyall remarks, "I've started to look at those communities within the queer community that still need help—and it's the trans community, it's definitely the nonbinary, the intersex kids, and then also the QTBIPOC kids—and them finding a voice." Lyall works with Lucia to produce Transmissions. "We strive for unapologetic transness," Lucia tells me when I ask about the vibe of the party. "What we did was created a space that also welcomes nonbinary people, and transmasc people, and intersex people, and people who are questioning their gender, and people who don't know what they are. They come downstairs, and they may not look femme at all, but they'll tell you their name's Susan, and that's completely fine. They're here to find out who they are. We're all on journeys." The emphasis on gender expansiveness is something that cis-identifying people, like Amelia, also appreciate about club nights. "I think it's really encouraging to see people creating spaces that specifically, in the tag line or in the advertising, have trans or nonbinary included," she says. Why is that important? I ask. "I think that's a direct acknowledgment of the fact that trans, or nonbinary, or gender nonconforming people—it's extremely difficult to feel safe still. I think that's why we need queer spaces."

Sitting on her couch, Rosie and I take a deep dive into nightlife politics in order to better understand the need for multiple centers and scenes. "I think there's something about this newer queer culture of being trans and nights that are trans-inclusive," she reflects. "They're more about people of color, trans people of color." After thinking for a moment, Rosie distinguishes an "older model" of nightlife, which includes gay bars, from club nights. The latter "have more up-to-date gender inclusion policies. They're more trans and nonbinary friendly. They'll have non-gendered toilets." These places are "privileging the bodies of people who don't normally get to go to a public space and be centered." Gaby, the organizer of Queerdirect, agrees. At club nights, "people will be more inclined to be genderqueer, or show a truer side to their self," they say. In contrast, gay bars "can often feel more oppressive" because of their gender norms. "Forms of femininity within men are shut down there." Back on the couch with Rosie, she summarizes these efforts as "a whole new culture of queer trans people organizing for themselves, putting on their own nights, creating their own communities"—reworking power, politics, and place along the way.

Gay bars have also experimented with gender, although generally through the medium of drag. In the years leading up to the pandemic, "it was subversive to do gender," Michael remembers. "Drag felt a bit underground in the city. Just putting on a look and being messy and wild was enough. That was exciting, and it was subversive. People would be like, 'Wow, you've got people in beards and dresses.'" The perceptions of drag changed once it entered the mainstream and became commercialized with shows like *RuPaul's Drag Race*. "In London and London's clubbing scene, it's not unusual to see that anymore at night," Michael shrugs. The ubiquity of drag in gay and straight bars has stripped it of some its insurgency. Consequently, an imaginative space has opened to rethink gender expression and inclusion in nightlife. "And so, the younger performers and the younger artists and younger promoters, a lot of the ones who I find interesting, are now trying to work out what the next subversive thing to do is. A lot of that is around gender more than just drag." What does that mean, gender more than just drag? I ask. "There are nights that are about being nonbinary or performances that are genderqueer. Or Sissy Scum," Michael replies, "which is this night that one of the drag queens just started once every couple of weeks, which is all about embracing femininity, and being fem, and trans people, and deconstructing gender."

Compared to gay bars, club nights engage with gender in ways that feel more inviting and safer for trans+ people. "When you go to a gay bar, you get drag queens being allowed to perform femininity," Lola says. "As someone that is visibly gender nonconforming, I'm not allowed to perform my gender in the same way." Others offer a similar observation. Prem identifies as nonbinary and has a South Asian and Polish background. They went out in Soho one night with a friend who also identifies as nonbinary. When they approached the bar, "the guy at the door whispered to me, 'You've got to tell him to take his lipstick off, otherwise he can't come in.'" Transphobia and misgendering are common at gay bars, whose staff "police their borders," Prem remarks—and as we saw before we went to Femmetopia. For these reasons, Gaby and his friends now avoid gay bars. "A lot of my friends who I know who are queer don't like to go to gay bars because they feel like their body, or their race, or their sexuality doesn't have a place in those spaces." As an alternative center, club nights have a more empowering vibe. "I feel like queer nights are often put on in reaction to gay bars, to what gay bars don't offer queer communities, which is a safe space for bodies, and genders, and sexualities across a whole spectrum."[5]

The desire to center genderqueerness motivated Ingo to name their event Wotever World. I ask about it. "When you're saying, 'How can I help you, sir?'—if you're standing opposite a person saying that, and you're not giving them anything [a response], then they're getting nervous." Ingo withholds a response every time someone misgenders them. "And then they're like, 'So, how can I help you, madame?' And you still don't give them anything." Your silence in these moments reveals the other person's attitudes about gender. "Then, suddenly, people around you in the queue waiting to order, they become nervous because you are not giving them what gender you belong to. And then the person is like, 'Oh, *whatever*.'" The story illustrates a recurring experience of gender bias that triggered for Ingo not retreat but an intentional desire to create more inclusive worlds. "It happened to me so many times," they share. "The whole 'Wotever' is coming from that: 'Oh, whatever.'" The word implies an approach: "We are all transitioning. Life is a journey, and 'wotever' stands for that."

In these discussions, I was intrigued by the specificity of how people talked about gender—or, to put differently, how infrequently they mentioned bodies that were female or identities that were lesbian. The category of a woman, when it did emerge, arose in two contexts: discussions about the threat of male violence, often heterosexual, made being a woman more salient, like Julia's belt buckle moments, or the category of a woman was associated with whiteness, as we heard from Nadine when they recounted the confrontation about the zine. The latter instance raises the prickly possibility that White women, including White lesbians, are seen by some as similar to White gay men—and thus some club nights form in opposition to them as well. It might also be the case that infrequent mentions of gender-as-lesbian are due to declines in, even concerns about the extinction of, people claiming lesbian identities.[6]

In contrast to female bodies and lesbian identities, people did talk about, and organize around, more expansive gender expressions. Some culture creatives center femininities in parties like Femmetopia, Sissy Scum, and others, although they often decouple feminine gender expressions from female-presenting bodies. Katayoun, the genderqueer Iranian we met before, is the organizer of Femmi-Erect, a club night that celebrates "the whole femme spectrum," as they say. When we chatted about gender in the context of club nights, they referenced "queer women" and "queer femme people" rather than lesbians: "There's a massive lack of queer women who are femme-identifying and queer femme people who DJ. It's really hard to find." Femmi-Erect creates its own center for people who identify in this way. "I want people who are queer, femme, and definitely prioritizing people of color. I want to make sure I prioritize trans people and people of color." Katayoun uses the party to fight femmephobia as expressed on a range of bodies and identities. "I wanted to give a platform to people that feel like they're excluded by the gay scene," they say. "Most of the time, femmes become objects of glamour. People will non-consensually touch you, and if you give them any attitude, you can expect to get called a bitch or even have drinks thrown at you. People can make you feel like you don't belong in their spaces, and try to get rid of you. These are all things I have experienced personally and know my friends have experienced too." Although many of these experiences—being called a bitch, for example—also happen to lesbians, it did not go unnoticed by me that Katayoun, like others, referenced gender as a way to address trans+ and queer issues.[7]

Femmetopia has a similar focus. I ask Kat, the organizer, why she created it and for which audiences. Her objective was to create "a femme space, so a place that isn't binary, for lesbians *or* for gay men. It's a femme-presenting queer space, so it's queer women, trans women, nonbinary people, and femme-presenting men." Here again, we encounter an expansive vision of femininity as decoupled from, and existing independently of, female bodies. Kat attributes this way of thinking about gender to a new wave of feminism. "The feminine is seen as lesser than the masculine on the binary forms of women and men. If we can address the fact that the feminine is seen as lesser, because women were always seen as lesser, then I feel like we're really starting to move forward at a faster pace than we're doing now with rights for women, rights for femme-presenting people, rights for feminine men."

If a femme space is not defined by gender binaries, then addressing femmephobia will necessarily involve an intersectional approach. "For Black, Brown, and East Asian femmes, it's even more difficult," Katayoun tells *gal-dem*. "Femmeness is harder to access if you have dark or non-western features—they're seen as unfeminine due to White beauty standards (not that femme necessarily means feminine). It's so much harder to claim a femme identity when you're not White, because we always have to try harder to be seen as beautiful or desirable." It is precisely this type of thinking which gives club nights their intentional ethos. "Also, inherent queerphobia is a big thing," Katayoun continues. "People often automatically assume someone who is Brown can't be queer. So, the intersection of both identities sometimes feels very suffocating."[8]

Butch, soft butch, transmasculine butch, and female masculinities are all in the midst of a moment too, seeing a resurgence in recent years as motivating underground scenes, with club nights called

Butch Please!, Soft Butch, Pillow Kings, and Lick. Butch Please!, which started in 2016 and set up a residence at the Royal Vauxhall Tavern, sells 1,000 tickets for each event. With roots in working-class lesbian communities in the United States from the 1940s and 1950s, butchness and butch appreciation are becoming popular and more visible once again (the heyday of butch identities, historians say, was in the 1980s and 1990s). "In 2023, the butch identity means different things to different people," Ella Braidwood writes in *The Guardian* about how the gender expression has traveled over from the United States. "For me, a twenty-nine-year-old in London, it is the merging of my sexuality with my female masculinity: a physical reflection of how I feel on the inside—that is, inherently masculine—via men's clothing, short hair, and the way I carry myself." Braidwood is careful to distinguish masculinity from the male body or a desire to be a man. "It is not that I want to be a man; I love being a woman." Braidwood and others talk about gender in specific ways without defaulting to traditional, binary conceptions of male or female, masculine or feminine. In the story, Braidwood speaks with Prinx Silver, a drag king and transmasculine individual who regularly performs at Lèse Majesté, a party we talked about earlier. "Butch is that queer identity that allowed me to reclaim my masculinity that I thought I wasn't allowed to have," Silver says. Rather than an approach to categorize the world into tidy little boxes, Silver sees butchness as worldmaking, an expansion of affect. "I see it more as a way of moving through the world, of being perceived, or like a feeling."[9]

Hearing these voices, I wonder whether the elision of gender-as-female, gender-as-lesbian, or masculinity-as-male is intentional, since it defines club nights as queer more than anything else. "I think the word queer allows for a bit more freedom and is a bit more inclusive of different gender identities," Lola explains. Queer is all these things—and so much more, as we'll see in the next chapter. For now, it is the queerness of club nights that makes being Black or Brown and being trans+ more salient categories, even though parties like Aprhodyki, "London's only Ancient Greek night" for lesbians, do also exist. But even they are rebranding from "a lesbian night," as *Time Out* described them in 2016, to a "night for queer women, trans and nb [nonbinary] lovaaahs," as they now call themselves on Instagram.

Accompanying the move from "lesbians" to "queer women" is an impulse that allows organizers to address gender in more expansive ways, beyond binary categories.[10]

No surprise, then, that nearly every organizer amplified a counternarrative as queer. When bias restricts the ability to be queer *and* Black, queer *and* Brown, or queer *and* trans+, QTBIPOC folks create club nights to celebrate their intersectional experiences in a spirit of joy and resistance. "It's just nice to have a community of people like myself," a reveler said to Braidwood about their reasons for enjoying Wile Out, a club night in Birmingham "that's all about no boundaries" and that attracts people of color. "I don't have to walk into the room and be the only Black person there." BBZ in London also cultivates a "culture of authenticity" so QTBIPOC people can "be their full selves," Tia says, and "learn how to love yourself." It's often a matter of survival. "There is no choice but to have a community; otherwise, you can't exist." Hence the reason Tia works hard to reorient nightlife. "We don't care about anybody else's gaze," she tells me. "We're creating a space for us." Lewis from INFERNO, the next party we're going to, echoes the message. Club nights are for "the most marginalized groups within the queer community," they say. The parties are "platforming them, and really giving them a voice." Nadine also agrees, strongly. In gay bars, "we're just being invited." But that's not enough. "We don't want to be invited anymore. We want to be in charge."

Taking Up the Whole Bed

Like so many people we have met, I too have felt an astonishing sense of belonging at club nights. But still, we should exercise caution amidst our enthusiasm for a few reasons. First, although there are many centers in nightlife, I don't know exactly how many. This brings us back to a disclosure I made in the opening pages about the absence of hard data. You won't be surprised, therefore, that I cannot tell you how many club nights are run by QTBIPOC individuals. I am equally uncertain about how many club nights are run by White gay men. Regardless, there is a far more important point worth making. Unlike other facets of LGBTQ+ cultures I have witnessed or studied, White men are not just in the minority, they are often not the priority. The constellation of club nights, though constantly shifting, was almost always shaped by the priorities of everyone else *but* White gay men.

Second, it might be easy to assume, from the rapturous good feelings we have felt and progressive politics we have heard, that everything is copacetic at club nights. Not true, since queer humans are still humans. What distinguishes club nights is not the absence of bigotry but the presence of unique response cultures. "I think my experience of race isn't different, necessarily, in a gay space than a queer space," Jonathan, who identifies as Mixed race, tells me, "but maybe my response to it is different." How so? I ask. "In queer spaces, even though there might be an experience of racism, it tends to be, for me, a space where I feel like it's something I can raise, whether it's with the staff, or even feeling safe enough to say to the person, 'That term is not acceptable.'" The difference, in other words, is not the naïve notion that racism is only present in one place but, rather, how different places affect our ability to respond when something does happen. "It's not the incident that's different, it's my response, and how I feel that I can respond to it." In a gay bar, Jonathan is "hesitant to presume that I would have the backing of staff, or the people that might overhear and don't know either of the people involved, that they would actually be on my side, or be like, 'Actually that's not cool,' whatever this person said or did." As I listen, I remember Nadine's story about the angry White woman, and then think about an innovative policy at Pxssy Palace. Volunteers called "badge bitches" make themselves known, roaming the party and chatting with revelers while providing opportunities for people to report any potential problems. As an example of a response culture, this is an extraordinary way to help people feel recognized, respected, and safe.

Third, despite their best efforts, some parties still end up with a mostly White crowd. "Conversations about race are happening," Zax remarks, "and people are questioning the lack of racial representation. But you go out sometimes and you're the only person of color in a night in this woke, artsy, supposedly interesting space." Gay bars can also surprise. "And occasionally, I go out in Soho, the supposedly normative space, and it's much more racially diverse, and I'm like, what is that little dichotomy?" Zax's observations defy easy explanations, and while they do not undermine aggregate patterns, they do warn us against overstating them.

Fourth, not all club nights are organized by QTBIPOC individuals. Meet Alex, who is twenty-nine years old and identifies as a cis White gay man. He co-organizes Knickerbocker, an "alt-pop, indie-dance and happy house" club night. It is hosted at different places throughout the year, although generally in a converted warehouse in Hackney Wick. Knickerbocker bills itself as "East London's friendliest queer dance party." This means, "as ever, no racism, misogyny, transphobia, homophobia, body, slut, or kink shaming will be tolerated."[11] Alex is aware that the progressive politics of the night misalign with the optics of the organizers. "We've been very conscious of being two White gay guys, cis White gay guys who put on another gay night that is for gay men." He also recognizes that the crowd is "mostly White, mostly male." The organizers manage this in their branding and programming efforts. About the first, Alex says, "We've always billed it as a queer night, not a gay night, and always been belligerent that we did not want it to just become a sausage fest." Actions can speak louder than words, and here too Knickbocker excels. "[We are] very proud of the diversity of our lineup," Alex adds. "I'd say at least 40 percent of the work we program, probably 50 percent, is people of color." This is how they "make space," Alex remarks. "We vigorously program radical alternative work, which is inevitably going to be coming from queer people of color, and especially in the performance art world. That feels like the right thing for us to do." From Knickerbocker we can see how the privileged profile of some organizers does not undermine their efforts to produce broadly inclusive platforms.[12]

One final reason to exercise caution: not all club nights are trying to make a political statement about nightlife or attempting to reorient it in any way. Adonis comes to mind. Founded in 2018, the collective organizes day parties, night parties, and after-parties that can last up to eighteen hours in a single stretch, all under the logo of a male phallus. But that's not what it's about. "It's not a literal way, that it's a night where we're all just obsessed with dick," Shay says. *Time Out* describes Adonis as "London's coolest queer club" (not a gay club, notice) and a "cult party."[13] Shay, who started it, speaks with me about what motivated him (spoiler alert: he wasn't trying to re-center the scene). "It wasn't like I set out to do it, but I had a studio directly across the road from Five Miles, the club that was just opening. It's like a no man's land in Tottenham. It's just warehouses and not really anything going on." That description reminds me yet again of crack capitalism. "I thought it was really cool that this club was opening there on the street that's a bit of a shithole, really. I thought it would be the perfect place for a party because there's nothing else around."

In our conversation, Shay does not make a single reference to racialized, gendered, or trans+ experiences, nor does he speak about efforts to prioritize any particular group. It was never about that for him. Instead, he wanted to replicate the rave scene in Berlin. "It just reminds you of those illegal Berlin raves that you'd go travel for miles to. And then it all flowed from there like, it just happened." There wasn't much of an idea beyond that. "I didn't really have a vision," Shay admits. "I just wanted to do a warehouse party and knew some good DJs that would be great at it. I'd love to say I had this elaborate thought-out plan for it, but I didn't, really." From Adonis we can see that White gay men like a good club night too.

I went to one of his parties. That night it was at The Cause, a warehouse far from Soho. Shay told me that "there's no dress code or anything like that. Just wear whatever you want. Get your fishnet tights on." The party didn't get started until around midnight. Bass-heavy techno and house music played, and I was surrounded mostly by men (I didn't wear fishnets to this party, like I did to Femmetopia). Shay alerted me in advance that the party "seems very mixed even though it's mainly male." It's still a reasonably diverse group of men, I think, in terms of race, ethnicity, and self-presentation. What I felt on the dance floor was consistent with what Shay told me: "It doesn't feel like a really masculine space." It didn't to me either, although presenting as male and identifying as such undoubtedly influenced my experiences. As a comparison, however, I note that it wasn't full of shirtless, hypermasculine men like I used to see at circuit parties in the 2000s. Instead, there were "a lot of snazzy outfits," like Shay told me to expect and which I observed with delight. I didn't count any of this, mind you, since those numbers would be mostly meaningless anyway.[14] Some of these guys did in fact wear fishnets, and many painted their faces.

The vibe was friendly, welcoming, a bit queer, and very frisky—and the entire time I was there, I never felt like an outsider, despite my darker skin. I'm not sure if I would call that party *my* center, *their* center, or *whose* center it was—just that it was fun, and I felt safe. No one asked me where I was from, or really from. It was easy to feel the appeal of Adonis, because all I saw was joy on faces, bodies adorned with bling, and a lack of inhibition in how those bodies moved. No wonder tickets sell out quickly every time.

Adonis felt different from Hungama and The Cocoa Butter Club. But then again, I can't help but wonder: does any one party represent the baseline? Surely not. As Erkan reminds us, "Sometimes, the incentive behind the party is not necessarily to center queer people of color." Yet these events are still fun and popular—and surprisingly diverse. "Ultimately, because they're good parties, or they have good DJs, they end up having loads of queer people of color there. Adonis is an example of that"—they drop the name without me saying anything about it or my experiences that night—"where the intention behind it may not necessarily be a political one, but the result of it ends up having some political nature to it."

None of these things are easy to measure. What I do know, however, is that Shay's party is extremely popular—and I had a great time that night. In fact, I hope to return the next time I'm in London. But still, I feel a little extra grateful for QTBIPOC events. Maybe it was me singing songs in Hindi at Hungama while I was surrounded by Black and Brown bodies that looked like mine that accounts for the difference. I'm reminded of Sara Ahmed's call for an "affinity of hammers," an approach to social justice informed by the experiences of people hammered by multiple vectors of power. "I think of the potential as atomic," Ahmed writes, "an attraction or force between particles that causes them to combine."[15]

Twenty-nine-year-old Aisha, who identifies as nonbinary and Pakistani Egyptian, discovered this atomic potential when they traveled to New York and saw "how diverse and bustling and abundant queer POC life is there." When I ask what they learned from their travels, Aisha invites me to feel instead. "It was less of a lesson and more of a feeling, and an invitation to desire certain things." I exhale as I listen. "It gave me the ability to dream. It opened my perspective on what's possible." Thinking about the force between atomic particles of people who look like Aisha, or like me, did make me wonder before I arrived at Adonis what that party would be like, even if I discovered that my worries were unwarranted.

As we feel our way through these ideas, Soof, who described nightlife earlier as radiating, even if some expressions exist out of our eyeline, shares another memorable image that I think captures the aspirational qualities of club nights, regardless of who you might find at the center. The organizers are looking to create "a space that allows you to starfish and stretch out." I repeat the phrase, telling Soof how much I like it. No two events that I attended were the same, but they all made me feel like I, too, could stretch out. "In most spaces, I don't necessarily feel I can starfish," Soof continues, but at a club night, "you feel at home, like you can just take up the whole bed." The image is so appealing—restful and full of joy.

INFERNO

Institute of Contemporary Art

It was nearly midnight on The Mall, and the streets were swarming with people. It felt energizing as I anticipated the world that awaited me inside the Institute of Contemporary Art (ICA), where I was headed. INFERNO, London's original queer party and performance art platform, had taken over the place for one of their events. The club night was the creative brainchild of Lewis G. Burton, the queen of the capital's underground scene. "Inferno was born out of frustration," Lewis once told a reporter. "The queer scenes at the time were dominated by White, cis, gay Muscle Marys. It wasn't queer at all. It was just gay . . . We were a rebellion against that."[1] With 750 people in attendance that night, the rebellion was jam-packed.

Queer and trans security guards greeted me at the door. This place was already different from the basements, railway arches, outdoor festivals, and converted warehouses where I had partied before, but it made sense in its own way. The ICA has a reputation for supporting radical art and genre-fluid programming, making me keen to see what this queer collaboration was going to look and feel like inside the doors.

After presenting my ticket (I paid £15 [US$19] in advance), I walked in and through the ICA's bookshop, passing by feminist manifestos, intellectuals, and left-wing philosophers. Up ahead was a long queue outside Cinema 1, one of the biggest rooms with a capacity of 150. Here, we were invited to view a selection of queer erotica curated by the Otherness Archive. I googled the group. "The Otherness Archive was created out of being othered, thus reimagining the term as a form of empowerment and celebration. The Otherness Archive defines the historic censorship of homosexual, trans and racial themes, and instead highlights them as representations of otherness that deserve equal, if not greater, recognition. Otherness acts as a route into complex narratives and subjectivities."[2] Tonight's screening was part of an interdisciplinary festival called "Uncensored," which presented art at the intersections of pornography and activism. If I had any uncertainty about the tone of the evening, that was now settled.

As I entered, I received a program with words penned by Ailo Ribas. "This selection of films is the product of research fueled by horniness: digging through porn archives and trawling the internet for obscure and obscene home movies, searching for those films that possess a sense of do-it-yourself smut: cruising, pulling, perving, rough-'n'-ready, intimate, fucking with your eyes and everything else. This section is an ode to queer sex, to its forced resourcefulness in needing to carve out moments and spaces for itself to exist, even if only in the shadows."

It took me a little while to find a seat; the room was dark and full of people lost in the moans emanating from the screen. As I took in the scene, an agitated grumbling caught my attention. "Why is there no dick in these porn movies?" I couldn't believe the question, hurled by three White gay men. In a spark of protest, a group of women stood up, blocking the men's view, and started making out. As the situation escalated, people around me started undressing in what appeared like an expression of solidarity. This is what it looks like to speak truth to power, I thought as I marveled at the spontaneous, desirously defiant scene.

I wanted to watch the gay men squirm—it's not something I often see—but I didn't want to miss out on anything else either. I quietly ducked out of the cinema and decided to explore the rest of the party. Passing through a set of thick black curtains off to the side of the bookshop, I now found myself following the sounds of stomping feet.

To locate the source, I had to walk by "Another World," an exhibition by Christopher Kulendran Thomas of giant sculptures lurking behind cages, illuminated with makeshift red lighting. Beyond them was a second room, a bar area, where I connected with Lewis, draped in a stunning floor-length, red-laced body suit.

After we exchanged air kisses, Lewis described the crowd as "beautiful freaks": club kids, weirdos, drag kings and queens and other things, transgender deities, fashion queers, and techno goths. One person scribbled "F-A-G" across their forehead, while others fit their mouth with muzzles. Painted faces, bodies, and hair all around me—reds and blacks and acid greens—and looks of shiny black rubber body suits, leather face masks, lots of chains, and sunglasses. Finding any binaries on these bodies was impossible. "It's so beautiful to see all these people from all different backgrounds, all different races, and genders, and sexualities together in one room just having a great time." Lewis's eyes lit up as we talked. "We can escape and be free from all of the confines that are in our normal day-to-day life. People are letting go and having the best time. It's really beautiful." After scanning the crowd, Lewis met my eyes again and repeated the sentiment: "It's really beautiful." I felt a lump in my throat as I heard the sentence twice. Lewis looked full of feelings too. "I actually get quite emotional when I have a look around." INFERNO felt escapist and edgy, an otherworldly celebration of queer spectrums.

Lewis and I squeezed through the crowd to a theater space beyond it, the third of three rooms at the party, from which we could hear the sounds of techno. While gay bars and nightclubs usually play pop, INFERNO featured a completely different style of music—and a visual feast of futurism and empowerment to accompany it, or at least that's how I would describe what I saw on a screen behind the DJ booth. Created by artist Karl Murphy, three banners draped down from the ceiling: ASCEND. AWAKEN. WITNESS.

In the middle of the room was a stage with a television and old analog equipment. Lewis told me that this was the setting for an upcoming performance by Sweatmother, a Latinx, trans-identifying visual artist who blends performance with self-recorded documentation and archival footage. All of a sudden, the music stopped and

▸ Meet Lewis, indomitable founder of INFERNO. Photograph by Roxy Lee on behalf of INFERNO.

an electro-inspired sound installation began. As Sweatmother took center stage, a projector screen illuminated the four corners of the room, like a cast spell. Lewis described what we were seeing: "A group of dykes, trans+ guys, and nonbinary babes are shouting down a microphone as sweat distorts their faces via a video synthesizer and intersecting it with capitalist logos."

As the performance continued, I realized that they were shouting brand slogans. The voices became louder and felt more aggressive until finally all the lights went off, seemingly flipped by a switch. It was anticipatory, a tease really, since as soon as the lights went out, a single beam shone on Sweatmother, who now stood up, removed their shirt, passed it to the person next to them—and then kissed that individual. The scene repeated, person after person and kiss after kiss, until a group of performers, some of whom were naked, entered the room, encircled us, and locked arms. I imagined watching this circle from above and witnessing what felt like a fearless celebration of anti-capitalism.

I lost track of time—the performance was gritty and gripping—and before I knew it, the bass began again, thumping us into the final chapter of the night. *Boom, boom, boom, boom!* The sound, curated by artists like Maze, NEUROM4NCER, and Wax Wings, featured industrial and rave beats, dark electro, and Gabba-infused techno. Tonight, there was also a special guest from New York, Jasmine Infiniti, who brought us the Black roots of the ballroom scene from Harlem. Lewis spun too, playing a killer set of hard remixes of tunes like t.A.t.U.'s "All the Things She Said," while dropping in some samples from The Prodigy to help us lose ourselves in the trance and transcendence of the floor. We moved our bodies until the ICA shut us down, just as the sun was rising. "Wow," I thought as I was greeted by the morning light outside. "That was one hell of a party."

6

The Room Feels Queer

Club nights vary enormously yet share some common qualities. Chances are: the surroundings are dark, the music thunderous. Chances are: the ceilings are high, the air acoustical. Whichever party you attend, it is likely not in the gayborhood but harder to find. The organizers have transformed an empty space into another world. This is not a fixed venue, available night after night, but an event that appears for a mere moment. The limited duration means that every occasion presents an opportunity for something new. Next time, if there is a next time, it might pop up somewhere else. This is less consumerist, more creative and communitarian. The tenor is ephemeral, the mood experimental. Say bye to Britney; this sounds more like Black Obsidian. Look around: there are no rainbow flags. Nothing about the vibe here is gay. If you've come this far, it should be no surprise that this room feels *queer*.[1]

We have glimpsed the visceral value of these episodic events from that very first cup of coffee we poured in the introduction. But I think it would have been difficult for us to ask questions about queerness any earlier than this moment, as there were more foundational matters we first needed to grasp. Now that we have immersed ourselves in the world of club nights, even when capitalism tries to crush nightlife scenes and despite the baked-in biases that shape us all, it's time to push further on this cultural component. We now can feel the feeling of club nights with renewed appreciation, from a more sophisticated vantage point, even if those feelings are not typically something we focus on in the social sciences (though humanists like Ahmed describe them as atomic).

The element of queerness and queer-feeling has surrounded us and kept us moving this entire time, like the air we breathe. But as with anything so significant yet subtle, it has sustained us without drawing much attention to itself, even while the word queer and its qualities animate club nights as distinct worlds and distinct centers in nightlife. Like we saw at INFERNO. When people have spoken with us about these parties, why did they so often associate the word queer with them? Why not call club nights gay? Similarly, when people talked about the closure epidemic, why did they describe at-risk places the other way around: as gay bars, but seldom as queer?

Anything but an accident, these semantic choices are meaningful patterns for us to consider, if only we can find a way to mine them, to think anew about a familiar theme. We will discover those meanings, again here as elsewhere, via place. It's time to reflect on that alluring word, to bring it from the background to the front as our main muse, and ask at last about the queer-feeling rooms where we have been partying.

Messy Queerness

When Aisha went to New York, recall how inspired they felt by QTBIPOC parties. Nothing specific stayed with Aisha when they returned home. "It was less of a lesson and more of a feeling. It gave me the ability to dream. It opened my perspective on what's possible." I return to these words because they remind me what is so compelling yet also elusive about queerness. For many minds over many decades, the idea of queerness has vexed and inspired, tortured and tempted. Much like club nights, queerness celebrates the realm of possibility and the refusal of fixity.

Remember Dan De La Motte? He leads walking tours in Hackney, Soho, and the East End. Given his knowledge of these many places, I ask him if queerness is like a compass. If I picked you up and put you in a city you've never visited, how would you know which places were queer? "That's a very difficult question," Dan replies. We banter for a bit about its expressions, including drag, architecture, and parties in Berlin, before Dan proposes, "Everybody's definition of queer is different to everybody else's, isn't it?" I ask him to think about his own experiences. "I have been in clubs in other cities in this country that you can just tell immediately are gay rather than queer." Still, Dan can't define it. What he can offer, like Aisha, is a feeling. "There is just something that you can kind of—you know when you go into a space, any space, and you feel at home. You feel that this is your tribe. I know that I feel comfortable and feel at home when I know that I'm in a queer space as opposed to a gay space. I just know. There's something in me that knows that."

Brooke and I also talk about these fuzzy matters. "It's kind of hard to say," they remark, like Dan. "There's just a feeling." We try to parse it out, though without much success. "I'm stuttering a lot because it's such a feeling that I can't necessarily generalize about what creates it." Jonathan advises against using any indicators for queerness. "There's nothing measurable," he says. I nod, remembering the same struggle I confronted about counting club nights. How do you measure the evanescent? Can queerness show us the way? Can it provide a methodology? We need to try our best to understand what English professor Heather Love describes as a "classic odd couple, uptight methods attempting to impose order on the slovenly queer." But I think opposites attract![2]

My next step comes in a conversation with Olimpia who, recall, was a graduate student when we met. "I've been writing a lot about messiness," she tells me. Olimpia, like so many of us, has struggled with the meaning of the word queer and its spatial expressions. "It's very hard to describe what a queer space is." She starts by ruling out what it is not. "It wasn't so much about identity. It wasn't the rainbow flag. It wasn't LGBT friendliness." What was it then? I ask. "It was the sense of messy queerness."

The mess, yes! That's where queerness lives. A word we use to talk about disorder ironically creates clarity in my mind. It is easy in these days when we prioritize hard data about people and populations to focus on precise measurements and the orderliness of identity politics—things like "pride and visibility," in Olimpia's words, or the rainbow flag as a symbol. A feeling of *messy queerness* points us instead to places that exist "very anarchically and very randomly," Olimpia adds—like a takeover of the Institute of Contemporary Art or a caravan that shows up in a parking lot. "I think that's what I mean by messy queerness, something that is quite anarchic and is totally at random." These qualities make queerness "hard to pinpoint," which is frustrating, but that's exactly the idea. To think through the differences between orderly gay and messy queer, Matt from Buttmitzvah offers a thought experiment. "You could be straight in a queer space, and that makes you slightly queer, and that's cool. But if a straight man goes into a gay space, are they slightly gay?"

Too often, we take a world that is messy and try to clean it up by creating categories. The world is full of gay or straight people, we say, men or women, and so on. Cognitive sociologists call this tendency "lumping and splitting." When we tidy up complexity, we "strip it of contingency, ephemerality"—the very things that make both queerness and club nights so compelling. We need to create space for the "ineradicable messiness" of queerness. I love what Love says about the mess: "When it comes to being messy, *we are*."[3]

To round out our conversation about club nights, let's sit in the middle of the mess and use that notion to consider what makes club nights queer. If something is messy, we seek to make sense of it. But rather than assigning fixed categories, I want us to focus on finding meanings. I call this quality *kinesis*, and it builds on our conversation about reorientations, an ongoing process of reflection and renewal in nightlife as we create more centers for more people. Queerness is that pursuit of *more*—more of many kinds, from intentions to representations, voices to bodies. One of the things that I appreciate about the biological definition of kinesis is that it describes movement without a clear sense of cause or effect. That movement is not a direct result of any initial action, and this quality makes it feel connected, in my mind, to the metaphor of messiness. We don't know exactly how things will go or what will result from any specific action—because life is messy, because momentum is constant, because our search for meanings never really ends.

The imagery of a mess raises another question: is there anything we can actually *see* in that mess? How do you see queer, in other words? The question invites us into a matter of optics. Symbols, like the rainbow flag, can create legibility of group membership and feelings of belonging for some people. When I see a rainbow sticker in a storefront, I feel like I might be a little more welcome in that place than somewhere else. Hence why certain parts of the city, like the gayborhood, are awash with rainbows. But, unlike gay identities, queerness is not represented by a single or all-encompassing symbol, even though the word attempts to do just that, especially when people describe it as an umbrella term. In terms of its visual representations, queer is less legible, intentionally and defiantly, and thus messier to perceive.

Links abound between our feelings (messy queerness) and these other themes of movement (queer kinesis) and visual aesthetics (seeing queer). I do not wish to suggest that the trio is comprehensive, or that the ideas fit together into a unifying framework. To do so would neaten the mess that I want us to celebrate! And so, allow me now to open the door and invite you inside. Take a look around and ask: why does the room feel queer?

Queer Kinesis

When I ask Angel, the organizer of Gayzpacho, about the differences between gay bars and queer spaces like his party (hold tight, we're headed to that tomato-wrestling blowout right after this chapter), he rubs his thumb and two fingers together and replies, "I think a queer space is more dynamic, and a gay space is more static." If a gay bar was a person, we would find that it is "constantly trying to define itself as something specific and clear." That makes the idea of "gay" feel stuck in motion or inactive for Angel. A queer space is "reactionary" against things like "time" and "what's going on in the world," he adds, pointing to a nearby newspaper article about bar closures. The spatial format matters too. "I think this is one of the things that I like about Gayzpacho, moving venues." What about it appeals? I ask. "You constantly have to adapt to whichever venue it is at."

A sense of momentum comes through in these words. "I see queer as more queering, as a verb," Olimpia similarly tells me. Notice the gerund, attaching "-ing" to queer as a way to make it move. She uses this strategy with great effect: "It's about questioning, and problematizing, and making trouble, and fucking with the norm, rather than opposing the norm, because who are we to assume that we could ever detangle ourselves from the norms?" As I process comments I hear from Olimpia and others, I notice the repetition of some ideas: queerness is moving, queerness is questioning, queerness is creating. A phrase comes to mind: *queer kinesis*.

The word "kinesis" means movement or motion, often in ways that are not determined by a single cause. In biology, as I mentioned earlier, kinesis refers to a type of action or propulsion that does not have a specific inciting source but instead can come from several possible stimuli. The energy embedded into the word builds from familiar imagery, like reorientations and multiple centers. Queer kinesis, then, seems to me like a good way to describe the kinds of creativity we have been observing all along. Unlike the emphasis on behavioral responses in biology, we will think about queer kinesis in the context of nightlife as an ongoing blend of active and reactive responses to the many things that people experience. It is a jumble of generative movements, the momentum of creative destructions side by side with cultural revolutions.

Still, the idea requires a point of contrast to appreciate whether we are, in fact, moving. Comparing generations is the most common way that people make that evaluation, since cohorts describe time and trends. "Every generation has their own thing," Lewis from INFERNO remarks. This creates a constant search for the next new thing. "We're still having conversations about what's new, what's next," Stuart, age thirty-six, says. These words—"what's new, what's next"—exemplify a kinetic logic. "A new scene is emerging," Charlotte, forty-three, remarks, "and it's coming out of people wanting those spaces where they can bring their whole self to it, and actually, it's encouraged. And I think that's very much with the younger generation." Charlotte is tuned into how nightlife expresses generations. Club nights, she says, are "emerging from people being more comfortable, and actually more fluidity in the whole spectrum of LGBTQI." Fluidity is a complex idea, and I ask Charlotte to explain what she means by it, especially as I am drawn to its sense of momentum. "People aren't just gay, lesbian, or bisexual anymore. There is a whole spectrum, and people are fluid within that spectrum." And then she offered the key point: "I think these spaces reflect that."[4]

I'm intrigued with how self-evident this all seems to Charlotte: that of course trends in nightlife reflect generational differences. It sounds so simple and so obvious when she says it, yet this assumption has implications about an idea that we generally treat as psychological and developmental. At twenty-three years of age, Koen is twenty years younger than Charlotte, but even he offers a similar observation. "One of the things that people say is that my generation—so, people around the age of twenty—that they don't go to gay spaces because they don't identify as gay."

This surprises me, as I recently read that rates of non-heterosexual self-identification have actually *increased* among younger generations. For instance, while 7.1 percent of Americans self-identified as something other than straight in 2022, 21 percent of Generation Z adults identify as such. This is almost twice the rate of Millennials, five times greater than Generation X, and eight times higher than Boomers.[5]

The numbers are slightly lower in Britain, but the trend is the same. According to the Office for National Statistics, in 2020 an estimated 3.1 percent of the UK population (sixteen years and older) identified as lesbian, gay, or bisexual. But within that population-wide statistic, differences between generations are clear: younger cohorts (16- to 24-year-olds) have the greatest rates of self-identification at 8.0 percent.[6]

We see similar trends for gender. In a 2021 global survey of twenty-seven countries conducted by Ipsos, those who describe themselves as transgender, nonbinary, nonconforming, or gender fluid make up 4 percent of Gen Z (born in or after 1997), compared to 2 percent of Millennial (born 1981–1996), 1 percent of Gen X (born 1965–1980), and less than 1 percent of Boomers (born 1946–1964).[7]

If younger people are more likely to self-identify as not heterosexual and not cisgender, then wouldn't we see more of them at gay bars? Koen suggests the opposite. People of his generation, he says, "identify much more either with no label or with queer," and this affects their social habits. "So, they will go to queer parties or queer spaces. They don't organize around the label of 'gay.'" Is that true for you personally? "I feel like the places where I would go to, it doesn't really matter that much which categories of sexuality you fall in. And that, I think, translates also in the way a space—how a space or a club is promoted, is marketed, and is recognized by other people. Maybe some people would recognize that particular space as ambiguous." Alan, who is fifty-seven, describes these trends as "a fluidity and a blurring," which he says impacts the "canon" of nightlife, or who goes out where: "I think there's an increasing number of spaces that aren't in the canon of the gay scene, using 'gay' for shorthand, that gay, lesbian, trans people, younger people would go to."

The reverse is also true: older people who were socialized in gay bars and came of age in them feel more comfortable there, as opposed to a queer space. Andrew is a thirty-eight-year-old gay man. He speaks frankly: "I guess queer spaces for me suggests something that is—this makes me sound really old-school and old now—I guess queer spaces for me are young spaces." Stuart, age thirty-six, grew up in a milieu defined by gay bars. "The places that I've always been when I started to come to London, and then I've developed with friend networks, I've always been in gay bars, predominantly male bars, gay men." Why is that? "I think it's an age thing," he replies, intuiting a generational pattern.

Many younger people do not prefer places that are populated exclusively by gay men. "I think young people no longer have the desire to go to an exclusively gay male space," Amir, twenty-three, says as he imagines himself in conversation with someone like Andrew. "There's a huge appetite for queer spaces, or spaces which are more plural in terms of representation, in terms of what they celebrate, in terms of their ethos." Sam, twenty-nine, conceptualizes the difference between gay and queer three-dimensionally. "The term 'queer space' is better than a 'gay bar' because a 'gay bar' sounds like it's just for gay men," he echoes. "We should all feel accepted and safe somewhere in the world. And if we can find one place that you can go out and have fun in as somewhere on the LGBT+ spectrum, up, down, left, right, wherever you want to identify yourself onto it, and be referred to as the term 'queer,' I think that's really good, a really good initiative and fight."

Individuals like Andrew are aware of these sentiments, but he also recognizes that he comes from a different era. "It's probably a loop I'm out of," he admits. "The people I met when I first started going out, that's not [queer spaces] what was talked about." Younger people today, however, take the association between queerness and particular places for granted. Amir explains, "I think young people would rather go and inhabit a space which maybe is temporary, in maybe a straight venue, but there's a queer event. They'd rather go to that, as opposed to something which is homonormalized and has become a gimmick of itself, if that makes any sense." Yes and no, I reply. What's the gimmick? "I think what I'm referring to is really the commercialized, sterilized gay bars that you'd find in Soho. I think they're not as fun. At least young people, myself or my peers, I just don't feel it's as exciting or as 'progressive,' quote-unquote, to go to a space like that." What Andrew likes, Amir rejects—even though they are just fifteen years apart.

As I listen, I sense slight tensions and subtle shifts. Previously, it seemed like a key difference between gay bars and club nights was between whiteness and QTBIPOC experiences. Now, the perspective expands to include generations. Even though queer spaces do not actively exclude people because of their age (apart from being old enough to legally enter), some individuals don't feel comfortable because they are older—and this suggests limits to queerness. "I think the word queer has its flaws," Michael, twenty-four, concurs, "but I think it's a wider group of people than gay." When we talk about gay bars, the words suggest to Michael "places that are tailored to gay men." This is why club night organizers do not call their events gay. "I think changing our language is really important because then we start making it feel, even on just a really basic level, as though that space is for people who aren't just gay men."

Arguments about generational differences, that they affect place preferences, who goes where, and their different vibes, emerged repeatedly in my conversations. "If it's a gay bar, you think gay man," Stefan, the thirty-two-year-old Canadian, explains. "That's it." Gay bars are "places where the gay men go," Chris, twenty-six, echoes. "It's like, well, you're not really broadening the horizons." Perceptions about a limited range of genders and sexualities can feel alienating if you identify as something other than a gay man. "If you are even part of a smaller minority," Sam, age thirty-four, begins to say, "you might feel like, 'Actually, I don't see anyone [like me],'" or "'I don't actually think I fit in with gay men at all,' because you might be a bisexual woman, or you might be transgender."

What do gay men who are young think about this generational divide? They straddle both groups, after all—they belong to the "gay man" group aligned with gay bars, as we just heard, but they also belong to the younger generation that is more attuned with queer cultures and identities. Because the generational theme arose unexpectedly, it did not always inform my conversations. But it did remind me that crossovers are common: gay men and lesbians, including those from White backgrounds, enjoy club nights, and QTBIPOC folks also enjoy gay bars—and the culture of those bars is evolving with time. I also remember how much I enjoyed Adonis, which had a mostly White crowd of gay men—but it still felt queer. We can revisit that experience and look at it now through a generational lens, which might help us appreciate why Adonis had that vibe. Even if a club night is organized by White gay men or women, like Adonis and Aphrodyki, the individuals who organize them and the revelers who attend are often younger and more politically progressive, they are more likely to identify as queer, and thus they contribute to the queer feeling of the place.[8]

Due to the younger demographic, queer places have a distinct political sensibility as well. Koen explains, "They transformed from being spaces that were promoted as gay or as lesbian, targeting a very, quite-specified group of the LGBT community, to places that promote themselves as queer, or as free, or as open." Older generations could also have identified as "free" or "open," like younger people today. Why the difference? I ask. "The older generation put a lot more emphasis on visibility politics, demonstrating that gay people were out there, demanding rights on the basis of that," Koen replies. "I can see how, for this type of politics, it is important to have gay spaces and to promote them as gay spaces."[9]

I'm guessing that some older gay men would agree with Koen, although they might add, as I heard informally, that the "problem with the younger generation" is that they do not want to sustain the activism the older generations started and fought so hard for. Think decriminalization, employment nondiscrimination, military access, and marriage rights, all massive fights and monumental victories. Personally, I think the concern is an overgeneralization: if you are not doing what we did, then you must be apolitical or irresponsible. It resembles conclusions like "nightlife is dying" that people make based on observations of only gay bars. We called that isomorphism, you might recall, or a tendency to examine a narrow range of expressions in a large field like nightlife.

The question is not whether younger queers engage in activism but what forms they prefer. Let me explain: the struggle for LGBTQ+ rights has been structured on a pluralist political system that relies on electoral or interest group politics that promote single-issue lobbying efforts as an avenue for legal change. Queer politics are different. They often use street-level provocations and parody, like a kiss-in, and they build intersectional alliances with other groups. The goal is not always legal change but cultural revision, or what we define as normal. That can range from heterosexuality to homonormativity ("something which is homonormalized," as Amir said). Whether we are talking about the closure epidemic or politics, the lesson is similar and worth slowing down for: we need to diversify our inputs, as there is always more than one way to think and feel—at a party and a protest.[10]

Reflecting on gay bars and queer club nights can move us, kinetically, from identity politics to "identity responsive spaces." The idea comes from Carla. "That's the term I use for what we do." Carla, thirty-two, is the managing director of The Outside Project, the UK's first LGBTQ+ community shelter, center, and domestic abuse refuge. "Queer people who live in squats and sofa-surf and that kind of thing, they don't go into the system, or they don't feel it's their place," Carla told *Vice* magazine, describing the idea behind the Project.[11] In our conversation, Carla describes identity-responsive spaces as a way to run a queer organization. "It's anyone who's part of our community. There isn't any kind of segregation. It's not like this is a women's space, or that's the men's space, that's for trans men, that will be for nonbinary people. It doesn't make sense. Everybody would have their own little box if you were to do that."

The vision, which Brooke describes as "radical inclusivity," is spreading across the nonprofit sector. Consider Open Barbers, a hairdressing service for all genders and sexualities. *Pink News* describes them like this: "The trans-led, nonprofit salon began as a pop-up that cut hair at queer events, which then grew into two chairs, one night a week, at a barber in north London, and then finally into its own light and airy barber shop and social space by Shoreditch Park."[12] Thirty-eight-year-old Greygory began the enterprise. "We very deliberately are not an exclusively LGBTQ+ space," they tell me. Open Barbers maintains a "safe spaces policy," but beyond that, its queerness is a function of "recognizing this is a space where we are actually all learning from each other." "The emphasis is not on identity silos or identity politics, but rather on identity-responsive spaces." If we push a bit further, we can appreciate its applications to club nights. "We don't want to make people feel like, when you come in the door, you need to meet certain criteria if you're going to be welcome here," Greygory explains. Eligibility is not a function of ticking boxes, you need to be this or that to be here or belong here. "It's just thinking outside of your own range," Peter, age thirty-six, says. Sam, twenty-nine, personalizes the message—"queer, for me, is a more conscious effort to include everybody"—while Aisha flags a feeling of authenticity apart from specific identities: "Queer has more space in it for, I think, people being whoever they are."

This is the vision to which many club nights aspire. Glyn imagines Sink the Pink as "label-less." He explains, "We weren't a night for drag queens, we weren't a night for gay men, we weren't a night for lesbians. We were a night for people that were ready to leave everything at the door, and come in, and just be free." The trend toward "wonkiness," as Olimpia calls it, is spreading across the field of nightlife. "I feel like clubbing now is less about the labels, and it's more about a way of thinking," Glyn adds. "That, to me, is what being queer is about." When he organizes a club night, Glyn's goal is to create a place "where we all come together . . . We're all just coming together in a likeminded way to share in our differences." What future do you desire? I ask. "I want to be with people from all different walks of life. I definitely want my work to reflect that, and I definitely think that that's the way clubbing's going." I don't know if Glyn's vision will pan out, but his determination, like that of so many other culture creatives, certainly leaves a positive impression. However the idea of queerness evolves, I think it will maintain a commitment to movement, no matter how messy the process may be, and a promise to engage with unmet needs—kinesis, in short.

Seeing Queer

The room feels queer with its messy and moving qualities, but what would we see once we step inside? And how are the aesthetics of queer club nights different from those of gay bars? "When I hear 'gay spaces,' I will think of the pride flag on the wall," Liam, twenty-six, mentions. Alex, age twenty-nine, calls this a "gay pride aesthetic of your average gay bar." Both of their words remind me of Koen, who similarly said, "Having a rainbow flag is a clear symbolics that this is a gay space or a gay bar." Queer spaces tend to steer away from explicit signs. "In queer spaces, you wouldn't have that clear symbolics." Let's follow these breadcrumbs and consider a classic symbol: the rainbow flag.

In 1974, Harvey Milk challenged Gilbert Baker to create a representation that would inspire the community, which was gaining national and international visibility. Four years later, Baker, with thirty volunteers, hand-dyed and stitched eight stripes of cloth into a flag for the 1978 San Francisco Freedom Day Parade. This was the unveiling of the now-iconic symbol; together, the different-colored stripes resembled a rainbow. Baker's creation earned him the nickname, "the gay Betsy Ross," alluding to the upholsterer credited for making the first American flag in 1870.[13]

The design was deliberate. Hot pink represented sex, red stood for life, orange for healing, yellow for the sun, green as serenity with nature, turquoise symbolized art, indigo for harmony, and violet represented the spirit. The colors combined to affirm diversity as united under a single symbol. Practical factors, like production costs and the lack of commercial availability for some colors, forced Baker to drop hot pink and turquoise from the design, while royal blue replaced indigo. The result was what we recognize today as the six-striped flag, sometimes referred to as "the freedom flag" or "pride flag." Following the assassination of Harvey Milk, the flag spread rapidly across the country, and soon the globe. It became the primary symbol of gay pride, replacing the pink triangle from earlier decades.

Today, the flag is featured in gay bars around the world—but it is noticeably absent in club nights. Why is that? The bars that fly rainbow flags operate on "an understanding of gender and sexuality as a cultural thing," Olimpia proposes, echoing Koen's comments about identity politics. Olimpia mistrusts mainstream uses of the flag as a "rhetoric of diversity," and thus "something that can be measured." Once we make identities measurable, they become a "manageable, commodifiable, packaged cluster of symbols, and images, and icons" that corporations use for "marketing purposes." I nod my head, visualizing the endless floats in pride parades sponsored by banks, businesses, and the like. The rainbow flag, for Olimpia, has lost its "anti-capitalist radical roots," and that's why some queer people do not identify with it. When an organization trots out a rainbow flag, "I think people are very suspicious and skeptical." Erkan is one of those people. "We're against the rainbow flag," they say. That flag represents "normative pride," "corporate pride," and a "commercialization of our identities, which is embodied within that very flag itself." Rainbows do not look or feel queer. "Flags are a reflection of this division of us versus them. Regardless of whether it's an inclusionary us, it still creates an us. I think that community identification can be a good thing, but it can also be like, 'We're this, and you're not part of it.' I think a lot of people want to deviate away from that."

Lola and I talk about what, other than the rainbow flag, you might see at a club night. "I think the rainbow flag for a lot of people is considered this gay thing," she begins, like others have also commented. "I've never seen one in those spaces [club nights], let's put it that way." Never a rainbow flag? I ask. "No," Lola replies. "I think occasionally there will be like a bi flag somewhere, or a trans flag somewhere." Why not a rainbow flag? "I think people don't include gender variant people under that rainbow flag. People think of gay men, and gay women, and lesbians. That's really what the rainbow flag is."

Tracing its history back to Baker does little to affect these perceptions. "Whether it was supposed to represent that all along or whether it's even supposed to represent it now, that's usually what people think of." Although "gay" was once an umbrella term, like queer operates today, it has not retained its perception as a broadly inclusive word, symbol, or idea. "It's a bit tricky," Lola adds, "because 'gay' was the word to describe everything in the first place."

It's interesting that club nights prefer particular flags rather than the more general rainbow flag. That decision is important for two reasons. First, as Lola noted, even though "gay culture" might sounds inclusive, it still feels alienating for many people. We talked about this at length in earlier chapters. Dwayne, thirty-five, mentions it again. "The younger generation wants inclusion," he says. "It's not enough anymore to just have a rainbow flag on it." Second, the choice to fly a bi or trans flag, rather than the rainbow flag, potentially contradicts the claim that queer culture is more inclusive than gay culture. By displaying only certain flags, is everyone else unwelcome? The answer is no, actually. The use of flags at club nights is not to exclude but to *expand*. People who identify as queer, even if not as specifically bi or trans, often feel more comfortable in places with these symbols, as they represent a politics of intentional inclusion, unlike the "rhetoric of diversity" that Olimpia mentioned before—performative inclusion, we might call it in contrast. More than just optics, a place that puts up a bi or trans flag will also have a set of policies about gender, consent, and safety, like the one I shared from Riposte. Amir notes, "Some of these parties put their safe space policy on the wall in terms of the classic 'no transphobia, no fat phobia, no ageism, no racism, no sexism.' That's one of the only iconographies or pointers that can identify a queer space from, say, a gay space." Riposte, I observed, posted additional flyers about their photo policy and playroom rules.[14]

This is where the organizational qualities of club nights meet the aesthetics of queerness. Lola remarks, "Because they don't tend to be permanent venues, you can't really do much [with the space]." Club nights make strategic use of a blank canvas, like a basement, parking lot, empty garage, or warehouse. By moving from place to place, one canvas to the next, organizers are less likely to display any symbols, since the infrastructure is impermanent. "What I can say," Amir offers, is that "they [club nights] operate under unfixed circumstances." What does that mean? I ask. "It means they have to operate like once a month here, or they pop up somewhere else in a different venue." Amir takes this familiar nomadic theme and connects it with our current question of optics. "That may be why there isn't as much iconography that you can physically see when you go to this queer space." DIY, policies taped to walls, everything is easy to take down—useful architectural features for parties on the move.

The disidentification from the rainbow flag, if not resistance to it, also applies to established venues that embrace a queer identity. Dan de la Motte mentions VFD, where we went for Femmetopia. "The outside of it is just a former shop, I guess, with a basement. The outside is just a grey—there's no—it's just grey, and there's three letters in neon, V-F-D, Vogue Fabrics Dalston. The window, because it used to be a former shop, changes, and it's a piece of installation art. Currently, there's a shopping trolley full of TVs. I don't know what that represents." To recognize it as queer, it helps to have queer networks. "I guess you have to be in the know to know what the queer spaces are." That's how Dan recognizes it. "I know that Vogue Fabrics is a queer space, and therefore, I know it's there. I've taken other people there for their first time, so now, therefore, they know it's there. One of my friends took me there for the first time, and that's how I knew it was there."[15]

VFD is not queer because of any flags it displays. "They're not going to be as brazen with their labeling because, by definition, that's not what they are about," Dan continues. "They're not trying to be known to a wider audience in that way, and so you need to be more learned in what you're looking for and more versed in what's on the scene." If there is any visual marker of queerness inside the space, it's certainly not "glittery walls" like you sometimes see at gay bars. "Those aren't reflective of the community," Samuel from The CAMPerVAN argues. "A very neutral, accessible space that can be adapted to any form of activity is the queerest thing you could build."

The obvious logistical reason for the lack of much iconography at a club night is the impermanent, irregular use of venues. But that is just one part of a more complex answer to the question of how we can see queerness at these events. I was captivated by Samuel's idea of being "neutral" as the "queerest thing you could build." What a statement! In addition to countering every homophobic stereotype of flashiness and flamboyance, it also suggests that club nights share an aesthetic. I can think of many ways to describe it: an aesthetic of neutrality, to riff off Samuel, aesthetic minimalism, or perhaps an aesthetic of emptiness, insofar as we can conceptualize something empty as expansive in its possibilities. The sparseness of the space, whether a warehouse or a dingy basement, is deliberate—not just because the organizers know that they have to clean out the space after the party, but also because the venue itself doesn't belong to them. They don't own it, rent it out regularly, or control it.

The room feels queer not because of what it looks like. Club nights are not about the décor but something deeper. I would venture to say that organizers keep the space empty in order for the people to fill it. An intentional emptiness enables a *people-led aesthetic*. Seeing queer is not about the symbols in the space but the people who are in it. It might be easy to assume, from the outside, that we should be able to identify something specific or obvious, some sign or symbol, like a flag. What is ironic though revolutionary about club nights, in terms of their optics, is that there really isn't much to see in the built structure. It is the feeling of the space, not the look of the space, that matters—and the people who fill the space imbue those feelings with queerness.

One Size Never Fits All

The word queer is a litmus test to gauge belonging in nightlife. Conversations about it, Em tells me, have divided LGBTQ+ people into two groups: "Those who knew how to speak about more recent developments in politics were 'good queers,' and then those who weren't up-to-date with vocabulary kept on putting their foot in it." She describes the new binary as "the good queer/bad gay division of people." This is how queer can become "exclusive" to particular people, Dan remarks. "It's woke, and it's cool to say 'I'm queer,'" Amir adds. "And this is happening even amongst straight people." All this affects who feels comfortable at club nights. "If you are queer, you can go to these spaces," Dan explains. "If you are gay, and you are, to use a term that's in popular discourse at the moment, 'basic,' then it is exclusive against you." It also affects who belongs. "People whose sexual identity—and this is fine, let's let them be them—but if their sexual identity is not politicized in any way," like gay identities apparently, "then nights like this are not going to be for them."

I find it curious that so many people equate "gay" as "bad," not "woke," normative, and apolitical. Historically, gay was much more inclusive—and progressive. Michael is one of the few people who recognizes this. "I think about how ten or twenty years ago, it was radical to go to a gay bar as a White gay man." Although Michael admits that he does not know for sure—"I wasn't around"—he imagines that being gay "was subversive, and it was probably dangerous. There were risks attached. To be an out gay man, an out White gay man, was still something that, you would see prejudice—and it still does today, but not to the same extent—you would face prejudice, and could be shunned, and could be beaten, and could be murdered, and could be assaulted. To walk into a bar that was gay, and was proud of that fact, was something."

It's true. Three years before Stonewall, activists in New York staged a "sip-in," similar to the lunch counter sit-ins made famous by the civil rights movement in the United States. The trio, as I described in the beginning of the book, walked into several bars, announcing at each place that they were gay, and waited to see if the bartender would serve them. Bartenders could legally refuse to do so in those days—and most did.

Gay was definitely radical when I came out. In the early 1990s, gay men were being attacked in broad daylight on downtown streets. I remember seeing safety alerts posted around campus at the University of Michigan in the liberal bubble of Ann Arbor. Listening to Michael takes me back to those moments, to those streets. I felt angry, and my rage motivated me to become an activist. The groups I joined had many members who were White gay men, yet they engaged with questions about power in critical ways. We marched down Main Street holding hands and signs that declared, "Gays Bash Back."

Gay bars—like the identities, like the word—were also radical places. As Amir reflects, "back then, the gay bar was really an underground space where only gay people would go." His words remind me of my first visit to a gay bar. I was eighteen, a freshman at Michigan. It was a Tuesday night. In fact, it was October 11, 1994—I still remember the exact date. Every Tuesday, the Nectarine (now the Necto) had a "gay night." I nervously paced back and forth outside, on the other side of the street, for half an hour before I found the courage to go inside. With rainbow flags everywhere, that room felt gay, not queer. But feeling gay back then was like feeling queer today.

Gay people would go to bars "out of necessity," Amir adds. "It was criminalized in the US to be gay, and gay men were actively subject to police brutality. I can understand the necessity, like the physical need: it was a spatial response to the fact that there were no gay spaces in the heterosexual city." To be openly gay was brave, sometimes even militant. We had to be, in the face of state-sponsored homophobia and flagrant anti-gay violence on the streets. And so, we went to gay bars for many of the same reasons that people go to queer club nights today: to feel safe, to celebrate, to mobilize, to love and be loved, to belong.

LGBTQ+ life now is quite unlike what it was that night I went to the Nectarine. "I think that the situation in which we're operating, the context in which we're operating, is different," Michael observes. "There are more ways to be privileged as a White gay man than there are if you are a trans person of color in this city, or a young lesbian woman, or an immigrant, or a twenty-four-year-old man who's bisexual. The challenges they face are greater than the challenges faced by middle-class White gay men across the board." Amir agrees. "I think now that we have reached a stage of assimilation, at least gay men, or middle-class majority White gay men have, or like cisgender men have achieved this social acceptance. There maybe isn't the same necessity to go to these underground gay bars, like the Stonewall Inn, as there was fifty years ago." Social life has changed, and that has altered what places mean. Simon, the producer of Duckie, wonders out loud: "As the closet gets smaller and the ghetto [gayborhood] gets smaller, what does the notion of gay culture offer us, and what does it offer young people?" Gay bars were once "underground" places—his word—but now club nights have taken on that same designation. This suggests that the closet has become smaller only for some of us, not all of us.

It all makes sense, but still, there is a question that keeps bothering me: why have gay bars not been able to maintain a subversive vibe? When I raise it with Dan, he cites a bar in Soho called Heaven. While it "played a really important role in terms of gay equality and liberation," many people today think it's "not cool" and "a touristy thing to do." But what about its history? I ask. Dan answers with a zinger: "Heaven's history is very important, but Heaven's history is not Heaven's present." Simon offers a similar distinction: "Queer and gay matters are a living, changing culture. It's not static. It's not in a museum. It's living, and it's changing." Club nights are related to gay bars, but they also represent significant departures, not uncritical continuities from one to the other.[16]

Not to say that club nights are perfect. "You can't ever build a space for everyone," Soof says. "I don't think it ever exists all-in-one-go, at the same time." What about you? I ask, curious about Soof's personal experiences. "I think queer spaces don't tick all my boxes because I've got so many other things that need ticking as well," they reply. "But that's okay." When club night organizers use queerness to strive for an intentionally inclusive ethos, they do not naïvely presume that one size fits all. "The moment you go, 'Yeah, this covers everyone,' is the moment it gets a bit dangerous and will unintentionally end up excluding someone." The way out of the good queer/bad gay binary, then, is to reorient how we think about nightlife: we must recognize its many cultural centers without privileging any one expression.

After pausing for a moment, Soof begins to smile. "I'll take a buffet," they say (from eyelines and starfish to buffets, I love the metaphors Soof uses to grapple with complex ideas). "I'm going to take that bit from that bit, that bit, and have an amazing meal." The wisdom of these words embodies the qualities of queerness: its messiness, its sense of movement, its people-led aesthetics. Club nights "can't solve every problem in the world," Soof admits, looking untroubled, "but they can solve this one particular thing for me."

Gayzpacho

Bethnal Green Working Men's Club

"Ever since we become adults, everything around us becomes more serious, more orderly, more logical," Angel told me. "At Gayzpacho, we try to do the opposite." Now was my chance to lock up the adult Amin at home and find a place to free the more playful side of me.

That night, I was with five hundred other people who paid £18 (US$22) each and flocked to Bethnal Green Working's Men Club, a venue in East London that supports diverse events, from the cultural and refined to wild good times, as they proudly proclaim on Instagram. This particular party occurs three or four times a year, and it offers exaggerated, nonsensical imagery full of belly-laughing fun every time as it celebrates queer Spanish heritage.

The night got started with a flamenco show, which worked like an opening ceremony. A guitarist, singer, and several dancers began to perform, subduing the din. The melody felt like it carried the ancestors of gypsy communities, although the voice that accompanied the music was full of hope. Some people turned to the stage to contemplate the performance, while others danced with their eyes closed.

"Flamenco has something special," Angel whispered in my ear. I turned to look at him, meeting his eyes and inviting him to say more.

Meet Angel, the incomparable co-creator of Gayzpacho. Photo credit: Manu Valcarce.

"It opens people's hearts, it humbles them, it gives rise to our best emotions, like connection, empathy, compassion, empowerment. I think it brings us closer." In that moment, I felt connected with the dancers, with Angel, and with everyone else in the room. By the end of the singing and the dancing, something had shifted: arms were now flung around shoulders. This club night was already special, and we just got started.

Angel and I went to the bar after the performance. As we waited, he connected the event with the Spanish queer diaspora in London—"to which I belong," he said. "Gayzpacho, being born of this diaspora, has evolved into an identity of its own," Angel tells me, "one that remembers its origin but that also embraces the place in which it exists." What does that mean? I ask, so I can better understand the culture of the party. "Gayzpacho is Spanish, but it is also British and pan-European."

With drinks in hand, we returned to the dance floor and moved for a bit. The night featured euro-electric beats, a little disco, and some carnival sounds, all of which was fun to dance to. Next came a collection of performances. Camille, a regular entertainer, walked onto

▸ Soulful sounds, soulful moves. Photo credit: Zbigniew Kotkiewicz.

Jonny Woo is on fire. Photo credit: Manu Valcarce.

a stage at one end of the room, the word "GAYZPACHO" written in all-caps and different colors inside a heart of red lights on the wall. At first, I thought she looked shy, but soon enough, her act transformed into a symbol of defiance. Camille removed her clothes, revealing a dominatrix look with a bewitching red wig and brazen buck antlers tattooed on her neck. I was mesmerized.

After Camille came Jonny Woo, a co-organizer of the party with Angel and another regular performer. Johnny startled the crowd by gripping a sparkler in his bum while a drag queen with a maniacal expression on her face lit it on fire! This was all par for the course, Angel told me in hysterics. "We have had processions carrying drag virgin Mary across the dance floor, naked performers spitting fire from their buttholes, and we have cruised each in a dark room under a giant bull's head lit up with candles." By this point, my eyes were watering from laughing so hard.

Some hours in, Gayzpacho unveiled its signature move, the outrageous moment for which it is best known: a tomato wrestling competition—on stage—set to Spanish music. Angel and Jonny invited six volunteers the night before, using social media to connect with

▸ Camille commands the stage at Gayzpacho. Photo credit: Zbigniew Kotkiewicz.

How the Gayzpacho gets made: tomato wrestling at center stage. Photo credit: Manu Valcarce.

A saucy celebration. Photo credit: Manu Valcarce.

them. The prep was exhilarating to observe: a group of volunteers emptied what looked to me like a hundred pounds of tomato passata (a puree) into a paddling pool, the kind that toddlers play in during a backyard barbecue. The wrestlers stared at the scene from the side with a mixture of delight and horror. One by one they would get in the pool—and slip and slide in all that passata.

"We wrestle shame with vulnerability," Angel told me as we studied the stage. The scene was definitely disarming: stripping down to your underwear and wrestling in a pool of pureed tomatoes, being silly and making a fool of yourself in public, everyone watching you with glee but without judgment. The goal was to wrestle until one person managed to push the other out of the pool. I watched one winner wrestle another until a sauce-covered champion stood alone, receiving boisterous ovations from fellow competitors on stage—and the rest of us applauding from a drier distance away.

There was no prize that night, not one that I saw, nothing beyond what I guessed was a moment of escape and freedom, an opportunity to play in a way most of us never even dare to dream. Some of the wrestlers stayed in their briefs and continued to dance, tomato-drenched, until the very end. I left the party that night with my heart looking like their skin, soaked in joy.

That Was Fun

In recent years, the closure epidemic was overshadowed by a viral epidemic and then, in short order, a global pandemic. As I write this, we find ourselves in a strange, twilight zone–like moment: we are post-COVID but not really, we are returning to some kind of normal but still far from what life was like before, and we are not entirely sure what comes next. I described the closure epidemic in these pages as a disruptive event—the pandemic, of course, has been a disruption par excellence—and both have forced us to think about the significance of places: what they mean and why they matter.

Gay bars and nightclubs faced profound challenges even before the pandemic—58 percent closed in London in between 2006 and 2016, and 37 percent vanished in the United States around the same time. Those numbers come from the "before times," as my friends and I describe the world before it flipped upside down. What happened after? And through it all—one day after another in our life, one page after another in this book—what did we learn?[1]

All LGBTQ+ nighttime venues in London, like every other business, had to close between March 2020 and July 2021—sixteen grueling months of anxiety and a massive loss of revenues—as Britons endured three national lockdowns. In that time, which was compounded by an inflationary crisis, the Night Time Industries Association, a not-for-profit group that represents businesses operating between the hours of 6pm and 6am, estimated that nightclubs across the country closed at a rate of one every two days, equivalent to the loss of 10.63 clubs every month.[2]

But none of this—not the closure epidemic, not the pandemic, not soaring inflation—portended the end of nightlife. Far from it. The closing of gay bars and nightclubs sparked a revolution of culture and creativity. To borrow from the British writer Samuel Johnson, my research revealed that there is in London all that nightlife can afford.[3]

The vast disruptions of the pandemic only proved what we already knew: nightlife is a place of belonging, proof of existence, and a joyful experiment in worldmaking. The creative genius behind the Opulence party, madison captured the essence beautifully: "To the why of queer nightlife, we are always looking for erotic release in the face of constant and daily annihilation." So many of our revelatory encounters emerge from the uncertainties of life. These past several years have offered the greatest uncertainty we have ever known, in fact, and they confirmed the monumental importance of nightlife. In our final moments, let's shoot for the stars and take stock of some of the gifts that queer nightlife offers.

Nightlife Is Belonging

Every step of the way, with each person we met and every party we attended, we danced with feelings of belonging. Proposed by psychologists in the 1990s, the "belongingness hypothesis" suggests that every one of us has a fundamental need to belong. We pursue that need by trying our best to form stable, positive attachments with other people. A generation of research in psychology has made it clear that no person is an island. But as a sociologist, I want to invite us to explicitly broaden the contours of this concept. After all, our connections with others do not happen in a social vacuum but as we interact with people in particular places. Acknowledging that dual reality—people in places, places with people—shifts our perspective from belonging in some vague sense to *belonging in place*.[4]

Think for a minute about your favorite gay bar or club night. Why do you love it? For Ingo, the producer of numerous events, the feeling is spiritual. "It's like our church," they say, drawing on more than two decades of experience in nightlife production. Damien uses the same word: "I felt like it was my church, and when I went there, I was praising who I was as a human being with others like me, so that was a congregational kind of collective experience." Gabriel and Othon, the co-founders of Papa Loko, explore the collective effervescence we experience in nightlife: "When people come to dance, they come with a much more open spirit, open heart," they tell me. "It's a great opportunity to use that state, when people are more open, when they're more receptive, so you can give them something beautiful, something full of light."[5]

I was surprised at how often I heard religious and spiritual references, like church and light, to describe the experience of belonging in nightlife. Laurie from The Chateau introduced me to something called the "queer third eye." He mentioned his friend Tam, who has been running venues for more than three decades, and how "Tam has this theory about the queer third eye, which is an idea of a higher being or a higher power for queer people." I find myself drawn to the concept. "It's like an energy, and it guides you in what you do."

Laurie's queer third eye opened once he started organizing club nights. "It was always my dream to be on stage," he says. "I wanted to be a singer. I wanted to be Freddie Mercury, as you can see, the poster." Laurie laughs as he points to an image taped to the wall that depicts him as Mercury in drag. "I was like, 'Oh my god, I'm not going to make it! What am I doing?'" It was then that he imagined using nightlife as an outlet for his creative ambitions. "As soon as I changed that tack of my life to try and create this space, everything has just flowed in such a natural way." Each step has come with affirmations. "To hear people say how much it means to them, to have a trans man come up to you and tell you that they took their top off in the space for the first time because they felt comfortable. Those little things that we experience, it is amazing. The energy of queer people is like nothing else you've ever felt." For Laurie, "it's a gift."

When our third eye opens, we feel like we are at our "cultural home," an analogy from both Liam and Kat. This idea, *nightlife emplaces belonging*, has been a book-tying thread for us. By shifting our focus from gay bars to club nights, we saw how that cultural home, and those feelings of belonging, can be emplaced without being place-bound. Club nights pop up around the city, after all, and they are not available every night.[6]

Nightlife is "where we do everything, and so it becomes our culture." I heard this from Glyn, the founder of Sink the Pink. The UK's largest queer clubbing extravaganza that ran for thirteen years, Glyn sold 150,000 tickets to his events; collaborated with Pink, Little Mix, and Mel C; and performed everywhere from the five-day Glastonbury

Festival to Times Square in New York. "That's why people feel so connected to it and so passionate about it—because it's our culture. A huge amount of our culture is in our nightlife." Revolutions erupt from cultural homes. "I feel like gay nightlife has—let's be honest, it's changed the world. It's changed pop culture. It's changed fashion. So much comes out of it, because it's a frenzied place of excess and creativity. It breaks down a lot of social stuff."

Belonging is abstract, an idea that is hard to measure. Yet the recurring analogies I heard—nightlife is culture or a cultural home, nightlife is church or congregational, nightlife is energy or spiritual—suggest that the places we go at night for fellowship, where we experiment with creating new worlds and new centers, shape who we are with a transcendent force. "I feel like people take club culture, queer club culture, seriously because that's the backbone of the community," Chester, the organizer of Little Gay Brother, tells me. That phrase, community backbone, is so vivid. It describes something central, constitutional, and connective. What makes nightlife so fundamental? Gideön, the mastermind behind NYC Downlow, can think of many reasons. "As a group of people, we get to pass down everything through music and culture." A lot of this happens in nightlife: "the way we communicate with each other, the way that we dance, the way we tell stories, the language we use, the fashion, the way we move, the way that we relate to each other." I sway as I listen, drawn to the rhythm of the words. As he watches me, Gideön proclaims his adoration for the underground scenes where club nights are thriving. "I'm laying claim over the spirit of the queer dance floor, underground gay culture—the thing that is like the magic ingredient for everything."

Nightlife Is Proof

When we go out, whether to a gay bar that has survived or a club night, we connect with our history, who we are, where we were, where we want to be. "It's nice to think of a party or a space as a way of organizing people's engagement with the past," Brooke shares with me. We like this feeling, Simon, the producer of Duckie, says:

"People like history. They like heritage. They like having a past, and hopefully a future."

Nightlife is important because it proves we exist. "We're all walking vessels of history," Damien, an education officer at Parliament, adds, "but sometimes we don't realize it unless we meet others, and we talk about it." We need to see ourselves through the lens of people and places. "And then you get ripples," Damien continues. "It's like a pond. Someone chucks in a stone, and you get all these ripples of memory and history, and you're swimming in that pool together."

London's institutional offerings, what it does and especially does not have, make nightlife feel extra special. "London's really shoddy for queer institutions," Ben Walters quips. How do you mean? I ask. "We don't have a museum at the moment," he replies, and then uses repetitions to express a larger point. "We don't have a community center at the moment. We don't have an AIDS memorial at the moment. We don't have any of these sites that affirm to queer people that we have been here in this city for a long time, forever, and that we matter, and that we have a stake in not just our own lives and the lives of the people that we love, and respect, and cherish—but in the city. The closest thing to that is nightlife venues."

Ben and I have spent a lot of time together during my visits to London, both one-on-one and on dance floors with friends. "Historically, the only spaces that are like institutional places with an institutional lineage of queer use are nightlife venues," he says. To feel a sense of continuity is powerful, and nightlife provides that. As I listened, I heard distant echoes of Descartes: we come together at night, therefore we are. Or more simply: *nightlife, therefore we are.*

The pain we feel when a place closes is further proof, visceral proof, of how important it was, how much we value and need places in general, and the link they provide between us, each other, and our histories. Zax, a museum assistant, told me about a project called "This Dancefloor Isn't Here Anymore." The performance art piece, held on Valentine's Day in 2018, portrays "acts of remembrance" which "summon up that history, the disappearance of spaces." On their social media page, Zax wrote: "Queers! Is this the end of London? Or is it the beginning? This is a one-night living archive of transient queer spaces and moments, through performance, through intimacy." Zax invites us to reflect on why nightlife matters. "Have you ever fallen in love on the dance floor? Can you still taste the freedom and fear the first time you kissed another queer person? Do you remember taking your first pill? Have you ever fallen in love with a room full of strangers all at once? Can you imagine, beyond surviving in London, what would it look like for us to thrive, to flourish?" The performance was about the "mourning of queer spaces that we have loved and lost," Zax tells me. They expressed grief as "a queer remix of the Kaddish," which is "the Jewish prayer that you would say over someone's dead body." By importing it into nightlife, "we say goodbye to spaces that we've lost." Even so, Zax can still imagine a more hopeful future. "We invoke or summon a new queer city" where queer nightlife can insist and persist.

Prem uses art to mirror life above ground, like Zax, but also to inspire gatherings below it. They are part of a collective of "London's finest young artists" who are "doubling up as party planners" to produce a club night called Anal House Meltdown, the "artiest-not-fartiest" underground party, "cult night," and "queer party with the best name," as *i-D* describes in multiple feature stories. Prem once did an exhibition at an art gallery "when Soho began to be very boarded up." The closure of bars, their meltdown, informed Prem's art practices. "Because I noticed that there was lots of shutter boarding on windows, and signs taken down, and empty venues, I tried to mirror that with the gallery space." The inside reflected the world outside. "I boarded the whole gallery up. I invited people to use the gallery as a meeting space. I just put benches in there, and it became a quite bleak view about the closure of spaces during that time because as you stood inside the gallery, you could only see the wood through the windows. There wasn't a view outside of it." Prem's gallery might sound grim, but it inspired them to create Anal House Meltdown. They express this motivation concisely: "Nightlife is part of our artmaking."[7]

So powerful are the feelings we have for nightlife that the closure of a beloved venue can feel like the loss of a limb, as it did for Jon. "When a place closes down, that's a loss. You lose a finger. You lose an arm. It's not very nice." The image is intense, and I can feel it in my body as he describes it. "When a place closes down, it's just part of you—I'm going to be dramatic now—part of you dies with that place."

Mourning, prayers over dead bodies, the loss of limbs, dying with a place: these are unforgettable metaphors for why nightlife matters—and the message is mighty. We feel a strong connection with the places where we gather, our cultural homes, and we grieve when they close. That sense of agony and anguish was felt even by those people who did not particularly like gay bars, or did not always feel welcome in them, attesting to the considerable power of nightlife more broadly. What I heard over and over again, implicitly and explicitly, is that nightlife provides proof of existence, evidence that we were here, evidence that we are *still* here.

Nightlife Is Joy

Ben invited me to join him one Saturday night at the RVT for Duckie, the UK's longest-running weekly club night. After twenty-seven years of bacchanal bashes, this famed, performance art–based party was taking a bow on July 2, 2022, the weekend of London's fiftieth anniversary Pride celebrations. My heart hurt when I heard the news. Duckie survived the pandemic, only to close after London reopened.[8]

Duckie began in 1995 when, as Ben writes in *The Guardian*, "six twentysomething mates in London were sick of never finding anywhere to go out that fitted their idea of fun, so they put on a night of their own at the RVT and called it Duckie." The party's raison d'être was a subversive opposition to the mainstream scene of the 1990s. Rather than "gym culture" or "strippers and pills," Duckie did something different with its "live-art vibe of the ICA, creating what it called 'homosexual honky-tonk.'" In short, Duckie was "less consumerist-aspirational gay, more sarky art-school queer."[9]

I arrived around eleven to a place that was already full of people, shoulder-to-shoulder, dancing and drinking, laughing. The bar, outfitted in chocolate brown wood paneling, was on the opposite end from where I entered. The interior was shaped like a crescent, mimicking the exterior architectural structure of the building. It took me several minutes to walk across the 1,500-square-foot room that, during the day, would take just seconds. Perpendicular to the bar was a raised seating area, and across from it was the performance stage. The entire space could accommodate around four hundred people. The cover charge that night was £10 (US$12). Many looked like regulars, I thought as I scanned the smiling faces, and I felt like I was at a family reunion. Saturday nights at Duckie, Ben tells me, have catalyzed "lifelong bonds." No wonder the party is "a queer night out that feels like home." For Ben, Duckie has been transformative: "It's a place where I learned how powerfully fun, challenge, and care can combine."

I watched these words on Ben's body as we raised our glasses in the air, toasted, and danced until two in the morning. That moment in time felt forever special to me. With each bump and grind, strut and shuffle, Ben and I were sharing cultural information with each other, "like the body's version of an accent or tone of voice." That's how Emma Warren describes dancing. Music, Warren says and as I experienced many times, "sounds better when it's danced, and when it's communal." Just as I celebrated club nights for their worldmaking (not statistical) qualities, so too does Warren make a similar point about dancing: "The day-to-day art of moving to music is not about quantifiable excellence; it's about coming as you are and contributing to the dance floor."[10]

Sitting down for breakfast the next morning, I slowly sipped my coffee, reflected on my night out, and thought: *that was fun*. Nightlife is an alchemical feeling—an intimate interlinking of having fun and feeling joy—that depends on us coming together in person, in places, in moments. Nightlife, Ben says, "needs to exist as physical spaces that people can come to and be together." Why is that? I ask. Why can't we do it online? "Because there are so many aspects of human engagement that you can only get when bodies are in rooms together," he replies. "Of course, there are other things that happen in other conduits as well," Ben quickly qualifies, "but that's really, really, really big, the things that happen when bodies are in rooms together." Co-presence in place is everything—it's "irreplaceable," Ben argues. "You can't have culture without knocking heads and knocking other body parts." People, places, moments. These, I think, are crucial elements for creating nightlife cultures. Ben continues, "People see each other, people look at each other, people feel each other, people pick up all the different signals: their pheromones, their looks, their sex." I nod and smile as he speaks. "There's laughter, there's crowds, there's dancing, there's arguments, there's humanity."

The Morning After

I have been struck while writing this book by how much we have to learn from people like the night czar, the producers of club nights, and those of us who flock to them. I would often wonder the next morning, after my very visceral and ebullient experiences, about the feelings that would stay with me. It was always joy, queer joy. That sensation I would savor, like a favorite drink. I felt it so frequently and so deeply—imagine writing a book about nightlife without feeling joy!—but are other researchers as keen?

Take the closure epidemic. Today, years after reports from the UK and the United States released early distress signals, gay bars still exist—alive and quite well in many places around the world—and yet we are still losing sleep about them and still not seeing a bigger picture about how nightlife is changing. To wit: Greggor Mattson, the author of the original American study on bar closures, tells *LGBTQ Nation*, an online news magazine, that "widespread alarm" about "the decline" of gay bars continues to this day (he gave the interview in 2022). "In most parts of the country, gay bars are the only public LGBTQ+ place," Mattson says. "In other words, they're the only place where queer people can reliably encounter other queer people in public."[11]

I find the standard story fatiguing, quite frankly, in its emphasis on loss and limited opportunities for fellowship. Existing arguments about LGBTQ+ nightlife, in public discussions as well as in the social sciences, often focus on one place, the gay bar—apparently, the "only place." If we see those bars through the lens of a closure epidemic, then it's no wonder we lose sight of joy! But we survived a global pandemic, and we came out the other side with incredible insights and innovations about people, places, and moments. Why wouldn't we make it through the closure epidemic in a similar way? Having come this far, I want you to leave my party with a more dynamic view of nightlife as still, and always, vibrant.

You can never step in the same river twice, the poet Heraclitus said. The culture creatives we met used bar closures to reflect on their experiences in nightlife and to reorient it in response. Not once did they turn a blind eye to real social problems in order to make room for more people and more places. Marginalized groups struggle and suffer—from the crushing forces of capitalism to a core of whiteness, belt buckle encounters and blackface, institutionalized homophobia and systemic inequalities—but they also find moments of joy.

Grappling with complex interpersonal and structural factors without denying our human capacity for joy was not an easy task! To guide us, we created a compass from three concepts. I first encouraged us to see nightlife as a larger landscape, like a cultural field, where gay bars are not the *only* place but *one* place among *other* places. Researchers use the word "isomorphism" to describe the trouble we can have recognizing other kinds of places, or other organizational forms, in that field. As the second concept in our compass, this idea also served us well. It ensured that we did not focus exclusively on the most familiar and visible expressions of nightlife—but without losing sight of them either. We heard about power struggles in gay bars, like the zine clash and the Hides/Jonz controversy, although we used those difficult moments to appreciate how creative prospects can emerge in a field from the ashes of conflict.

But still, gay bars *are* closing in startling numbers, they *are* very important places (even if also fraught), and we *did* have to account for them. Bar closures were the start of our story, however, not its end. And that brings me to the final concept in our compass: we conceptualized bar closures as a disruptive event. Disruptions, the management scholar Letian Zhang notes, can be "either anticipated, such as a merger, or unexpected, such as a natural disaster." Either way, they "dramatically alter the opportunities available to different groups." We examined disruptions as at once a social problem—statistics about bar closures are undeniable and undeniably troubling—and an encourager of revolutions in nightlife scenes.

Each concept in our compass is popular among organizational and cultural sociologists, although we used them to explore new ways of thinking about how disruptions affect urban nightlife. These areas of study are seldom in conversation, yet blending them revealed a picture that few others have seen or studied: gay bars are closing, yes, but a greater number and variety of club nights are emerging at the same time. Ritualistic gatherings, even if they are nomadic or occasional, provide joyful moments of contact that can inspire us to create new worlds. It doesn't matter that those moments are fleeting. The time I spent at club nights in London made me forever fall in love with nightlife, with the city, and with its people. Intermittent interactions can leave indelible impressions.

Joy is foundational to this book, as it is to human existence, but some researchers are allergic to it. This is noticeable in sociology, where there is a full-on "joy deficit," as stef m. shuster and Laurel Westbrook call it. Scholars are preoccupied with the negative, focusing on inequalities, trauma, bigotry, and discrimination. Mine is a problem-oriented discipline, and so I suppose what Eve Tuck describes as "damage-centered research," work that documents our pain and brokenness, makes sense. Too often, we assume that joy is the opposite of social problems, and to focus on it must involve a neglect of those concerns. That makes centering joy pointless, at best, or else irresponsible. But the notion of a "problem" is neither simple nor self-evident. Problems can be a topic of study, but they can also be an analytic approach. In other words, we can think critically about joy, asking why it matters and about its collective consequences, just as we can address social problems with a sense of hope and agency.[12]

Damaging experiences are inevitable in an unjust world. But, as shuster and Westbrook say, they are "only part, not the whole" of our life. If we focus entirely on "negative experiences and outcomes," then "misery and oppression become erroneously magnified, while the aspects that make lives livable become obscured." Too often, journalists and academics describe the experiences of minority groups using tropes of suffering and misery—the doom and gloom narratives that Lewis cautioned us against right away.[13]

Consider this: in late 2022, the sexualities section of the American Sociological Association was welcoming a new chair who circulated an email to the entire section of more than six hundred scholars. I sank in my chair as I read that "vulnerabilities abound," "we are in a moment of crisis theorizing," "more trouble is coming," and an "unraveling" is "happening at both the planetary scale and at the smaller scales of our communities." How do these words make you feel?[14]

The crises are many. It's true. And yet, I think we do ourselves and the world a disservice if we allow crisis theorizing to become our *only* theorizing. What about our capacious capacity for joy? Even those humanists who succeed in expanding conversations about nightlife to "the variety of permanent, temporary, stable, and mobile sites" somehow still see only limited slices of what those places can provide. People go out "to get relief from the pressure of everyday life," they say, but also, I would add, to feel joy.[15] Club night organizers see the closure crisis and the viral crisis—how could they not?—but they respond by putting pressure on the pillars of power that prop it up—and *still* they manage to laugh and play.

We cannot breathe in joy if our air is filled with particles of pain. To be clear, I am not minimizing the injuries we suffer, nor am I diminishing the agony that is the architecture on some streets of our life. We need places of respite, and we need to recharge. Instead, I am acknowledging what I was told again and again: when life brings pain, nightlife counters with moments of relief, a little rhapsody, and a lot of joy.[16]

When I was eating bagels at Buttmitzvah, cleansing myself of patriarchy at Femmetopia, dancing behind converted Victorian brick railway arches at The CAMPerVAN, swooning over the sultry sounds of cabaret at The Cocoa Butter Club, singing Bollywood hits at Hungama, feeling erotic energies at Adonis, admiring the power of queer activism during a porn screening at INFERNO, giggling as I watched tomato wrestlers at Gayzpacho, or connecting with the familial crowd at Duckie, my heart was so happy that I thought it might burst! Our neglect of joy, the recognition that it can come from pain but still motivate us to create something beautiful, constitutes an ethical and intellectual failure. Being an engaged citizen of the world, or a serious scholar, does not require us to evict joy from our mind or from our pen. I refuse to punctuate my book with pain.

When we started, I called fun a gateway drug, a way we work out how to be together, how to express the world in intentional and radically inclusive terms. Let me bring us full circle and allow fun to have the final say, as it did the first. “Fun matters,” Ben tells me. “Fun is worth taking seriously.” Having fun at night makes life more livable, I reflect back. “Fun is really important,” he adds, although it “tends to be trivialized.” It sure does, I say. “Fun is basically how we rehearse all the things that we do in life.” It gestures to a future defined not by closures but by commencements.[17]

When I returned to London after what felt like an eternity of lockdowns and social restrictions, I wanted desperately to have fun again, to feel joy again. That urge—surely you felt it too—is a valuable lesson we can take from that brutal period of our lives. Because even when we are not in the midst of a global pandemic, we still need to have fun. We still need joy. Alluring, indomitable things, those feelings. *Nightlife is fun. Nightlife is joy.* Three simple words in each instance that show us ways of changing the world.

The fun we have on a dance floor—like I did, like I hope you do—provides what Ben calls “a place to experiment with low stakes.” Those stakes may be low, yet the end result is anything but. “It’s powerful,” he affirms. I ask why, anticipating that some readers may want to dismiss having fun and feeling joy as hedonistic or trivial. “Even though it looks or feels disposable and inconsequential, fun models and rehearses values, behavior, and interactions that have wider ethical and political consequences. The fun you have says a lot about the world you want.” I wonder what you think.

What fun do you have?

What joy do you feel?

What world do you want?

The Crew

Bar Owners, Party Producers, DJs

Name	Age	Sexuality	Gender	Race/Ethnicity	Club Night
Aisha	29	queer	nonbinary	Pakistani Egyptian	Misery
Alex	29	gay	cis male	White British	Knickerbocker
Amy	32	queer lesbian	female	Welsh	Lèse Majesté
Angel	35	queer	male	Spanish	Gayzpacho
Angelica	34	queer	femme woman	White British	Choose Your Own Adventure
Cassie	28	lesbian	female	Welsh and St. Lucian Mixed Race British	The Cocoa Butter Club
Chester	27	gay/queer	cis male	White British	Little Gay Brother
Dan	40	gay	male	White British	Chapter 10, Disco Bloodbath, Dalston Superstore
Dwayne	35	gay	male	Black British	Lèse Majesté
Eden	26	bisexual	male	White and Arabic	Riposte
Gabriel	41	gay	male	Venetian Italian	Papa Loco
Gaby	25	queer	genderqueer	French Arabic	Queer Direct
Gideön	41	gay	male by birth	White British and Jewish Lithuanian	NYC Downlow
Glyn	39	gay/queer	male	Borderless White British	Sink the Pink

Ingo	56	queer	nonbinary	Swedish	Bar Wotever, Club Fuck, Female Masculinity Appreciation Society, Nonbinary Cabaret, Wotever World
Kat	26	queer	female	White British and American	Femmetopia
Laurie	28	gay	cis male	White British	The Chateau
Lewis	27	queer	nonbinary/genderqueer	White British	INFERNO
Lucia	22	queer	trans woman	White British	Transmissions
Lyall	51	no labels	no labels	Maori	VFD
madison	36	queer	male (all pronouns)	African American	Opulence
Matt	30	gay	male	Jewish American	Buttmitzvah
Nadine	29	queer femme	undecided	Scottish Pakistani	Pxssy Palace
Othon	39	gay	male	Greek	Papa Loco
Prem	35	gay/queer	nonbinary	South Asian and Polish Mixed Race British	Anal House Meltdown
Ryan	32	queer	male	South Asian Canadian, British, and Asian	Hungama
Sadie	27	queer lesbian	female	Black British and Zambian	The Cocoa Butter Club
Samuel	27	queer	cis male	White Jewish British	BUM.P, The CAMPerVAN, HOWL
Shay	36	gay	male	White British	Adonis
Simon	51	gay/queer	male	White British	Duckie
Tia	25	queer	female	Black British	BBZ

Activists, Artists

Name	Age	Sexuality	Gender	Race/Ethnicity	Occupation
Brooke	30	queer lesbian	nonbinary	Italian American	book dealer
Carla	32	queer	genderqueer	White British	nonprofit director
Dan de la Motte	27	queer	cis male	White European	performer and tour guide
Dan Glass	34	queer	male	Jewish	activist
Erkan	24	queer	genderqueer	Middle Eastern British	curatorial resident
Greygory	38	queer	trans	White British	barber
Peter	36	queer	male	White British	project manager
Rosie	36	lesbian	female	White British and Sephardic Jewish	filmmaker
Zax	28	queer	genderqueer	Black and Hungarian Mixed Race British	museum assistant

Government Officials, City Employees

Name	Age	Sexuality	Gender	Race/Ethnicity	Occupation
Amy Lamé	47	lesbian	female	White Other	night czar
Edward Bayes	26	heterosexual	male	White British	culture-at-risk officer
Elliott	44	gay	male	White British	city planner
Rishi	36	gay	male	Asian-Gujarati British	councilor

Nightlife Researchers

Name	Age	Sexuality	Gender	Race/Ethnicity	Occupation
Ben Campkin	41	gay/queer	cis male	White British	professor
Ben Walters	41	gay/queer	male	White and Jewish British	independent researcher
Em	32	lesbian	female	White British	teaching fellow
Mark	33	gay	male	White British	professor
Olimpia	23	queer lesbian	female	Italian	graduate student

Revelers

Name	Age	Sexuality	Gender	Race/Ethnicity	Occupation
Alan	57	queer	male	White British	teacher
Amelia	26	lesbian	cis female	White British	journalist
Amir	23	gay	cis male	Swedish and German Egyptian	policy analyst
Andrew	38	gay	male	White British	manager
Andy	52	gay/queer	male	European	massage therapist
Ashley	46	lesbian	female	White British	engineer
Charlotte	43	gay woman	female	White European	HR manager
Chris	26	gay	male	White and Mexican Mixed Race British	video producer
Damien	35	gay/queer	male	White British and Irish	education officer
James	30	gay	male	White British	advertising

(continued)

Joe	26	gay	male	White British	teacher
Jon	45	gay	male	Basque	human resources
Jonathan	30	gay	male	White British	finance
Jonathan	35	queer	male	Mixed Race	tutor
Julia	34	lesbian	female	Mixed Race	architect
Katayoun	22	queer	genderqueer	Iranian	union organizer
Kenny	39	gay	male	Scottish	advertising
Koen	23	gay	male	Dutch	student
Liam	26	gay	male	White British	professor
Lola	33	bisexual queer	gender nonconforming cis female	African British	fundraiser
Manuel	37	gay	nonbinary	Spanish	civil servant
Matthew	30	gay	male	Black British	manager
Michael	24	gay	male	White British and Jewish	journalist
Rachel	30	lesbian	female	White British	manager
Richard	38	gay	male	White British	diplomat
Ryan	41	gay	male	Native American	professor
Sam	29	gay	male	White British	accountant
Sam	34	gay	male	Mixed Race British	fundraiser
Soof	26	queer and asexual	gender nonconforming	Pakistani British	graphic designer
Stefan	32	gay	male	White Canadian	manager
Stuart	36	gay	male	White British	magazine editor
Tom	30	gay	male	Irish	advertising

(continued)

Acknowledgments

This book was an accident. When my friend Ryan invited me to join him at the London School of Economics and Political Science (LSE) for my sabbatical in 2018, I had no intentions of studying nightlife—or even going to London. But for reasons I still cannot explain, I followed my feelings and landed at Heathrow.

Then came a series of surprises—people, places, and moments—that effloresced into this book. Each was an opportunity that manifested unexpectedly, like magic or metaphysics, to guide my pen.

The Seeds of Something. My deepest gratitude to Ryan Centner for that initial invitation, and to his colleagues in the geography department for nurturing the beginnings, before there was even an idea. Claire Mercer, Alan Mace, Kasia Paprocki, Austin Zeiderman, and Sam Colegate made me feel welcomed right away at St. Clements.

It is true that there is in London all that life can offer—and I longed for more. Thanks to LSE sociology for supporting my return a year later in 2019 and then again in 2022. Rebecca Elliott, Sam Friedman, Suzi Hall, Monika Krause, David Madden, and Fran Tonkiss gifted me with their colleagueship and friendship.

Thank you to the staff at High Holborn residences for allowing me to stay in the same flat each year; it became my beloved British home. Jubilee Hall kept my body strong as I made demands on my mind. I give thanks to Julien Bertherat for training sessions where I could process ideas and Riz Niwaz, the resident chef, for healthy, protein-packed meals. Pub crawls with Gary Coulson, Richard Lee-Smith, Dwayne Clark, Jonathan Cole, Tommy Grimshaw, Amit Nigam, Gerulf Rieger, and Michael Segalov provided the elixir of laughter and levity.

This research was undertaken, in part, thanks to funding from the Canada Research Chairs Program. The initiative establishes federally endowed research professorships across the country for a diverse cadre of world-class researchers. I hold a Canada Research Chair in

Urban Sexualities. I thank the Government of Canada for awarding me one of these prestigious positions and financially supporting me in my pursuit of research excellence.

Everyone I met in my three years of fieldwork in London engaged with an open mind and heart. One conversation led to another until I met 112 people from all walks of nightlife. I thank each of you for your generosity of time and spirit. (And Paula Kamen and Margie Porcella for their transcriptions of this treasure trove of ideas.) You Londoners deserve credit for all that sparkles, and I alone for anything that does not.

A few people were especially revelatory in helping me formulate arguments, and some went above and beyond with kindness: Amelia Abraham, Dan Beaumont, Laurie Belgrave, Simon Brooksbank, Olimpia Burchiellaro, Lewis G. Burton, Tia Campbell, Ben Campkin, Simon Casson, Peter Cragg, Damien Arness Dalton, Samuel Douek, Matt Feczko, Dan Glass, Kat Hudson, Ryan Lanji, Cassie Leon, Mark McCormack, Aisha Mirza, madison moore, Angel Samuel Perez, Amy Roberts, Amir Salem, and Ben Walters. Without you, these pages simply could not and would not be.

Each goodbye harder than the last, I loved how London would break my heart at the end of each visit. Alas, all good things, as they say. Or was it something about the closing and opening of doors? Opportunities that look like windows? No cliché can capture the effect that doing this work has had on me—and for that, I am forever grateful to you, London.

Centering Joy. The pandemic was an utterly abnormal period. When life went into lockdown, Ellen Berrey in Toronto, Page Nolker in the Pocono Mountains, and I in Vancouver formed a group called "Trinity." We met every two or three weeks on Zoom for moments of spiritual fellowship. Trinity cued me into joy, a concept-feeling that became our muse and meditation. Joy is a form of activism, we would say, a way of elevating the consciousness of the planet. I thank Ellen and Page for this precious gift. That's how joy found its way to the heart of my book.

The Architecture of Ideas. In January 2019, Jean Beaman reached out and asked if I would pen a piece for the journal *Metropolitics*. With her guidance, I wrote "Culture and the Nighttime Economy," the first essay in which I attempted to make sense of some of my initial data. Jean did not know then that I was working on a book, but I thank her, for she helped me to realize the interlaced economic and cultural significance of nightlife: it has a unique economy, and it constitutes a core part of a city's cultural infrastructure.

And then time stopped. The year 2020 is a blur, a memory hole, yet those months prompted in me a sense of urgency. Lockdowns and social isolation were a brutal reminder of our need for life. As the haze lifted a little in February 2021, the sociology department at Brown invited me to speak about the connective power of organizations for the study of cities, cultures, and sexualities. Although my doctoral degree was in a joint sociology and organizational behavior program, I had not considered that theories about organizations could help me understand queer nightlife—but that's exactly what I came to realize as I prepared my lecture. Conversations with Janet Blume, Dan Hirschman, Micheal Kennedy, David Lindstrom, Josh Pacewicz, Mark Suchman, and Nicole Gonzalez Van Cleve helped me clarify my thinking about the generative possibilities of disruptive events.

Robust intellectual foundations are often multilayered and, for me, sometimes a matter of luck. To celebrate their fiftieth anniversary, Jan Willem Duyvendak, the brilliant director of the Netherlands Institute for Advanced Study (NIAS), invited me to deliver a keynote address over Zoom in June 2021 on the subject of belonging. I thank him for the generous gift. A year later, in the summer of 2022, I was in residence at NIAS in beautiful Amsterdam. Rousing conversations over lunch with Jan Willem and in queer spaces with Aidan McGarry, a charming former fellow, refined the introduction and the conclusion, which for me were some of the hardest pieces to write.

I did not anticipate any of these invitations, yet each birthed a big idea—culture and economics from *Metropolitics*, organizations from Brown, and belonging from NIAS. I am grateful for the interplay of industry and luck, my guides as I crafted the architecture of ideas for this book.

From Private to Public. For reasons I do not fully understand—perhaps my decision to foreground joy in a problem-centered discipline, or the psychic damage that critics have done to me over decades of work—I have been extremely private about this research. Only a few people saw the book before you did. All were charitable with their time, reading every page, taming every anxiety. Meagan Levinson, executive editor extraordinaire at Princeton University Press, was the first. She was elated by the prospects of this book from the beginning, and her sharp viewpoints, alongside her soothing smile, restored my faith each time I lost it. Meagan was wise in her selection of reviewers, and I thank them for their comments.

And then there's David Lobenstine, my developmental editor. David is a wonder. Thinking with him, word by word, transformed the book. I felt an odd sense of withdrawal after we completed our work together, a testament to the power of ideas to connect us, me on the west coast of Canada and he on the northeastern seaboard of the United States. Thank you for the three-peat, David.

Family and friends knew I was staying up late studying nightlife, and they aided my transition from private and cautious to public and celebratory. The people closest to me gave me space, shared a meal, or filled my glass—on a boat or on the beach, at home or at the bar—and for their daily grace, I am deeply grateful. Letta Page, a word wizard, tinkered in bold and beautiful ways that made me smile as the book was on its home stretch.

Last but certainly not least, I embrace my partner Gary. You I cannot thank enough, my indefatigable champion, patiently bearing witness to the six-year-long birth of this book, with significant absences from home, and especially as I retreated into "monk mode" in the last year. I raise my effervescing glass and express my most sincere gratitude for your love and support.

People, places, moments. Do you see? Serendipity defines our lives, like it did my pages—unscripted flashes of time, undeniably full of joy.

Partying as a Professor

We know where this story begins: in 2017, Ben Campkin and Lo Marshall from University College London (UCL) published a report that set off alarms across London. Between 2006, a year after civil partnerships were introduced in Britain, and 2016, 58 percent of bars, pubs, and nightclubs that catered to LGBTQ+ people shuttered. The "closure epidemic," as Samuel Douek calls it, created a staggering net loss: at the start of the observation period, there were 125 venues; by the end, only 53 remained. The impact was most acute in London's city center, although eleven local authority districts (the British term for boroughs, which provide the majority of day-to-day services for local residents), lost all their bars (figure 1).[1]

Why are gay bars closing? This is the most immediate, the most obvious, and the most urgent question to ask. No surprise, then, that it has received considerable attention by the municipal government, members of the media, and researchers. Bar closures are where everyone's story begins—and often where their inquiries end, the outcome most people seek to explain. While our night out had the same starting point—"the gay bar is in trouble" is how I opened the book—I have taken us along roads less traveled. My interest was in the phenomenology of club nights, rather than the causes of bar closures, and that epidemic of closures provided a point of departure for us to find underground places that illustrate the remarkable variety of organizational forms in nightlife. But to get there, we had to alter our frame of reference in fundamental ways. I did not want to ask the well-rehearsed question: why are gay bars closing? (We have many compelling answers.) Instead, I encouraged us to ask something else: how are people responding? That simple shift, designed to accent human agency, rejected baked-in assumptions of loss. By posing it, we opened up avenues to think in new and generative ways. *How is nightlife changing? How is it persisting? Where do new joys await?*

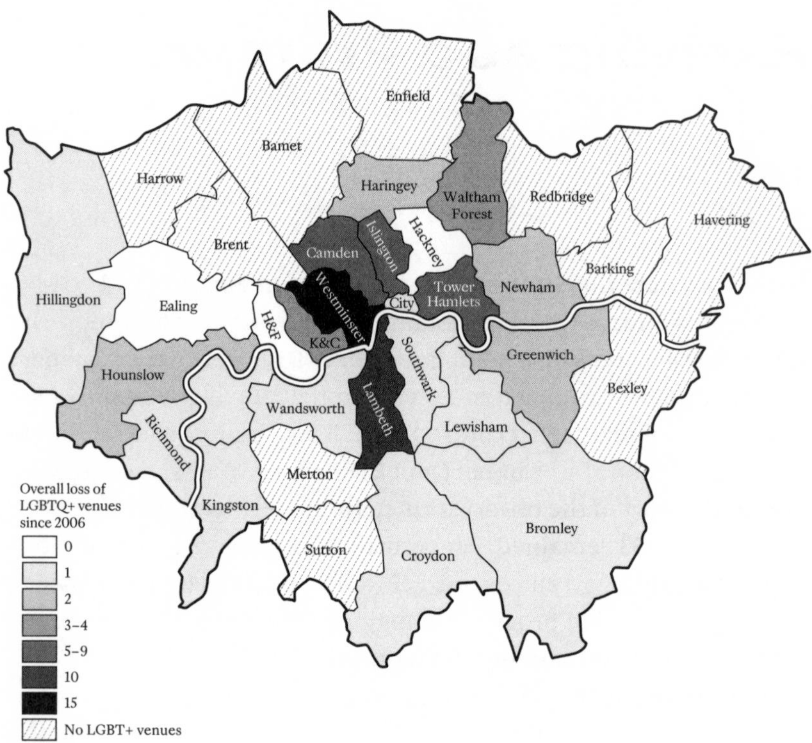

Figure 1. Source: Based on a map published by James Manning for *Time Out London*, reporting data from Campkin and Marshall (2017) and the Greater London Authority.

The Place of the Party

London is a global center of culture and creativity. Many people frequently move between it and other cities. This makes London a site of dense transnational connections and exchanges; ideas move seamlessly into and out of the city. Although London receives considerable coverage in sociology and in other disciplines, I would not call it a canonical case for the study of urban sexualities or urban nightlife. The city is unique in Britain in terms of its size and its significance as a financial, political, and cultural capital, not to mention that its population is more diverse than the country in general. London also has a particular history that distinguishes it from other European and international cities. These qualities make London more a liminal than a model case, a research site that is neither privileged nor ignored. This, I think, is a great strength: a case at once familiar yet also strange, allowing us to appreciate its unique and shared qualities without taking either for granted. The patterns I found here are neither isolated instances nor idiosyncratic occurrences, evidenced by the numerous connections to other cities that I made throughout the book. As you read, I invite you to reflect on the portable qualities of this place, how ideas travel from London to where you live.[2]

Now that we are in London, and understand why we are here, how do we study its nightlife? The most common strategy is to count bar listings in travel guides, like *Yelp* or *Damron*. This approach has been a methodological feature of the literature for decades. While imperfect, like all data, bar listings do establish statistical trends about closures. Unfortunately, no such data exist for club nights—their existence is shaped around itinerance and impermanence—and thus it is impossible to make direct comparisons. That club nights are episodic or ephemeral, existing for a couple of months to a year or longer, poses additional challenges in identifying quantitative trends. Despite these difficulties, it is clear from my many interviews and from the mayor's policy reports that the number of club nights was growing during the same period that gay bars were shuttering.[3]

We can say with certainty that club nights are becoming more prominent as gay bars are closing, but we cannot establish a causal relationship. In other words, it is tempting to say that bar closures caused club nights to form, but such a relationship is impossible to establish. Instead, I believe it is more accurate to say that bar closures *prompted* or *encouraged* club nights to increase in number and variety. I prefer these descriptions because they suggest a relationship without reducing its complexity or fixing its form.

Hence also the utility of "disruptions" as our principal frame for interpreting the closure of gay bars. That image does not require a causal relationship because disruptions by definition are messy. They have a variety of consequences, not all of which are intended, expected, anticipated, or predictable. Disruptive events "shake up old hierarchies" and "force substantive changes," often with a "sense of urgency." In the context of field-level disruptions in nightlife, a situation that can feel both ambiguous and overwhelming, people of all kinds began telling stories about the closure epidemic as a way to make sense of it, to figure out what they could do about it, and to motivate responses to it.[4]

To understand the complexities of how nightlife is changing in the context of a disruptive closure epidemic, I relied on a lot of data, including ethnographic observations, interviews, and municipal reports. I use all of it to fully understand the contours of my case—not in the pursuit of generalizability but, rather, to uncover new insights and add nuance to our knowledge about queer nightlife. As my guide, I followed a strategy called "cognitive empathy," which directed me to inquire into the perceptions and feelings, meanings and motivations of the people who are actually involved in this dynamic social world.[5]

The People at the Party

How do city officials think about and address the large numbers of bar closures? This question establishes the baseline for how a problem is framed, how solutions are proposed for it, and what the prevalent assumptions are that we make about it. To answer it, I used two dozen reports published between 2016 and 2022 by the mayor's office, local planning authorities, and independent policy centers. These reports, which range from 30 to 525 pages, describe how municipal authorities tried over the last decade to change our attitudes about nightlife away from a focus on crime, disorder, and conflict toward a notion of nightlife as an essential part of a city's culture. The reports I read outlined the tenets of nightlife as an economy, the importance of the creative sectors for the nighttime economy, London's aspirations as a twenty-four-hour city, responses to an affordability crisis, thinking about nightlife as cultural infrastructure, development strategies, and a unique LGBTQ+ venues charter.[6]

While the city's analysis of nightlife was informative, it was colorless in comparison to people's lived experiences. To learn about those experiential aspects, I interviewed 112 individuals (using a combination of snowball and sampling for range), including the night czar, culture-at-risk officer, ordinary Londoners, bar owners, and club night organizers (table 1). The data for this last group include a subsample of thirty-five interviews with people who produce forty-two remarkable events (table 2). I continued to collect interviews until I achieved what's called "saturation"—people were repeating the same themes and explanations.[7]

As with the municipal reports, I once again deliberately gathered a large sample, not to make statistical inferences about representativeness but logical inferences about the meanings that structure how people think about and participate in nightlife. Despite not being able to report numerical trends about club nights, this goldmine of a dataset provides great confidence in the validity of the claims I can make about how and why nightlife is changing.

Most of my respondents are in their twenties and thirties (unsurprisingly, given a focus on nightlife), although ages still range from twenty-two to seventy years. The sample also represents a wide variety of sexual orientations, genders, and races. In each instance, I followed queer methodological protocols and asked respondents to tell me the word or words they use to talk about their identities, rather than forcing them to select from a limited number of preexisting categories. The sample also includes diverse educational backgrounds, residential tenures, and boroughs.[8]

I was torn about whether to add descriptor-laden parentheticals after each person's name (age, gender, sexuality, race) every time we meet them in the book. The purpose of this information is to make the interviewees a bit more known to you, the reader—to help you flesh them out and to show you the incredible variety of everyone you are meeting. The disadvantage, however, is that they can be bulky and distracting (parenthetical descriptors, like this one, pull you out from the narrative). As a way to maximize the first while minimizing the second, I introduce the core crew in a separate table, using a mix of pseudonyms and actual names, depending on what each person requested. Like a cast of characters in a play about actual events, these are the people I refer to in the book by name and who speak to us directly about how nightlife is changing. The list includes eighty-one individuals from all kinds of backgrounds. The others shaped my thinking too, of course, even if they are not named or quoted.

Interviews averaged an hour each, ranging from 16 to 100 minutes. I organized the questions around six major themes: London (history, politics, urban design); nightlife (options, opportunities, importance);

Table 1. Sample Demographics

Total Sample (N)	112	(100%)
Age		
Average	34	
Range	22–70	
20s	41	(37%)
30s	46	(41%)
40s	16	(14%)
50s	8	(7%)
60s	0	(0%)
70s	1	(1%)
Sexual Orientation		
Gay	51	(45%)
Queer	28	(25%)
Lesbian	13	(12%)
Gay/Queer	8	(7%)
Lesbian/Queer	5	(4%)
No Labels/Spectrum	2	(2%)
Asexual/Queer	1	(1%)
Bisexual	1	(1%)
Bisexual/Queer	1	(1%)
Bisexual/Sexually Fluid	1	(1%)
Heterosexual	1	(1%)
Gender Identity		
Male/Man	56	(50%)
Female/Woman	21	(19%)
Cis Man	11	(10%)
Nonbinary	11	(10%)
Genderqueer	6	(5%)
Trans/Transgender	3	(2%)
Cis Woman	2	(2%)
None/Genderless	1	(1%)
Undecided	1	(1%)

Race		
White British	48	(42%)
White European	16	(14%)
Mixed Race	13	(12%)
Asian, South Asian, Middle Eastern	10	(9%)
White Jewish	9	(8%)
Black British or African American	7	(6%)
Latin, Spanish, Mexican	4	(4%)
White American or Canadian	4	(4%)
Native/Aboriginal	1	(1%)

Highest Degree		
High school	9	(8%)
BA or BSc	53	(48%)
MA or JD	33	(29%)
PhD or MD	17	(15%)

Years in London		
Less than 1 year	6	(5%)
1–5 years	20	(18%)
6–10 years	23	(20%)
11–20 years	20	(18%)
20+ years	43	(39%)

Residence		
East	49	(44%)
Southeast	16	(14%)
North	15	(14%)
Southwest	11	(9%)
Northeast	7	(6%)
West	6	(5%)
Central	4	(4%)
Northwest	2	(2%)
South	2	(2%)

geographic and residential logics (distribution of LGBTQ+ spaces); bar closures (awareness, reactions, explanations); club nights (awareness, reactions, explanations); and power (belonging, resistance, representation).

I recorded all the conversations (on two different devices, just to be safe) and transcribed them verbatim. This produced 1,558 pages of single-spaced textual data. I uploaded this dataset into NVivo and analyzed each interview line by line. In the coding process, I stayed open to surprises (an abductive approach) as a way to identify commonalities of perspectives as well as departures and discrepancies. To call something a surprise, I checked empirical statements against existing theories and implicit assumptions. I created codes to capture explanations for bar closures; survival and adaptation strategies that gay bars use; explanations for the emergence of club nights; features of club nights; survival and adaptation strategies that club nights use; and general remarks about placemaking, including mobility (why club nights move from place to place) and temporality (the significance of occasional gatherings).[9]

Despite my best efforts to maximize representation, the proportion of backgrounds among my interviewees is not perfectly balanced. Remember, however, that a core argument I make is about efforts to reorient nightlife in ways that produce multiple centers of belonging. To achieve an argument like this, I had to engage in a dual analysis of my data for content and vantage point, engaging in a constant comparison of perspectives based on sample characteristics. I like to imagine my approach as a qualitative counterpart for weighting, a technique that quantitative researchers use to adjust their datasets to account for the population they are studying. A similar process informed my selection of the crew I mentioned earlier and thus my decision to quote most people but not everyone. This procedure of *cultural weighting* made me more mindful, analytically and philosophically, about not theorizing from any one vantage point, while continually crosschecking the positions being expressed.

I supplement my interviews with ethnographic observations to understand how nightlife is experienced consciously, affectively, and somatically from a first-person point of view. What does it feel like to participate in a club night? To answer this question of direct experience, I draw on ten months of fieldwork distributed over three years (five months in 2018, three months in 2019, and two months in 2022). As I mentioned earlier, I arrived in London in January 2018 as part of my sabbatical. It was during this time that a key informant directed me to underground events. The invitation, I later learned, came from my positionality—because I am a QTBIPOC researcher.

Over the next two years, I partied as a professor by adopting the role of participant-as-observer, going to gay bars and club nights across the city while disclosing my identity as a researcher during my interactions. I also attended organizing meetings with activists who were fighting against the closure of some particularly beloved bars, like the Joiners. Along with interviews, observations at these events expanded my focus from explaining why gay bars are closing to an analysis of how the larger field of nightlife is changing and persisting.

As my face became more familiar, I was introduced to more club night organizers. Rather than speaking with them extemporaneously at their events, I arranged to meet later for a formal interview. Pairing observations and interviews enabled me to compare people's expressed attitudes with what I saw directly. As additional robustness checks, or efforts at quality control, I evaluated what I saw and what I heard with what I read in municipal reports. Across all this data, I regularly asked if my findings were consistent or conflicting, isolated or recurring.

I use my analytic approach to make four interventions. First, my findings redirect the epistemological foundations of nightlife away from deficit (bar closures) to an asset-based model of agency and linked destinies (worldmaking). To see the glass as half full, I needed to shift my conceptual focus away from an isomorphic study of gay bars to other organizational forms of nightlife that are seldom featured in the social sciences. Second, instead of thinking about gay bars as uncontested sites of community-building, I considered their intersectional failures, where one form of inequality, like sexuality, overrides the others, especially race and gender. Third and related, focusing on club nights revealed how intersectional achievements are accomplished, often with intention and programmatic mindfulness. Finally, by elevating QTBIPOC voices, I am responding to calls by Aldon Morris, the former president of the American Sociological Association, to critically interrogate racial hierarchies in our research.[10]

Table 2. Club Nights

1. Adonis	22. Hungama
2. Anal House Meltdown	23. INFERNO
3. Aphrodyki	24. Knickerbocker
4. BBZ	25. Lèse Majesté
5. Block9	26. Little Gay Brother
6. Bar Wotever	27. Mighty Hoopla
7. Bum.P	28. Misery
8. Buttmitzvah	29. Nonbinary Cabaret
9. The CAMPerVAN	30. NYC Downlow
10. Chapter 10	31. Opulence
11. Choose Your Own Adventure	32. Papa Loco
12. Club Fuck	33. Pxssy Palace
13. Cocoa Butter Club	34. Queer Direct
14. Duckie	35. Queer Fayre
15. Female Masculinity Appreciation Society	36. Riposte
16. Femmetopia	37. Savage
17. Femmi-Erect	38. Sink the Pink
18. Gayzpachio	39. Strange Perfume
19. Glitterbox	40. The Chateau
20. Hard Cock Life	41. Transmissions
21. Howl	42. Wotever World

After the Party

Even after you finish this book, you will have more questions, or at least I hope you do. Being curious does not undermine what we have learned but, rather, affirms that the knowledge you have acquired about nightlife has become a new base or foundation on which you seek to build even more insights. Some of your questions I can anticipate, and for them, I can also offer preemptive responses. Club nights have little of that hard data I have mentioned many times, even if social scientists tend to champion it. I can read hundreds of pages of reports, speak to more than a hundred people from all kinds of backgrounds, and return year after year to London but still, I cannot tell you when the very first club night occurred; how many parties are organized, on average, every month or year; or the lifespan of a club night. I also cannot tell you how many parties are organized by QTBIPOC people; establish correlations with neighborhoods; or detail the types of venues that host club nights. The absence of numerical data makes it hard for me to tell you which came first, a certain threshold of bar closures or the emergence of more club nights. Questions about origins are especially tricky given a long legacy of queer gatherings outside formal institutional structures, like Ruth and Babe's house parties for Black lesbians in postwar Detroit.[11]

Despite all the data I collected and analyzed, there are still so many unanswered questions! In this regard, what I said when we started out is worth re-stating once more. Club nights thrive on improvisation. The worlds they create are synonymous with the underground and thus defined in blurry ways on purpose. Club nights are hard to quantify, but so what? The people who produce these parties, and those of us who attend them, are there to imagine new ways of being, new ways of feeling, and new worlds of belonging—not new ways of counting.

Even the broader and bolder curiosities will outpace our answers, regardless of the data or methods we use. Will club nights confront the same problems that affected gay bars as they aged? Will a hybrid version of nightlife emerge, combining roving events and a dedicated space? How many organizational forms can we identify on a continuum from the more temporary to the fairly fixed? The list of questions goes on. The only way we will get satisfying answers is if we first establish club nights, like nightlife, as worthy of serious study. Humanists are already on board. Sociologists: join the conversation!

In writing this book, my hope was to establish a research program about club nights—their organizational forms, cultural qualities, politics, and economic models. These pages, in other words, are not exclusively about particular events. My arguments are designed to move us from the specific to the general so that, thinking ahead, we are poised to make systematic comparisons between nightlife events and across places. This is just the beginning, not the last word. Let a thousand theses and follow-up studies bloom, both on local permutations and multinational patterns!

I had similar ambitions when I wrote about gay neighborhoods. While geographers and historians were penning pieces about these urban districts, sociologists, again, had little to say. With the publication of *There Goes the Gayborhood?*, also with Princeton, I put "the gayborhood" on the map for sociologists. In the years since, many scholars in my discipline have written about them, examining them in ever-nuanced ways. Gayborhoods are an intellectually fertile area of study—I maintain that today as fervently as I did a decade ago—and I am delighted to see so much interest in them now. I hope for the same outcome with club nights and other forms of nightlife that can teach us about temporary urbanisms and a sociology of occasions.[12]

I would like to offer advice to readers piqued by the prospects. Too often, young scholars are taught that building your reputation means ruthlessly attacking the foundations of a field, whether that's gayborhood studies, nightlife studies, club night studies, or anything else. I disagree. Critique can be limiting, a vacuum of the generative, and it is emotionally draining, attacking ideas as soon as they appear. Developing your scholarly voice should be a joyful, not pugilistic or pompous, experience. The academy perpetuates the idea that our work must be a hardship, that the competition is fierce, and that achievement is zero sum, winner takes all. Do not replicate the joy deficit!

Knowledge is collective and cumulative, with incremental advances and an occasional revolutionary burst. Let us reach spiritedly across the aisle, both to members of our own fields and to distant disciplines. Embrace an ethos of intellectual generosity. Be kind. Because when we do all this, when we create effervescent moments of scholarly copresence, we have the chance to truly change the world with the gifts of our mind.

Notes

The Closure Epidemic

1. "Living Joyously Is a Radical Act: Why America's Gay Bars Still Matter," by Dominic Rushe. *The Guardian*, June 25, 2019 (https://www.theguardian.com/lifeandstyle/2019/jun/25/america-gay-bars-stonewall-at-50-pride-lgbtq). The writer estimates that listings for gay bars in the United States fell by 16 percent between 2014 and 2018.
2. "The Death of the Gay Bar," by Samuel Clowes Huneke. *Boston Review*, February 18, 2021 (https://bostonreview.net/articles/samuel-clowes-huneke-death-gay-bar/).
3. "The Number of Gay Bars Has Dwindled," by Casey Parks. *The Washington Post*, December 10, 2021 (https://www.washingtonpost.com/dc-md-va/2021/12/10/lesbia-gay-queer-bars-return/). "Gay Bars Are Under Threat but Not from the Obvious Attackers," by Adam Smith. *The Economist*, December 24, 2016 (https://www.economist.com/christmas-specials/2016/12/24/gay-bars-are-under-threat-but-not-from-the-obvious-attackers). "New York Gay Bars Are Declining—and COVID Isn't All to Blame," by Ben Steverman. *Bloomberg*, June 24, 2022 (https://www.bloomberg.com/news/articles/2022-06-24/new-york-city-gay-bars-struggle-to-open-amid-red-tape-general-decline). "Is London's Gay Scene Dead?" by the editorial staff. *i-D*, February 27, 2015 (https://i-d.vice.com/en_uk/article/bjzvdw/is-london39s-gay-scene-dead-us-translation).
4. "Shuttered by the Coronavirus, Many Gay Bars—Already Struggling—Are Now on Life Support," by Greggor Mattson. *The Conversation*, April 14, 2020 (https://theconversation.com/shuttered-by-the-coronavirus-many-gay-bars-already-struggling-are-now-on-life-support-135167). "'We'll Die': Gay Bars Worldwide Scramble to Avert Coronavirus Collapse," by Rachel Savage, Matthew Lavietes, and Enrique Anarte. *Reuters*, May 13, 2020 (https://www.reuters.com/article/us-health-coronavirus-lgbt-nightlife-trf-idUSKBN22P1Z5). For numbers about pandemic lockdowns, see: "Did Nature Heal During the Pandemic 'Anthropause'?" by Emily Anthes. *New York Times*, July 16, 2022, p. 1 (https://www.nytimes.com/2022/07/16/science/pandemic-nature-anthropause.html).
5. For the UCL study, see (Campkin and Marshall 2017). The GLA is a governance body which consists of an elected mayor and an assembly that holds the mayor to public account.
6. See Douek (2016) for the "closure epidemic." For research on closures around the world, see (Eeckhout, Herreman, and Dhoest 2021; Rosser, West, and Weinmeyer 2008). For American studies, see (Mattson 2019; Morgan 2019). The rate of decline was first reported in the *New York Times* and then published by Branton (2021). Mattson counts gay bar listings in the *Damron Guide*, a national travel guidebook of LGBTQ+ places. *Damron* was produced annually between 1964 and 2017 and then once more in 2019.
7. See (Sassen 2001) for global cities, see (Currid 2007; Mears 2020) for global cities as cultural hubs, and see (Oakley et al. 2017) for London. Studies that examine nightlife as entertainment networks include (Grazian 2008; Grazian 2009; Lloyd 2006; Lloyd and Clark 2001). For an example of a policy intervention that targets nightlife, see (Lovatt 1996). For figures about the value of London's nighttime economy and its expected growth, see (Ghaziani 2019b;

Greater London Authority 2017). For UN reports, see https://unctad.org/news/creative-economy-takes-center-stage and https://www.g20-insights.org/policy_briefs/creative-economy-2030-inclusive-and-resilient-creative-economy-for-sustainable-development-and-recovery/.

8. Ben conveyed the first quoted sentence in our interview. He wrote the other arguments about fun on a blog post. See https://duckie.co.uk/events/queer-fun.
9. shuster and Westbrook 2022.
10. Muñoz (2009) writes about the utopian qualities of queerness. The chapters focus on many analytic sites, including stages, gestures, memories, protests, public sex, and performances. I extend his arguments into the context of nightlife. The quotes are from the first page. For moore's notion of being fabulous, see (moore 2018), and for a sociology of fun, see (Fine and Corte 2017). A similar shift from deficit to asset is happening at last in queer studies as scholars pivot from arguments about death drives, the disruptive negativities of queerness, its endemic failures, and visions for a future that is not necessarily better (Edelman 2004; Halberstam 2011) toward future-oriented projects (Muñoz 2009) of hopeful worldmaking (Muñoz 1999).
11. Researching Black queer women in Chicago, Adeyemi (2022:5) "refuses the urge to narrativize black queer (night)life as a utopian outlet." Rather than having fun or feeling good, this argument provides an alternative view about nightlife as "full of frustration and disaffection," including tedium, disillusionment, dullness, boredom, and failed expectations, all of which permeate the dance floor (ibid.). The goal of going out is not always to "feel good," Adeyemi asserts, but to "feel right," a sensation that some Black queer women experience in certain moments of nocturnal co-presence. Although this argument is vital, and vitally important to acknowledge, my commitment to joy compels me to walk along a different analytic path.
12. Kat's comments in this section appeared in *Light After Dark*, an art exhibition she curated in 2017 to celebrate the past, present, and future of LGBTQ+ nightlife in London. See https://www.kathudson.co.uk/light-after-dark. The quotes are from Room 2: A Modern Utopia. Worldmaking efforts are in the service of "making life livable," as Judith Butler describes it in an interview (Ahmed 2016b). For more on specifically queer worldmaking capabilities, see (Ghaziani and Brim 2019b; Muñoz 1996).
13. The perceptual shift from deficit to asset is an important framing device that I use throughout this book, bringing some ideas more clearly into view. "[L]ike a picture frame," sociologist Bill Gamson argues, "a frame directs our attention to what is relevant; like a window frame, it determines our perspectives while limiting our view of the world; like the frame of a house, it is an invisible infrastructure that holds together different rooms and gives shape to the edifices of meaning." Gamson is quoted in (Creed, Scully, and Austin 2002).
14. Muñoz (2009:108) argues that nightlife is "transformative" for LGBTQ+ people, especially for racialized groups. For additional arguments about worldmaking in nightlife, see (Adeyemi 2022; Hunter 2010b; Thorpe 1996). Arguments about "intersectional failures" (Crenshaw 2012:1450; Moore 2012) are compatible with the notion that, while being queer is often uncomfortable in heterosexual spaces, it does not follow that "all queers always feel comfortable in queer spaces" either (Ahmed 2014:151). This observation requires us to remain sensitive to uneven experiences of belonging (Centner and Neto 2021).
15. For reframing nightlife from crime to culture, see (Eldridge 2019), and for the twenty-four-hour city, see (Roberts and Turner 2005). See "Partying as a Professor" at the end of the book for details about the dataset.
16. The British Museum Library holds records about this incident in its general collection. The descriptions come from an essay by Maddy Smith, the curator of the Printed Heritage

Collections. See https://blogs.bl.uk/untoldlives/2020/06/remembering-the-vere-street-coterie-a-story-of-gay-community-a-police-raid-and-library-censorship.html.

17. See Nick Sibilla in *Reason:* https://reason.com/2015/06/28/how-liquor-licenses-sparked-stonewall/.
18. This discussion blends insights from Sibilla in *Reason* with those offered by Tracey Tully in the *New York Times*: https://www.nytimes.com/2021/06/29/nyregion/nj-gay-bars-liquor-laws-.html.
19. For the Stoumen case, see (Ossei-Owusu 2021). The quotes are from pages 716–717. For the development of a national political consciousness among lesbians and gay men, see (Ghaziani 2005; Ghaziani 2008).
20. The National Park Service describes the sip-in here: https://www.nps.gov/articles/julius-bar-1966.htm. Quotes from the court case are reported in *Smithsonian* magazine: https://www.smithsonianmag.com/smart-news/new-york-citys-longest-running-gay-bar-gets-landmark-status-180981272/. For an interview with the protesters, see: https://www.npr.org/templates/story/story.php?storyId=91993823. For the illegality of gay bars, see (Fellows and Branson 1957), and see (Canaday 2009; Chauncey 1994) for practices of state surveillance.
21. For the postwar emergence of gay bars, see (D'Emilio 1983). Scholars who write about these bars argue for their singular importance. Bars were "the only public" (Kahn and Gozemba 1992:92) if not "the only place in town" (Armstrong 2002:34) for LGBTQ+ people to meet. In fact, "gay bars have operated as the most visible institutions of the LGBTQ+ community in the United States for the better part of a century, from before gay liberation until after their assumed obsolescence" (Hilderbrand 2023, quoted on the back jacket). Kennedy and Davis (1993:29) say they provided relief from "crushing isolation." See (Harry 1974:238) for gay bars as "central institutions" and (Kennedy and Davis 1993:80) for bars as "the single most important public manifestation of the subculture." See (Ghaziani 2014b) for gayborhoods and (Martel 2018) for global gayborhoods. For bar districts, see (Mattson 2015), and see (Mattson 2023) for a discussion about their importance today.
22. See (Achilles 1967) for early research: page 182 for blinking lights; 179 for familiar bars closing; and 180 for galaxy of social types and types of bars.
23. The data for Harry's (1974) study includes 1,980 gay bars in the United States listed in a directory called the *Guild Guide*. This strategy, using bar listings and telephone books to study urban nightlife, is a methodological feature of nightlife studies. See (Israelstam and Lambert 1984; Knopp and Brown 2021; and Mattson 2019) for examples. See page 243 in Harry (1974) for bar types, and page 246 for diversifying institutions. See (Israelstam and Lambert 1984) for the next iteration.
24. References in this section include: bear bars (Hennen 2008), leather bars (Castells 1983; Rubin 1998), lesbian (Faderman 1991; Podmore 2013) and dyke bars (Brown-Saracino 2021; Brown-Saracino and Ghaziani 2009; Casey 2004), Black bars (Johnson 2011; Tolliver 2015), drag bars (Rupp and Taylor 2003; Rupp, Taylor, and Shapiro 2010), suburban gay bars (Podmore and Bain 2020), and post-gay bars (Baldor 2020; Hartless 2018). To learn more about what it means to be post-gay, see (Ghaziani 2011; Ghaziani 2015a). See also house parties (Kennedy and Davis 1993), bookstores (Liddle 2005), record companies (Taylor and Whittier 1992), and music festivals (Gamson 1997).
25. Shootings in the United States and bombings in the UK have triggered discussions about the importance of gay bars. On June 12, 2016, Omar Mateen, a 29-year-old man, killed 49 people and injured another 53 in a mass shooting inside Pulse nightclub in Orlando, Florida. Five years later, US president Joe Biden signed a law that designated the nightclub a national memorial site. He said, "Just over five years ago, the Pulse Nightclub—a place

of acceptance and joy—became a place of unspeakable pain and loss, and we'll never fully recover from it, but we'll remember." In his remarks, Biden called Pulse nightclub "hallowed ground." See the statement from the White House: https://www.whitehouse.gov/briefing-room/statements-releases/2021/06/12/statement-by-president-joe-biden-on-the-5th-anniversary-of-the-pulse-nightclub-shooting/. Located on Old Compton Street in London's Soho gayborhood, you will find the Admiral Duncan. Near the entrance of this gay bar, a blue plaque reads "Queer Heritage: 3 People killed, 70 injured, neo-Nazi nail bomber, 30 April 1999." Over three weekends during April 17–30, 1999, homemade nail bombs detonated across London. One was inside the bar. Each bomb contained 1,500 nails, and each of those nails was four inches thick. The explosion killed three people, including a pregnant woman, and injured 140 others, four of whom lost their limbs. All the bombings were carried out by David Copeland who, as BBC describes, is "a self-confessed racist and homophobe." See https://www.bbc.com/news/uk-england-london-47216594. These discussions define gay bars as safe spaces and suggest that LGBTQ+ people need them in response to homophobia and violence.

26. For Soho, see (Collins 2004). For demographics of gay neighborhoods, see (Doan 2007; Nero 2005; Spring 2013).
27. For Black and Latinx gay men in DC, see (Greene 2022:139, 155), and for Jim Crow, see (Grazian 2009:911).
28. Over the years, gay bars have struggled with many challenges, including the commodification and assimilation of once-radical sexual cultures (Chasin 2001; Rushbrook 2002), gentrification (Knopp 1990), drug and alcohol misuse (Slavin 2004), racism (Caluya 2008; Hunter 2010a; Teunis 2007), misogyny (Johnson and Samdahl 2005), ableism (Butler 1999), ageism (Betts 2021; Casey 2007), and trans exclusions (Doan 2007). These concerns have sparked creative responses, like I discussed in this section and will continue to show throughout the book.
29. Institutional theorists write about disruptions (Zhang 2021) and exogenous shocks (Corbo, Corrado, and Ferriani 2016). The idea is shared by social movement theorists, who also write about exogenous shocks (Fligstein and McAdam 2011), organization theorists writing about environmental jolts (Meyer 1982), and cultural sociologists who write about unsettled times (Swidler 1986). My interest is not to explain why change occurs in institutional, organizational, or cultural contexts. Instead, I borrow the concept to explore diverse expressions of nightlife. The conventional approach assumes that functional adaptation is the ultimate goal (Meyer 1982), whereas I focus on creativity in its many forms: experiential, economic, cultural, and organizational.
30. See (Zhang 2021:381–382) for arguments about disruptions requiring "urgency" and "quick response" with a goal of getting things "back on track." For the night czar as a form of urban governance, see (Seijas and Gelders 2021). For isomorphism, see (DiMaggio and Powell 1983). The idea explains why things look the same, or the constraints that produce similar forms. There are three types of constraints: coercive (formal and informal pressures), mimetic (we prefer imitation in times of uncertainty), and normative (working conditions) (pages 67–74 in ibid.). The disruption of gay bars is a mimetic constraint that creates a preference for preserving existing bars and creating new ones. "Institutional reproduction" (Mahoney 2000:515) is a related idea in the literature.
31. Frost (2014:72) calls this a "politics of singularity." The imagery of tracks is inspired by Weber's ([1915] 1946:280) famous argument: "Not ideas, but material and ideal interests, directly govern men's conduct. Yet very frequently the 'world images' that have been created by 'ideas' have, like switchmen, determined the tracks along which action has been pushed by the dynamic of interest."

32. Scott (1994:207–208) defines a field as "a community of organizations that partakes in a common meaning system." DiMaggio and Powell (1983) conceptualize it as a collection of organizations. They use fields to explain "an inexorable push toward homogenization," or "why there is such startling homogeneity of organizational forms" (p. 64). I use fields in the opposite way: to make *heterogeneity* more transparent. This is also why I prefer the definition from Scott (1994), who points broadly to a community of organizations. Both are considered classic treatments. Other scholars consider the location of individual actors in a social space, where they compete for material and symbolic benefits (Bourdieu 1984). Although I am not interested in the location of individuals in a Blau space (McPherson and Ranger-Moore 1991; McPherson 1983) characterized by sociodemographic variables, homophily (the organizing force of that space) is relevant when we think about who interacts with whom in nightlife. This can lead to arguments about "sexual fields," or arenas of social life where people seek intimate partners and compete for sexual status (Green 2014). But to be clear, I am not using this concept from organization sciences in the context of nightlife so that I can re-theorize fields. I use it as an application, a way to diversify how we think about the variety of nightlife forms. See Khubchandani (2020:27) for arguments about a "more capacious" view, and Grazian (2008:6) for calls to see a "larger landscape."
33. See (Wynn 2016:276) for a tendency to see all kinds of events—weddings, music festivals, religious ceremonies, football games, and club nights alike—as "sociological epiphenomena." He curates work on events under the umbrella of a "sociology of occasions." See page 282 for the quote on copresence. My argument to prioritize events is motivated by Erving Goffman, one of the most influential sociologists of the twentieth century. Goffman (1967:2) argued that rituals must be a "subject matter in their own right." Howie Becker (1982:270) also argues that events are a "basic unit of sociological investigation." For an assessment of Goffman as "arguably the most influential American sociologist of the twentieth century," see (Fine and Manning 2003:34). And see (Bailey 2013; Khubchandani 2020; Livingston 1990) for humanist arguments about the transatlantic, diasporic, and Indigenous cultural legacies of ephemeral events. The underground nature of these events means that there are few academic studies, especially in the social sciences, about them. In two articles, my graduate student and I use the word "pop-ups" to describe a North American version of club nights, specifically in Vancouver (Ghaziani and Stillwagon 2018; Stillwagon and Ghaziani 2019). Another study documents the use of nightlife events among expatriate queer men in the Middle Eastern city of Dubai, United Arab Emirates. These events occur in places from "penthouses to nearby desert locations" (Centner and Neto 2021:99), rather than in gay bars. Similar to club nights, this work also shows the creative construction of community in the midst of social occlusion. Other examples are documented in newspapers and magazines. For Toronto, see https://www.blogto.com/music/2022/12/toronto-nightlife-far-from-dead-just-evolving/. For Los Angeles, see https://www.verygoodlight.com/2020/05/28/queer-asian-americans-in-la-are-making-space-for-their-identities-and-redefining-cool/. For Chicago, Pittsburgh, New York, and DC, see https://mixmag.net/feature/6-party-crews-redefining-the-gay-underground. For a club night called the Flower Factory in DC, see https://www.washingtonpost.com/lifestyle/2023/03/11/flower-factory-lgbtq-dance-party/.
34. Compared to social scientists, humanists do a better job of examining nightlife events other than gay bars (e.g., Adeyemi 2022; Bailey 2013; Buckland 2002; Khubchandani 2020; moore 2016). For Houlbrook's study, see (Houlbrook 2017:2).
35. Houlbrook offered this description in a blog post for *The Trickster Prince*. See https://tricksterprince.wordpress.com/2013/04/02/a-call-for-help-edgware-road-in-the-1920s/.

See also a similar discussion at the National Archives: https://blog.nationalarchives.gov.uk/kisses-and-kind-thoughts-queer-networks-and-letters-between-men/.

36. Nightlife researchers use the phrase "subcultural capital" to describe the idea of being in the know in order to access information about events (Thornton 1996). Houlbrook's quote comes from page 3 of his book.
37. See (Chauncey 1994) for details. Especially powerful threat and greater wealth quotes are from page 349, and the multiple audiences quote is from page 351. Houlbrook (2005:79) describes similar "pansy cases" in London in the 1930s. He notes that "exclusive venues were few and far between until after the Second World War" (Houlbrook 2017:3). Both historians agree that the audiences were sexually mixed but politically progressive. Houlbrook describes British crowds as "cosmopolitan," while Chauncey calls them "bohemian" in New York. Interestingly, occasional parties were more popular among privileged groups in early New York. In London today, underground parties largely draw the opposite: QTBIPOC folks and others who are marginalized by multiple vectors of power.
38. Beemyn 2004:504.
39. Cunningham 1995.
40. Ibid. Harlem has been the center of the underground ballroom scene since the 1920s. See https://www.esquire.com/entertainment/a19733315/the-ballroom-revolution/. Today, there are ballroom scenes in most American cities, large and small. For studies about those parties, see (Adeyemi, Khubchandani, and Rivera-Servera 2021; Bailey 2013; Ghaziani 2022; Stillwagon and Ghaziani 2019).
41. See (Thorpe 1996). The quote about the center of lesbian communities is from page 41. See page 48 for the quote about White women, page 42 for the costs of attending, and page 44 for the quote about a house where queers go.
42. Ibid. See page 60 for Ronnie and Thorpe's quotes.
43. See (Lane 2015). The definition of scene spaces as "transient events" is on page 220. For a discussion about the drivers for this scene, see the same page. See page 223 for a discussion about White landscapes, and page 222 for the quote about desires and experiences. In writing about lesbian, bisexual, and queer women's experiences in the city, other scholars describe fragmented and fleeting geographies called "constellations" (Gieseking 2020), including lesbian nights that occur once a week in bars across the city, while still others describe how sexual identities vary in different places, rather than remaining constant across geographical contexts (Brown-Saracino 2015). See (Adeyemi 2022) for a study about Black queer women in Chicago today. The capacity to feel pleasure is thwarted by "the difficulties of forging Black queer life in a city that severely (and often violently) restricts their physical and affective capacities" (p. 4).
44. Uniqueness is fetishized among social scientists. The idea of being unique is a compelling piece of an argument, of course, and so it makes sense that researchers focus on it. But I'm not sure that it is so urgent, which is why uniqueness is not a cornerstone of my argument. Instead, and as I discuss in this section, I think about club nights as *uniquely influential* and *uniquely revelatory* in capturing how urban sexualities and urban nightlife are changing in the time and place in which our lives are located right now. Still, I offer in my discussion six potential distinctions of club nights compared to gay bars and earlier historical gatherings.
45. The emergence of malleable, flexible, and adaptive urban expressions like club nights are part of a broader conversation called "temporary urbanisms." This research examines urban practices and policies that leverage spatial and temporal adaptability, including the popularity of short-term events and other temporary uses of space. For reviews, see (Ferreri 2021; Madanipour 2017). The literature has grown quite vast, leading some to

argue that we have too many terms to examine similar research objects, including guerrilla urbanism, everyday urbanism, pop-ups, DIY urbanism, tactical urbanism, the temporary city, and the more general notions of short-term or temporary use (Andres and Zhang 2020; Hou 2020).

46. Some readers may want to dismiss short-term engagements as trivial, with no lasting value. I think that's a mistake. In this book, I challenge orthodox ideas about time in urban development and planning. Strategies of short-term use—the "makeshift city" as Tonkiss (2013) calls it—have material effects: they set the terms for what can happen later, and they inform our thinking about how cities work by revealing the longevity of temporary engagements. The makeshift city is a collection of urban strategies that illuminate "a politics and practice of small incursions in material spaces that seek to create a kind of *durability through the temporary*" (emphasis added). Tonkiss is not alone in this thinking about time. A "temporary turn" has been emerging in recent years in urban (Stillwagon and Ghaziani 2019:874), economic (Hirschman 2021), and sexuality studies (Muñoz 2009). This interdisciplinary literature examines places based on their temporal structure. Still, words like "temporary" and "permanent" are hard to define. A provisional definition of the former is a "finite period of time with a defined beginning and end" (Bishop and Williams 2012:5). The notion of permanence has preoccupied some of the earliest thinkers in my home discipline of sociology. For Durkheim, permanence poses "*the* fundamental problem for society" since it is "precarious." For Weber, modernity represents the "institutionalization of permanence." It is "unproblematic" because it is "built-in," although it comes with the cost of disenchantment. From these theoretical origins, Lizardo (2022) concludes that "everyone recognizes" temporality, even if it is "hiding in plain sight." This makes it hard to fix analytically. My interest is not to create a typology of temporality but to use rough distinctions between time-limited durations, relative permanence and relatively temporary events, to shift the conversation from bar closures (more permanent) to club nights (more temporary). Organizers recognize that the groups they center continue to exist after the party ends. This creates a Durkheimian emphasis on renewal and reintegration as something we need to perform in ritualistic gatherings. The concepts of permanence and temporariness are also important for urban theory and practice. If cities are a collection of buildings and activities that are in many ways temporary, Bishop and Williams (2012) challenge urbanists to move beyond our focus on permanence, much like our preoccupation with gay bars. Temporary forms have many advantages, after all. They are spatially adaptable and efficient, unlocking the potential of physical places now rather than becoming mired in "the slow and siloed conventional city building process," like planning procedures (Lydon and Garcia 2015). Temporary forms can also better manage economic uncertainties. For example, short-term leases have fewer financial risks and costs.

47. https://www.bnnbloomberg.ca/the-american-gay-bar-is-down-but-don-t-count-it-out-just-yet-1.1280367.

Chapter 1

1. Questions like these—what does something mean for people who actually experience it?—provide the basis for an analytic strategy that elsewhere I call "street empirics" (Ghaziani 2021). Researchers debate structural variables, like gentrification, redevelopment, and assimilation, as they try to explain the closure epidemic. Similar to work in gayborhood studies, nightlife researchers are also at risk of eliding "matters of meaning, interactions,

impressions, and interpretations" (p. 90) in their analysis. What nightlife means and why it matters is not reducible to statistics, nor is it only a function of macro-level forces. Nightlife is a collection of sentient people, after all. To understand its significance, we need to ask people why they are drawn to it, and in the context of a closure epidemic, how they think about its changes as they live through those changes.

2. In this chapter, I focus on the threats that gay bars face, while Mattson (2023) and Hilderbrand (2023) explore in greater detail their cultural significance and history, respectively.
3. The mayor's *Cultural Infrastructure Plan* details the national planning system, business rates, funding, licensing, and land values (Greater London Authority 2019:25–31). For a discussion about the history of business rates and how these taxes can harm enterprises, see https://www.standard.co.uk/comment/comment/business-rates-are-killing-high-streets-in-london-it-s-time-for-a-rethink-a3913076.html. The mayor's office estimates a 45 percent increase in taxes overnight, which negatively impacts cultural businesses like gay bars operating on smaller profit margins. On page 29, the report states, "The average London pub faces a business rates bill of nearly £15,000 (US$18,945), and the average nightclub nearly double that."
4. https://www.theguardian.com/politics/2009/apr/26/david-cameron-conservative-economic-policy1.
5. https://www.somersethouse.org.uk/whats-on/uk-gay-bar-directory-hannah-quinlan-and-rosie-hastings.
6. To learn more about the figures reported in this discussion, see (GLA Economics 2018:5–6). To learn more about the culture-at-risk officer, see https://www.london.gov.uk/what-we-do/arts-and-culture/cultural-infrastructure-toolbox/culture-and-community-spaces-risk and http://www.worldcitiescultureforum.com/case_studies/culture-at-risk-office. Today, the role has access to a £2.3 million (US$2.9 million) Culture-at-Risk Business Support Fund for London's creative and cultural industries, including grassroots music venues, LGBTQ+ venues, artist workspaces, and independent cinemas. See https://www.theculturediary.com/stories/mayor-london-launches-£23m-culture-risk-fund-and-resources.
7. For classic treatments about how the size, density, and heterogeneity of cities affect their variety of cultural offerings, see (Fischer 1975; Wirth 1938).
8. The nighttime economy is formally defined as the "number of workplaces and employees working in industry sectors that operate in the evening or night." It includes the following Standard Industrial Classification 2007 (SIC 2007) industries: cultural and leisure activities; activities which support nighttime cultural and leisure activities; twenty-four-hour health and personal social services; and activities which support wider social and economic activities. See data compiled by the Office for National Statistics: https://data.london.gov.uk/dataset/london-night-time-economy. For academic research about governance at night, see (Roberts 2016; Seijas and Gelders 2021). For research on the challenges of building twenty-four-hour cities, see (Roberts and Turner 2005). For statistics about tourism, see (GLA Economics 2018:7). See also London's workforce at night (GLA Economics 2018:90); total number of jobs in the nighttime economy (Greater London Authority 2017:9); and the value of the nighttime economy (ibid.:209). Estimates about its increase by 2026 from https://www.egi.co.uk/news/dawn-of-midnight-for-londons-night-time-economy/. Forty percent figure from (Greater London Authority 2017:8); and £2bn (US$2.5bn) in additional growth by 2030 from (ibid.:9). For comparisons, consider first the value for the nighttime economy of the entire UK, which the BBC estimates at £66bn (US$83.3bn). See https://www.bbc.com/news/business-49348792. Consider next the nighttime economy of New York City. In 2020, it brought US$35.1bn a year (as of 2020), and it

has created 300,000 jobs. See https://blog.mipimworld.com/investment/how-the-night-time-economy-helps-build-cities/.

9. The discussion at City Hall was reported by the BBC: https://www.bbc.com/news/uk-england-london-36332868.
10. https://www.london.gov.uk/press-releases/mayoral/mayor-reveals-uks-first-ever-night-czar.
11. For Milan, see https://bloombergcities.medium.com/rise-of-the-night-mayors-945a4fee5110. For convening power, see https://www.kpsrl.org/publication/building-bridges-of-knowledge-the-platforms-convening-power.
12. For the appointment of a nightlife mayor in New York, see https://www.nytimes.com/2018/03/07/nyregion/nyc-nightlife-mayor.html. We must not be too quick to make comparisons across all these cities. London's population is three times that of Berlin, and it is four times greater than the population of Paris. Based on the logic of population size, comparisons to New York or Tokyo are more logical.
13. For numbers of venue declines, see (GLA Economics 2018:20). For Khan's interview in *The Independent*, see https://www.independent.co.uk/news/uk/home-news/london-night-czar-sadiq-khan-night-life-job-24-hour-city-tube-a7206796.html. For Lamé's interview in BBC, see https://www.bbc.co.uk/news/newsbeat-37879183.
14. For the post-gay thesis, see (Ghaziani 2011; Ghaziani 2014b; Ghaziani 2015a; Kampler and Connell 2018; Seidman 2002). For applications to gay bars, see (Baldor 2018; Hartless 2018).
15. Elmer and Leigland 2013:6–7.
16. https://www.theartnewspaper.com/2021/05/07/its-officialgermany-declares-its-nightclubs-are-now-cultural-institutions. For more on Klubcommission, see https://djmag.com/news/Berlin-officially-declare-nightclubs-cultural-institutions. For the BBC and clubsterben, see https://mondointernazionale.com/en/i-club-berlinesi-diventano-istituzioni-culturali. "Forever be dying" quote from https://www.exberliner.com/berlin/keeping-the-night-alive/.
17. For Schobeß, see https://www.nme.com/news/music/berlin-clubs-to-be-declared-cultural-institutions-to-safeguard-their-future-2934978; for VAT, see https://www.theartnewspaper.com/2021/05/07/its-officialgermany-declares-its-nightclubs-are-now-cultural-institutions.
18. https://www.bloomberg.com/news/articles/2019-01-02/london-clubs-and-nightlife-need-berlin-style-attention.
19. The relationship between culture and planning seems self-evident when we are talking about cultural institutions, like music venues. But it arises in very different circumstances as well, such as proposals for concrete cladding for a building's finished form (Smith 2022).
20. https://www.theguardian.com/cities/2017/apr/21/lgbt-london-venue-closures-capital-future-night-tsar.
21. For a copy of the charter, see https://www.london.gov.uk/sites/default/files/lgbt_venues_charter_2017.pdf.
22. For my work on gayborhoods, both in Chicago and nationally in the United States, see (Ghaziani 2010; Ghaziani 2014b; Ghaziani 2015a).
23. In my other work, I talk about the plural places we call home, neighborhoods in a city other than the gayborhood where there are additional concentrations of same-sex households. I call these "cultural archipelagos," and I describe specific clusters for households with children, lesbians, and queer people of color (Ghaziani 2019a).
24. For lesbian geographies, see (Adler and Brenner 1992; Brown-Saracino 2011; Browne and Ferreira 2018; Ghaziani 2015b).

25. On contemplating art, Keats writes that great thinkers are "capable of being in uncertainties, Mysteries, doubts, without any irritable reaching after fact and reason." Brooke's ability to see death and existence at once, without a move toward resolutions, reminds me of Keat's musings on existence. For a summary of negative capability, see the Poetry Foundation: https://www.poetryfoundation.org/learn/glossary-terms/negative-capability.

Femmetopia (In a Basement)

1. https://origin.dazeddigital.com/life-culture/article/41287/1/femmephobia-xxl-gay-clubs-door-policy.

Chapter 2

1. Given my interest in thinking about nightlife as a field, it makes sense that there would be more than two forms, gay bars and club nights. In this discussion, I talk specifically about nightclubs and not gay bars, but I think about them in similar ways. They are both fixed, emplaced establishments—and both are under threat. The reason I organize my comparison of club nights with nightclubs is semantic: similar words yet distinct experiences. The reversal—from nightclub to club night—provides a vivid learning opportunity.
2. https://www.cnn.com/style/article/sink-the-pink/index.html.
3. This discussion draws our attention to the importance of names. Researchers who think about the politics of naming practices generally focus on conflicts that occur in neighborhoods, what David Madden calls "toponymic conflicts." Debates about names and struggles to create new names—what Pierre Bourdieu calls "the power to name" and "the power to nominate"—provide a window into urban politics. The variety of naming practices, from neighborhoods to nightlife, all have "the power to shape the world" (Bourdieu 1985:729, 731; Madden 2018:1601).
4. The language we use to talk about nightlife has often changed. "Gay discos" and "discotheques" were popular in the 1970s and '80s, "club kids" and "squat parties" emerged in the '90s, and circuit parties were booming in the 2000s (Ghaziani and Cook 2005). The word "rave" became more common in England in the late 1980s, after Detroit techno and Chicago house DJs crossed the Atlantic to perform for British audiences. Like club nights, raves were also underground gatherings, and they often occurred at repurposed spaces, like a warehouse or farmyard. Many were illegal (because they defied licensing rules), "renegade in spirit," and designed to "engineer an alternative reality for a few hours." See https://www.newyorker.com/books/page-turner/raving-co-opted-and-reimagined. And don't forget about the drags, rent parties, and balls from earlier decades! As well, given the centrality of the city in the evolution of nightlife and club cultures, places like Chicago and Detroit have become associated with certain sounds, as I alluded earlier—like house and techno music in the 1980s (Salkind 2019). Other cities, like Berlin, have acquired a reputation as a "mecca for nightclubbing." See https://stuarte.co/2021/a-short-history-of-clubbing/. See also (Hebdige 1979) for how subcultures and nightlife scenes are built on specific sounds, musical styles, and dance, as well as a discussion of specific British subcultures, like teds, mods, skins, hippies, and punks.
5. https://greggormattson.com/2022/04/13/chapter-the-changing-role-of-gay-bars-in-american-lgbtq-life/.

6. For examples of research that count bar listings, see (Campkin and Marshall 2017; Israelstam and Lambert 1984; Knopp and Brown 2021; Mattson 2019). The attempt to understand the perceptions, meanings, and motivations of the people involved in a social world constitutes an approach called "cognitive empathy" (Small and Calarco 2022:27).
7. Ghaziani 2014a; Miles et al. 2021.
8. A working men's club is a membership-based organization that offers cheaper drinks than are offered at pubs. They have dwindled over the years as the price of alcohol has decreased and as gentrification has affected areas that traditionally were working-class in composition. The best-known is Bethnal Green Working Men's Club. Historically a working men's club that dates back to 1887, today it hosts events from club nights to cabaret. See https://londonist.com/london/drink/london-s-working-men-s-clubs.
9. Thomas and Thomas 1928:572.
10. For the original study on the strength of weak ties, see (Granovetter 1973). For the BBC report about it, see https://www.bbc.com/worklife/article/20200701-why-your-weak-tie-friendships-may-mean-more-than-you-think.
11. Oral histories are a type of performance, and when we perform our life's history for someone, they affirm who we are in the interaction. The interlocutor bears witness to the story we tell, and by telling it, we feel like we belong to ourselves, to our story, and to the person who listens. See (Johnson 2019), especially the discussion on page 58. Social movement scholars also describe the power of storytelling. Telling a story and getting it right matters because it has political consequences. Story*telling*, the things we say to each other after an event has occurred, is as important as what we say about it. That act can create a sense of belonging by challenging the status quo (Polletta 2006).
12. https://www.vam.ac.uk/event/rqkENAbG/club-nights-and-the-queer-revolution.
13. Muñoz 1996:6.

Chapter 3

1. For a study of changing drinking habits, see (Oldham et al. 2020). For media coverage, see https://www.bbc.com/news/magazine-12397254.
2. In the 1950s and '60s, the gay bar represented the center of communal life for many people, especially White gay men. However, police raids, arrests, legal fees, the loss of jobs, blackmail and extortion attempts, and physical harm all created an economic burden associated with being gay. It was widely understood that bar owners catered to people who were stigmatized or perceived by society as criminals (homosexuality was not yet decriminalized). In exchange for the promise of freedom inside the bar, owners paid for protection from the police or the Mafia, whom they would pay off. This made buying a drink at a gay bar more expensive, since bar owners had to recover those costs. Despite their centrality in these earlier decades, gay bars were often black-market operations: they did not employ gay people, nor did gay people own their own bars. Straight owners more often reaped the profits and the income generated by gay and lesbian customers. And so, the "bars, despite their importance as homosexually oriented business activities, actually contributed little to the creation of the gay and lesbian community's own economic surplus" (Escoffier 1997:128). For business rental costs in Soho, see https://www.thestorefront.com/search/london/soho.
3. For crack capitalism, see (Holloway 2010:8–9). As I discuss in the chapter, this idea resembles arguments about marginal urbanisms and interstitial spaces of the city (Tonkiss 2013:317), as well as notions of enclosures (Hodkinson 2012).
4. Lefebvre 1968:151.

5. Tonkiss 2013:317.
6. Ibid.: 312.
7. References to free and discounted tickets are included under the FAQs on their website: https://www.pxssypalace.com/faq. For pay it forward tickets, see https://ra.co/events/1496679.
8. For the interview in *Resident Advisor*, see https://ra.co/news/76994. The *Daily Mail* broke the story: https://www.dailymail.co.uk/news/article-10462283/Party-club-blasted-112-man-tax-t.html.
9. https://www.advocate.com/business/2022/2/03/party-charged-white-straight-men-6-times-much-lgbtq-attendees; https://www.dazeddigital.com/life-culture/article/55361/1/why-pxssy-palace-are-charging-straight-cis-men-six-times-more.
10. https://www.pxssypalace.com/our-policy; https://www.dazeddigital.com/life-culture/article/38887/1/this-club-night-is-making-sure-trans-people-of-colour-get-home-safely.
11. Bivens 2016; Lindert 2017.
12. Community interest companies and social enterprises have regulatory and compliance requirements set by the government. Individuals who register their businesses are required to meet certain expectations, including the use of profits to benefit the community. In this conversation, Dan uses the idea both literally and analogically, a way of positioning club nights as similar to the enterprise. See https://www.gov.uk/set-up-a-social-enterprise; https://www.sumup.com/en-gb/invoices/dictionary/community-interest-company/; and https://www.simplybusiness.co.uk/knowledge/articles/2022/05/what-is-a-community-interest-company-uk/.
13. https://reader.acehotel.com/music/dan-beaumont-takes-five/.
14. Andersson 2009:64.
15. For the Roberts interview, see https://www.powertochange.org.uk/case_study/friends-of-the-joiners-arms/#. Biggs was quoted in *The Guardian*: https://www.theguardian.com/world/2017/oct/12/joiners-arms-redevelopment-must-include-lgbt-nightclub-council-rules. We know that cities breed contention—a fact well-established in the voluminous right-to-the-city literature—yet scholars seldom notice that planning hearings, which are gatherings of councilors (elected local representatives) who review the details of a proposed building project, can set the stage for protest actions. For an exception, social movement scholarship that does address planning, see (Souza 2006).
16. https://www.uk.coop/resources/community-shares-handbook/2-society-legislation/21-bona-fide-co-operative-societies/211.
17. https://www.crowdfunder.co.uk/p/friends-of-the-joiners-arms-community-shares-offer.
18. https://www.theguardian.com/uk-news/2022/jun/17/crowdfunder-launched-for-uk-first-community-run-lgbtqi-venue; https://www.crowdfunder.co.uk/p/friends-of-the-joiners-arms-community-shares-offer.
19. To learn about Lyall, see https://www.curionoir.com/pages/lyall-hakaraia and https://www.lyallhakaraia.co.uk/love-magazine.
20. The two-decade-long study reports results based on US mortgage lending data (Sun and Gao 2019)—but the general trend of economic inequality is global. President Jim Kim from World Bank remarked that LGBTQ+ people are overrepresented in the bottom 40 percent of class brackets (https://blogs.worldbank.org/governance/lgbti-people-are-likely-over-represented-bottom-40). Sexual and gender minorities experience lower socioeconomic outcomes due to discrimination, with the at-risk-of-poverty rate increasing from 16 percent to 20 percent for those who experience discrimination (https://www.worldbank.org/en/topic/sexual-orientation-and-gender-identity).
21. For research on the class-inflected nature of gay identity, see (Valocchi 1999). Some studies have shown that adopting an openly queer identity may be the result of economic *privilege*, conferred by greater rates of attending university. Higher SES may afford people

the ability to identity as queer and/or nonbinary. See (Goldberg et al. 2020), especially the discussion on page 110. Still, LGBTQ+ people and couples are more vulnerable to conditions of poverty in general, as compared to heterosexual individuals and couples. See the discussion about "sexual orientation and gender diversity" on the website of the American Psychological Association: https://www.apa.org/pi/.

22. Amy and Peter offered these quotes in an interview with *Dazed*: https://www.dazeddigital.com/life-culture/article/39174/1/the-joiners-arms-is-coming-back-as-the-first-community-run-lgbtqi-pub.
23. https://www.london.gov.uk/sites/default/files/meanwhile_use_for_london_final.pdf.
24. https://centreforlondon.org/publication/meanwhile-use-london/.
25. See page 24 of the business plan: https://www.friendsjoinersarms.com/.

Chapter 4

1. For ethnosexual adventures, see (Nagel 2003:18).
2. In addition to the empirical question of what concerns people raise without prompts, I focus on race in this chapter for two other reasons. First, I want to locate club nights in a context of globally networked movements asserting that Black Lives Matter (Francis and Wright-Rigueur 2021). It is no accident that these parties are becoming visible at the same time as there is a global reckoning around race. Second, my prioritizing race, alongside intersectional concerns, also responds to calls issued by the former president of the American Sociological Association to interrogate White supremacy and racial hierarchies in our research—to let the subaltern speak (Morris 2022).
3. Lang 2017.
4. Naeem provided this perspective in an interview with *Dazed*: https://www.dazeddigital.com/life-culture/article/45561/1/queer-clubs-lgbt-safe-space-report-inclusion-exclusion.
5. PBS/NPR poll: https://www.pbs.org/newshour/nation/a-majority-of-americans-say-policing-should-be-reformed-but-most-white-people-still-dont-think-police-treat-black-people-differently; Pew poll: https://www.pewresearch.org/social-trends/2019/04/09/race-in-america-2019/.
6. https://www.aljazeera.com/news/2021/5/24/black-lives-matter-activist-critical-in-hospital-after-shooting.
7. https://theconversation.com/how-racist-is-britain-today-what-the-evidence-tells-us-141657.
8. The research that I report examines "the outcome rather than the motivations of the employer or landlord so we can't be sure that they are acting on racist beliefs—but in law it is the outcome that matters. Unequal treatment of applicants is illegal, whatever the motivation." See https://theconversation.com/how-racist-is-britain-today-what-the-evidence-tells-us-141657. For the replication by *The Guardian*, see https://www.theguardian.com/uk-news/2018/dec/03/flatshare-bias-room-seekers-with-muslim-name-get-fewer-replies.
9. https://www.ons.gov.uk/peoplepopulationandcommunity/populationandmigration/populationestimates/articles/populationestimatesbyethnicgroupandreligionenglandandwales/2019.
10. Bonilla-Silva 2013:1.
11. Cheryan and Monin 2005:727.
12. Political philosopher Charles Mills (2017:49) coined the term "white ignorance" to talk about the willful sense of unknowing or unknowingness that White people often express about race, race relations, and racial inequality—a kind of racial unknowing, in other words. White ignorance leaves racial hierarchies unchallenged and thus resistant to positive change.

13. These findings come from the 2021 Census. In that year in London, 36.8 percent of the population identified as White British and 17 percent as White Other (these groups include English, Welsh, Scottish, Northern Irish, or British; Irish; Gypsy or Irish Traveler; Roma; and "any other White background"). In addition, 20.7 percent of the population in the capital identified as Asian (which includes Indian, Pakistani, Bangladeshi, Chinese, and "any other Asian background"), 13.5 percent as Black (which includes Caribbean, African, and "any other Black, Black British, or Caribbean background"), 5.7 percent as Mixed (which includes White and Black Caribbean, White and Black African, White and Asian, and "any other Mixed or multiple ethnic backgrounds"), and 6.3 percent as Other (which includes Arab and "any other ethnic group"). For general trends, see https://www.ethnicity-facts-figures.service.gov.uk/uk-population-by-ethnicity/national-and-regional-populations/regional-ethnic-diversity/latest. For the measurement of ethnic groups, see https://www.ethnicity-facts-figures.service.gov.uk/style-guide/ethnic-groups. According to census takers, "In England and Wales, there is an agreed list of ethnic groups you can use when asking for someone's ethnicity. The groups are usually those used in the Census, which happens every 10 years." One notable change in the 2021 census, compared to prior counts, is that the "Roma" group was added under the "White" ethnic group.
14. Erkan's observation also preoccupies researchers who ask if racism can exist without racist people. For these and other debates about color-blind racism, see (Berrey 2015; Bonilla-Silva 2013).
15. https://www.pinknews.co.uk/2015/12/14/blackface-drag-act-dropped-from-royal-vauxhall-tavern/.
16. https://www.theguardian.com/tv-and-radio/2021/mar/18/rupauls-drag-race-down-under-contestant-apologises-for-past-performances-in-blackface.
17. For arguments about the intersectional composition of gay neighborhoods and gay bars, see (Duffus and Colliver 2023). For arguments about the intersections between whiteness and queer studies, see (Kennedy 2014). Kennedy's quote is from page 120. For intersectional failures, see (Crenshaw 2012:1450; Moore 2012).
18. Duggan 2002.
19. For a review of "gayborhood studies" as a literature, see (Ghaziani 2021).
20. Dantzler, Korver-Glenn, and Howell 2022; Robinson 1983.
21. What Julia describes here is something that sociologists call habitus, the internalized habits of mind and body that subconsciously shape our movements (Bourdieu 1984).
22. The Roestone Collective (2014) argues that the idea of safety undergirding popular notions of "safe spaces" is relational, context dependent, heterogeneous, and socially constructed through the collective interpretations of its members.
23. For post-gay debates, see (Dean 2014; Ghaziani 2011; Kampler and Connell 2018; Savin-Williams 2005; Seidman 2002).
24. While attitudes about sexuality are liberalizing, these trends are sometimes performative and accompanied by new forms of discrimination (Brodyn and Ghaziani 2018). Arguments about "tolerance" further misdirect our attention to a lower bar for civil rights (Walters 2014). For reports of discrimination, see (Singh and Durso 2017).
25. Bailey 2009:259.

Hungama (In a Converted Warehouse)

1. https://www.vogue.in/culture-and-living/content/a-new-crop-of-south-asians-is-redefining-the-uk-underground-music-scene-youthquake.

Chapter 5

1. Gayatri Spivak explores the factors that obstruct a capacity to be heard among individuals who occupy the periphery. What does it mean to have political subjectivity and agency when these are your socio-spatial conditions? The work raises questions about the politics of margins and centers. See (Spivak 1988). In his presidential address, Aldon Morris revisits the idea and develops its sociological implications (Morris 2022).
2. My argument follows Bourdieu (1993) and other field theorists who describe "core" (insider, incumbent) and "peripheral" (outsider, dissident) actors in "cultural fields." Although Bourdieu focuses on literary and artistic works, I think that nightlife constitutes its own distinct cultural field, or a system of social positions and scenes that are structured by power relations and characterized by a struggle for dominance among its members. As we are seeing in this book, the field of nightlife has a unique set of organizational forms, values, discourses, symbols, rituals, and rules. Some actors in the field defend and reproduce their views while others challenge the taken-for-granted assumptions of dominant groups (Cattani et al. 2014). The analytic value of thinking about nightlife as a field is that the framework enables both structural (deterministic) and agency-oriented (subjective, charismatic) views.
3. https://www.buzzfeed.com/adeonibada/cocoa-butter-club-cabaret-black-queer-lgbt (emphasis in original).
4. https://www.dazeddigital.com/fashion/article/43426/1/trans-inclusive-activists-transmissions-gender-representation-london-fashion.
5. Gaby recognizes the importance of gay bars. "Gay bars need to be visible because when you first come out, or you want to experiment with your own gender identity, you have to go somewhere to see for yourself, and I feel like a gay bar is often the place." Why is that? I ask. "Just because you don't know any other things. You don't know about underground queer nights." Gaby offers a measured though vital view: gay bars provide an entry point for general feelings of fellowship. From there, people can seek more specific networks and connections.
6. Lesbian identities have acquired a multiplicity of meanings over the twenty-first century. That variation and variety of meanings, along with a greater recognition of differences between lesbian-identifying individuals, has undermined a sense of belonging in lesbian communities (Hagai 2023). Based on observations about the disappearance of lesbian bars, writers like Katie Herzog ask, "Where have all the lesbians gone?" In the *Washington Post*, the humanities scholar Lynne Stahl argues that "extinction anxieties"—notions that lesbians are "going extinct"—have "long fueled nationalist, fascist, and white-supremacist movements and often beget eugenicist agendas." For Stahl, assertions about lesbian extinctions represent "the latest form of transphobia." See https://www.washingtonpost.com/outlook/the-latest-form-of-transphobia-saying-lesbians-are-going-extinct/2021/03/18/072a95fc-8786-11eb-82bc-e58213caa38e_story.html. For academic debates about declines in the term lesbian, see (Forstie 2020). For broader public discussions about these issues, see an essay in *Slate* entitled, "For Many Young Queer Women, *Lesbian* Offers a Fraught Inheritance": https://slate.com/human-interest/2016/12/young-queer-women-dont-like-lesbian-as-a-name-heres-why.html.
7. In my mind, the move to decouple femininity from female bodies resembles "female masculinity," a notion that disentangles masculinity from male bodies (Halberstam 1998).
8. https://gal-dem.com/16504-2/.
9. https://www.theguardian.com/society/2023/mar/08/tell-me-about-it-stud-the-rapturous-return-of-the-butch-lesbian-scene.

10. See Instagram to learn more about Aphrodyki (their name is their handle). For the *Time Out* story, see https://www.timeout.com/london/clubs/aphrodyki. There are other women- and lesbian-focused club nights in London, including Lick, Gal Pals, and Big Dyke Energy. Commentators about these events make similar observations as I do: "History hasn't been kind to lesbian club nights." Over the years, "the most prominent examples keep being closed." See https://crackmagazine.net/article/long-reads/levis-queer-britain-crack-magazine-lgbt-history-clubs/. For efforts to commemorate bygone lesbian club nights, like the Robin's Nest in Cambridge, Ontario, in documentary films, see https://www.cbc.ca/news/canada/kitchener-waterloo/lgbtq-lesbian-gay-queer-bar-nightclub-1.6767686.
11. These quotes come from their Facebook page: https://www.facebook.com/knickerbockerparty/ and event page: https://theyardtheatre.co.uk/music/events/knickerbocker-6/.
12. But even this is complicated, Alex tells me: "That has opened us up to potential accusations that, particularly with the racial diversity of the people we've had performing, that we have a very White crowd, and that it's actually not cool to have people of color coming and being 'performing monkeys,' in inverted commas, for a White male audience. We thought a lot about that, and the way that we sell what our night is to those performers so that they feel safe in our space, because we are still a queer night. It's the queerness that binds us rather than necessarily race, or creed, or color."
13. Coolest club: https://theface.com/life/adonis-lgbtq-club-night-london-volume-4-issue-3; cult party: https://www.timeout.com/london/clubs/adonis.
14. The quantification of qualitative data, or assigning numerical values to observational data, is a misguided effort, although there are conditions under which it can be useful. Howie Becker (1970:81) calls the use of numbers in a qualitative context "quasi-statistics," a practice designed to support approximations of aggregate claims about themes, like some, most, many, or few of the attendees at a party are White. There is a large literature on these matters. Two of my favorite pieces include Maxwell (2010) and Small and Calarco (2022). These provide insights about how to think about qualitative research without depending on quantitative epistemologies. In qualitative research, statements like "half the interviewees mentioned X" do not imply that we would find that theme proportionally represented in the population. Such statements support the centrality of concepts, not central tendencies. The intuition is important: by transforming qualitative data into numerical expressions, we lose the centrality of concepts, which is the heart of qualitative approaches. Representation of population quantities is not always the goal—it certainly isn't mine in this discussion. Instead, my goal is to reflect theoretically on the salience of concepts, and to examine variation within them, between them, and other major ideas that resonate for my respondents.
15. Ahmed 2016a:33; Ghaziani and Brim 2019b:13.

INFERNO (Institute of Contemporary Art)

1. https://www.tmrwmagazine.com/features/music/behind-the-decks-lewis-g-burton.
2. https://othernessarchive.com/; see also an interview in *Into*: https://www.intomore.com/culture/otherness-archive-makes-past-present/.

Chapter 6

1. Black Obsidian Sound System (BOSS) is a QTBIPOC collective consisting of eleven members. BOSS "challenges the dominant norms of sound-system culture across the African

diaspora through club nights, art installations, technical workshops and creative commissions." See https://www.frieze.com/article/black-obsidian-sound-system-2021.

2. For the odd couple quote, see (Love 2016:346). To ask if queerness can "show us the way," as I do in this discussion, is to inquire about a branch of study called queer methods. For writings that engage with queerness as a method, see (Brim and Ghaziani 2016; Browne and Nash 2010; Compton, Meadow, and Schilt 2018; Ghaziani and Brim 2019a; Ghaziani and Brim 2019b), For writings that deal with the ambiguity and amorphousness of measuring cultural matters in general, see (Fine 1979; Ghaziani 2009).
3. For lumping and splitting, see (Zerubavel 1996). For Love, see (Love 2016:346). The idea of a mess resembles the notion of "wonkiness." Ahmed (2006) imagines queerness in this way: "unintelligible by the 'straightness of normativity.'" Try it: close your eyes and say out loud the word "straight." When you hear it, what do you see? Straightness, Olimpia tells me, is "an effect of things lining up with the straight line." Now close your eyes and say "wonky." How does the line change? Wonkiness is "an effect of things coming 'out of line' with the 'straight line': one is 'wonky' when one is 'oblique' and/or 'off-line.'" See (Burchiellaro 2021:34) for an article she published with these reflections.
4. See treatments on sexual fluidity in women (Diamond 2008) and in men (Carrillo and Hoffman 2018).
5. https://www.forbes.com/sites/carlieporterfield/2022/02/17/gen-z-drives-surge-of-more-americans-identifying-as-lgbt/.
6. https://www.ons.gov.uk/peoplepopulationandcommunity/culturalidentity/sexuality/bulletins/sexualidentityuk/2020. British statistics are from 2020, which was the most recent report available.
7. https://www.ipsos.com/sites/default/files/ct/news/documents/2021-06/LGBT%20Pride%202021%20Global%20Survey%20Report_3.pdf.
8. For research on age-related differences in the adoption of queer identities, see (Goldberg et al. 2020; Morandini, Blaszczynsky, and Dar-Nimrod 2017). For research on how the culture of gay bars has changed over time, see (Mattson 2023; Hilderbrand 2023).
9. Koen's perspective is consistent with research on identity politics (e.g., Armstrong 2002; D'Emilio 1983; Ghaziani 2005; Ghaziani 2008).
10. For homonormativity, see (Duggan 2002).
11. For The Outside Project, see https://lgbtiqoutside.org/. For the interview with *Vice*, see https://www.vice.com/en/article/a37mbe/homeless-lgbt-people-face-a-unique-set-of-challenges.
12. For more information about Open Barbers, see https://openbarbers.com/. For the feature in *Pink News*, see https://www.pinknews.co.uk/2021/03/31/open-barbers-trans-community-10-birthday-transgender-greygory-lane-felix-vass/.
13. For the history of the rainbow flag, see (Ghaziani 2008). For a discussion about the movement gaining national visibility in the United States, see (Ghaziani 2005).
14. Entire books wait to be written about the role of sex in gay and queer spaces, including how club nights create unique opportunities for sexual exploration and experimentation in the context of corporeal diversities. This is what the Riposte flyer states about their playroom: "Darkrooms have been a source of gay liberation for decades, and have an important history in our community. However, these dark rooms have historically catered to mostly men and the cruising culture associated with it, and community within such is sometimes non-verbal. At Riposte, we cater to something different. Although we are not a play party [a sex party], we have a queer playspace *for people of all genders and sexualities*. It is important for everyone to get acquainted with the rules before entering, so everyone can be on the same page and play safely. Every playroom/party/club has its own rules.

Please take the time to read Riposte rules before entering" (emphasis in original). The key component of the rules is consent.

15. The phrase "you have to be in the know to know" is an example of subcultural capital (Thornton 1996) applied in the context of queerness and club nights.
16. This discussion illustrates the pitfalls of what researchers call "path dependence" (Mahoney 2000).

That Was Fun

1. Campkin and Marshall 2017; Mattson 2019.
2. For stats on club closures post-COVID and in the added context of an inflationary crisis, see https://www.theguardian.com/business/2022/nov/03/one-uk-nightclub-closing-every-two-days-over-soaring-costs-night-time-industries-association-warn. For the Night Time Industries Association, see https://www.ntia.co.uk/. Not a single gay bar or nightclub closed permanently during the lockdowns in London. McCormack and Measham (2022) attribute this remarkable outcome to the Culture Recovery Fund, a £1.57 billion (US$1.95 billion) government grants package created to protect arts and cultural organizations, like museums and theaters, from the economic impacts of COVID-19. The Greater London Authority, known colloquially as City Hall, announced an additional £2.3 million (US$2.9 million) Culture-at-Risk Business Support Fund to help nighttime venues, including gay bars, which were not covered by existing government support systems yet were also at imminent risk of closure. The pandemic necessitated huge and sudden infusions of government assistance in these forms—and it will likely never be the norm. Still, these utterly abnormal last few years of our lives do reveal how a more engaged government can bolster the cultural infrastructure of our cities. They also show the value of reframing nighttime venues as part of that cultural infrastructure, and defining bar closures as a cultural risk rather than just a business loss. In my other work, I show how the pandemic presented new opportunities for gay bars, like consolidating mutual aid networks (using bars to distribute face masks), innovating interior designs (installing Plexiglas inside the bars to enable safe socializing), and discovering new institutional anchors (like club nights). See (Miles et al. 2021). To learn more about institutional anchors, see (Ghaziani 2014a). To learn more about the effects of pandemics, especially AIDS, on the interior design of gay bars, see (Andersson 2019). For details about the Culture Recovery Fund, see https://www.artscouncil.org.uk/CRFgrants. For details about the Culture-at-Risk Business Support Fund, see https://www.londoncouncils.gov.uk/our-key-themes/culture-sport-and-tourism/arts-and-culture/support-arts-and-culture-sector-during.
3. On September 20, 1777, Johnson was chatting with biographer James Boswell about whether Bosewell's affections for the city would wane if he lived here full-time, rather than the zest he felt on his occasional visits. Nearly two and a half centuries later and worlds apart, the words, which I feature with pleasure on the dedication page, resonate for me: "Why, Sir, you find no man, at all intellectual, who is willing to leave London. No, Sir, when a man is tired of London, he is tired of life; for there is in London all that life can afford."
4. See the belongingness hypothesis (Baumeister and Leary 1995), no person is an island (Donne 1975), and forming attachments with others in specific places (hooks 2009; Putnam 2000). Our knowledge about belonging is often based in the context of globalization, nationalism, and citizenship, or else on the experiences of immigrants, refugees, asylum seekers, and colonial subjects (DuBois 1903; Wekker 2016; Yuval-Davis 2011). The history, struggles, and perspectives of LGBTQ+ people are absent from this story (Ghaziani 2022).

To think about nightlife as a place of LGBTQ+ belonging, we have to confront the diasporic specter of not belonging, or un-belonging (Ahmed 2007; Rosenberg 2021). Being made to feel like a stranger in a place where you think you should belong is an awful experience, like sitting by yourself in a school cafeteria. But sometimes, exclusions can empower us, making us agents as we write bold new narratives.

5. To use "collective effervescence" to describe nightlife is to intentionally draw an analogy with religious experiences. See (Durkheim 1912).
6. The idea of belonging as emplaced without being place-bound provides, I argue, a distinct contribution to the temporary turn in urban studies (Bishop and Williams 2012; Tonkiss 2013; Wynn 2015), economic sociology (Hirschman 2021), sexuality studies (Muñoz 2009; Stillwagon and Ghaziani 2019), and social theory (Wynn 2016).
7. Finest young artists: https://i-d.vice.com/en/article/papngv/get-ready-for-an-anal-house-meltdown; artiest party: https://i-d.vice.com/en/article/papngv/get-ready-for-an-anal-house-meltdown; cult night: https://i-d.vice.com/en/article/gy85dw/meet-the-accomplished-artist-behind-cult-night-anal-house-meltdown; best name: https://i-d.vice.com/en/article/j5n88d/roxy-lee-shoots-the-wonderful-and-wild-people-of-anal-house-meltdowns-pride-party.
8. Duckie will continue to produce one-off parties, just not at the RVT. According to producer Simon Casson, "There are differences between Duckie and RVT management that we haven't been able to resolve, and that's why we're leaving . . . Our business practices and our cultural values are different. We want different things. I can't say they want money and we want art because everyone wants money. We want money as well. But we also want art." See https://www.nottelevision.net/duckie-is-closing/.
9. https://www.theguardian.com/music/2022/jun/05/cheerio-duckie-regulars-lgbtq-club-vauxhall-tavern; Ben offers history about the RVT in his article. "Around 1860, the pub was the first building to go up when Vauxhall's notorious pleasure gardens, home to early cocktails, pop songs and classless cruising, closed. The RVT became a space of gay socialising after the war and was central to London's 60s drag boom. In the 80s, its prominent community role at the time of AIDS and Section 28 provoked police raids, one involving resident drag act Lily Savage. The RVT hit a lull in the 90s, open just two days a week until the Duckie gang moved in and proved an instant hit."
10. Warren 2023; the quotes come from a review in *The Guardian*: https://www.theguardian.com/commentisfree/2023/mar/19/isolated-humans-dance-together-demise-clubbing.
11. https://www.lgbtqnation.com/2022/06/gay-bars-decline-nationwide-according-new-study/.
12. For joy deficit, see (shuster and Westbrook 2022). For damage-centered research, see (Tuck 2009).
13. shuster and Westbrook 2022:15.
14. A couple of months later, section members received a newsletter, the first from the new chair, that amped up the anguish: "the world swirls around us, fraught and freighted with racial capitalism, maiming, genocide, climate dystopias and other slow, less spectacular modes of necropolitics that render certain populations more vulnerable to death." The newsletter is from Fall 2022, and the quotes come from the first page.
15. Adeyemi, Khubchandani, and Rivera-Servera 2021:3.
16. What I think is a much-needed shift from the negative to hope and joy is happening in queer studies as scholars begin to pivot from arguments about death drives, the disruptive negativities of queerness, its endemic failures, and visions for a future that is not necessarily better (Edelman 2004; Halberstam 2011) to future-oriented projects (Muñoz 2009) of hopeful worldmaking (Muñoz 1999).
17. The quotes combine my interview with Ben and his writings (Walters 2017).

Partying as a Professor

1. See *The Guardian* for a closer look at the numbers: https://www.theguardian.com/world/2017/aug/04/you-must-open-a-gay-venue-in-office-complex-planners-tell-developers.
2. London is a global city (Sassen 2016) of culture (Currid 2007) and "transnational connections" (Houlbrook 2005:9). See also model cases (Krause 2021) and how facts travel (Guggenheim and Krause 2012). See Houlbrook (2005) again for London's particular history and character.
3. For examples of using bar listings as data to make inferences about nightlife, see (Israelstam and Lambert 1984; Knopp and Brown 2021; Mattson 2019). For mayoral claims about growing numbers of club nights, see (Campkin and Marshall 2017:32).
4. For research on disruptive events, see (Zhang 2021). The quotes are from pages 376 (old hierarchies), 378 (substantive changes), and 381 (urgency). For research on the effects of storytelling for motivating action, see (Polletta 2006).
5. Small and Calarco 2022.
6. For research on reframing nightlife from crime to culture, see (Eldridge 2019). For research on the twenty-four-hour city, see (Roberts and Turner 2005).
7. References: sampling for range (Weiss 1994), saturation (Small 2009:24), logical inferences (Mitchell 1983:200), and cultural meanings (Ghaziani 2018; Ghaziani 2019c; Lamont and Swidler 2004). The interviews were approved by the Research Ethics Committee of the London School of Economics and Political Science.
8. For queer methods, see (Brim and Ghaziani 2016; Compton, Meadow, and Schilt 2018; Ghaziani and Brim 2019a).
9. For abduction, see (Timmermans and Tavory 2012). They focus on the importance of crosschecks with existing theories and implicit assumptions on page 169. For additional arguments about the potential of surprises, see (Miles and Huberman 1994:270).
10. For research on the linked destinies of minority groups, see (Hunter and Robinson 2018:xiii). For arguments about isomorphism, see (DiMaggio and Powell 1983). For intersectional failures, see (Crenshaw 2012:1450; Moore 2012). For Morris's call to action, see (Morris 2022).
11. For Ruth and Babe's house parties, see (Thorpe 1996).
12. For temporary urbanisms, see (Andres and Zhang 2020; Ferreri 2021; Madanipour 2017). For a sociology of occasions, see (Wynn 2016).

References

Achilles, Nancy. 1967. "The Development of the Homosexual Bar as an Institution." Pp. 228–44 in *Sexual Deviance*, edited by J. Gagnon and W. Simon. New York: Harper & Row.

Adeyemi, Kemi. 2022. *Feels Right: Black Queer Women and the Politics of Partying in Chicago*. Durham, NC: Duke University Press.

Adeyemi, Kemi, Kareem Khubchandani, and Ramón H. Rivera-Servera. 2021. *Queer Nightlife*. Ann Arbor: University of Michigan Press.

Adler, Sy and Johanna Brenner. 1992. "Gender and Space: Lesbians and Gay Men in the City." *International Journal of Urban and Regional Research* 16:24–34.

Ahmed, Sara. 2006. *Queer Phenomenology*. Durham, NC: Duke University Press.

——. 2007. "A Phenomenology of Whiteness." *Feminist Theory* 8:149–68.

——. 2014. *The Cultural Politics of Emotion*. Edinburgh: Edinburgh University Press.

——. 2016a. "An Affinity of Hammers." *TSQ: Transgender Studies Quarterly* 3:22–34.

——. 2016b. "Interview with Judith Butler." *Sexualities* 19:482–92.

Andersson, Johan. 2009. "East End Localism and Urban Decay: Shoreditch's Re-Emerging Gay Scene." *London Journal* 34:55–71.

——. 2019. "Homonormative Aesthetics: AIDS and 'De-generational Unremembering' in 1990s London." *Urban Studies* 56:2993–3010.

Andres, Lauren and Amy Y. Zhang. 2020. "Introduction: Setting-Up a Research Agenda for Temporary Urbanism." Pp. 1–12 in *Transforming Cities Through Temporary Urbanism*, edited by L. Andres and A. Y. Zhang. Cham, Switzerland: Springer Urban Book Series.

Armstrong, Elizabeth A. 2002. *Forging Gay Identities: Organizing Sexuality in San Francisco, 1950–1994*. Chicago: University of Chicago Press.

Bailey, Marlon. 2013. *Butch Queens Up in Pumps: Gender, Performance, and Ballroom Culture in Detroit*. Ann Arbor: University of Michigan Press.

Bailey, Marlon M. 2009. "Performance as Intravention: Ballroom Culture and the Politics of HIV/AIDS in Detroit." *Souls* 11:253–74.

Baldor, Tyler. 2018. "No Girls Allowed? Fluctuating Boundaries Between Gay Men and Straight Women in Gay Public Space." *Ethnography* 20:419–42.

——. 2020. "Acquainted Strangers: Thwarted Interaction in Digitally Mediated Urban Gay Bars." *Social Problems* 69:58–73.

Baumeister, Roy F. and Mark R. Leary. 1995. "The Need to Belong: Desire for Interpersonal Attachments as a Fundamental Human Motivation." *Psychological Bulletin* 117:497–529.

Becker, Howard S. 1970. *Sociological Work: Method and Substance*. New Brunswick, NJ: Transaction Books.

——. 1982. *Art Worlds*. Berkeley: University of California Press.

Beemyn, Genny. 2004. "US History." Pp. 501–36 in *Trans Bodies, Trans Selves*, edited by L. Erickson-Schroth. New York: Oxford University Press.

Berrey, Ellen. 2015. *The Enigma of Diversity: The Language of Race and the Limits of Racial Justice*. Chicago: University of Chicago Press.

Betts, David. 2021. "Excluding the Queer Unwanted: Perspectives from Older LGBTQ+ Adults in New Zealand." *Journal of Gay and Lesbian Social Services* 33:475–92.

Bishop, Peter and Lesley Williams. 2012. *The Temporary City*. London: Routledge.

Bivens, Josh. 2016. "Progressive Redistribution Without Guilt." Economic Policy Institute, Washington, DC.

Bonilla-Silva, Eduardo. 2013. *Racism Without Racists: Color-Blind Racism and the Persistence of Racial Inequality in America*. Lanham, MD: Rowman & Littlefield.

Bourdieu, Pierre. 1984. *Distinction: A Social Critique of the Judgement of Taste*. Cambridge, MA: Harvard University Press.

——. 1985. "The Social Space and the Genesis of Groups." *Theory and Society* 14:723–44.

Bourdieu, Pierre. 1993. *The Field of Cultural Production: Essays on Art and Literature*. Edited by Randal Johnson. New York: Columbia University Press.

Branton, Scott E. 2021. "Negotiating Organizational Identity: The Communicative Resilience of Small-Town Gay Bars." *International Review of Qualitative Research* 13:497–521.

Brim, Matt and Amin Ghaziani. 2016. "Introduction: Queer Methods." *WSQ: Women's Studies Quarterly* 44:14–27.

Brodyn, Adriana and Amin Ghaziani. 2018. "Performative Progressiveness: Accounting for New Forms of Inequality in the Gayborhood." *City & Community* 17:307–29.

Brown-Saracino, Japonica. 2011. "From the Lesbian Ghetto to Ambient Community: The Perceived Costs and Benefits of Integration for Community." *Social Problems* 58:361–388.

——. 2015. "How Place Shapes Identity: The Origins of Distinctive LBQ Identities in Four Small U.S. Cities." *American Journal of Sociology* 121:1–63.

——. 2021. "The Afterlife of Identity Politics: Gentrification, Critical Nostalgia, and the Commemoration of Lost Dyke Bars." *American Journal of Sociology* 126:1017–66.

Brown-Saracino, Japonica and Amin Ghaziani. 2009. "The Constraints of Culture: Evidence from the Chicago Dyke March." *Cultural Sociology* 3:51–75.

Browne, Kath and Eduarda Ferreira. 2018. *Lesbian Geographies: Gender, Place and Power*. New York: Routledge.

Browne, Kath and Catherine J. Nash. 2010. *Queer Methods and Methodologies*. Farnham, UK: Ashgate.

Buckland, Fiona. 2002. *Impossible Dance: Club Culture and Queer World-Making*. Middletown, CT: Wesleyan University Press.

Burchiellaro, Olimpia. 2021. "There's Nowhere Wonky Left to Go: Gentrification, Queerness and Class Politics of Inclusion in (East) London." *Gender, Work & Organizations* 28:24–38.

Butler, Ruth. 1999. "Double the Trouble or Twice the Fun? Disabled Bodies in the Gay Community." Pp. 199–215 in *Mind and Body Spaces: Geographies of Illness, Impairment and Disability*, edited by R. Butler and H. Parr. London: Routledge.

Caluya, Gilbert. 2008. "'The Rice Steamer': Race, Desire, and Affect in Sydney's Gay Scene." *Australian Geographer* 39:283–92.

Campkin, Ben and Laura Marshall. 2017. *LGBTQ Cultural Infrastructure in London: Night Venues, 2006-Present*. London: UCL Urban Laboratory.

Canaday, Margot. 2009. *The Straight State: Sexuality and Citizenship in Twentieth-Century America*. Princeton, NJ: Princeton University Press.

Carrillo, Héctor and Amanda Hoffman. 2018. "'Straight with a Pinch of Bi': The Construction of Heterosexuality as an Elastic Category among Adult US Men." *Sexualities* 21:90–108.

Casey, Mark. 2004. "De-Dyking Queer Spaces: Heterosexual Female Visibility in Gay and Lesbian Spaces." *Sexualities* 7:446–61.

Casey, Mark E. 2007. "The Queer Unwanted and Their Undesirable 'Otherness.'" Pp. 137–49 in *Geographies of Sexualities: Theory, Practice, and Politics*, edited by K. Browne and J. Lim. London: Routledge.

Castells, Manuel. 1983. *The City and the Grassroots: A Cross-Cultural Theory of Urban Social Movements*. Berkeley: University of California Press.

Cattani, Gino, Simone Ferriani, and Paul D. Allison. 2014. "Insiders, Outsiders, and the Struggle for Consecration in Cultural Fields: A Core-Periphery Perspective." *American Sociological Review* 79(2):258–281.

Centner, Ryan and Manoel Pereira Neto. 2021. "Peril, Privilege, and Queer Comforts: The Nocturnal Performative Geographies of Expatriate Gay Men in Dubai." *Geoforum* 127:92–103.

Chasin, Alexandra. 2001. *Selling Out: The Gay and Lesbian Movement Goes to Market*. London: Palgrave Macmillan.

Chauncey, George. 1994. *Gay New York: Gender, Urban Culture, and the Making of the Gay Male World, 1890–1940*. New York: Basic Books.

Cheryan, Sapna and Benoît Monin. 2005. "'Where Are You *Really* From?': Asian Americans and Identity Denials." *Journal of Personality and Social Psychology* 89:717–30.

Collins, Alan. 2004. "Sexual Dissidence, Enterprise and Assimilation: Bedfellows in Urban Regeneration." *Urban Studies* 41:1789–1806.

Compton, D'Lane, Tey Meadow, and Kristen Schilt. 2018. *Other, Please Specify: Queer Methods in Sociology*. Berkeley: University of California Press.

Corbo, Leonardo, Raffaele Corrado, and Simone Ferriani. 2016. "A New Order of Things: Network Mechanisms of Field Evolution in the Aftermath of an Exogenous Shock." *Organization Studies* 37:323–48.

Creed, W. E. Douglas, Maureen A. Scully, and John R. Austin. 2002. "Clothes Make the Person? The Tailoring of Legitimating Accounts and the Social Construction of Identity." *Organization Science* 13:475–96.

Crenshaw, Kimberlé W. 2012. "From Private Violence to Mass Incarceration: Thinking Intersectionally About Women, Race, and Social Control." *UCLA Law Review* 9:1418–72.

Cunningham, Michael. 1995. "The Slap of Love." *Open City* 6. Available online at: https://opencity.org/archive/issue-6.

Currid, Elizabeth. 2007. *The Warhol Economy: How Fashion, Art, and Music Drive New York City*. Princeton, NJ: Princeton University Press.

D'Emilio, John. 1983. *Sexual Politics, Sexual Communities: The Making of a Homosexual Minority in the United States, 1940–1970*. Chicago: University of Chicago Press.

Dantzler, Prentiss, Elizabeth Korver-Glenn, and Junia Howell. 2022. "What Does Racial Capitalism Have to Do with Cities and Communities?" *City & Community* 21(3):163–172.

Dean, James Joseph. 2014. *Straights: Heterosexuality in a Post-Closeted Culture*. New York: New York University Press.

Diamond, Lisa. 2008. *Sexual Fluidity: Understanding Women's Love and Desire*. Cambridge, MA: Harvard University Press.

DiMaggio, Paul J. and Walter W. Powell. 1983. "The Iron Cage Revisited: Institutional Isomorphism and Collective Rationality in Organizational Fields." *American Sociological Review* 48:147–60.

Doan, Petra L. 2007. "Queers in the American City: Transgendered Perceptions of Urban Spaces." *Gender, Place, and Culture* 14:57–74.

Donne, John. 1975. *Devotions upon Emergent Occasions*. Montreal, QC: McGill Queens University Press.

Douek, Samuel. 2016. "The Eradication of London's Democratic Queer Pubs." Pp. 182–91 in *A Gendered Profession: The Question of Representation in Space Making*, edited by J. B. Brown, H. Harriss, R. Morrow, and J. Soane. London: RIBA Publishing.

DuBois, W.E.B. 1903. *The Souls of Black Folk*. Chicago: A.C. McClurg & Co.

Duffus, Melindy and Ben Colliver. 2023. "Gender, Sexuality and Race: An Intersectional Analysis of Racial Consumption and Exclusion in Birmingham's Gay Village." *Sexualities*. doi: https://doi.org/10.1177/13634607231157068.

Duggan, Lisa. 2002. "The New Homonormativity: The Sexual Politics of Neoliberalism." Pp. 175–94 in *Materializing Democracy: Toward a Revitalized Cultural Politics*, edited by R. Castronovo and D. D. Nelson. Durham, NC: Duke University Press.

Durkheim, Emile. 1912. *The Elementary Forms of Religious Life*. New York: Free Press.

Edelman, Lee. 2004. *No Future: Queer Theory and the Death Drive*. Durham, NC: Duke University Press.

Eeckhout, Bart, Rob Herreman, and Alexander Dhoest. 2021. "A Gay Neighborhood or Merely a Temporary Cluster of 'Strange' Bars? Gay Bar Culture in Antwerp." Pp. 221–38 in *The Life and Afterlife of Gay Neighborhoods*, edited by A. Bitterman and D. B. Hess. New York: Springer.

Eldridge, Adam. 2019. "Strangers in the Night: Nightlife Studies and New Urban Tourism." *Journal of Policy Research in Tourism, Leisure and Events* 11:422–35.

Elmer, Vicki and Adam Leigland. 2013. *Infrastructure Planning and Finance*. New York: Routledge.

Escoffier, Jeffrey. 1997. "The Political Economy of the Closet: Notes Toward an Economic History of Gay and Lesbian Life before Stonewall." Pp. 123–34 in *Homo Economics: Capitalism, Community, and Lesbian and Gay Life*, edited by A. Gluckman and B. Reed. New York: Routledge.

Faderman, Lillian. 1991. *Odd Girls and Twilight Lovers: A History of Lesbian Life in Twentieth-Century America*. New York: Columbia University Press.

Fellows, Will and Helen P. Branson. 1957. *Gay Bar*. Madison: University of Wisconsin Press.

Ferreri, Mara. 2021. *The Permanence of Temporary Urbanism*. Amsterdam: Amsterdam University Press.

Fine, Gary Alan. 1979. "Small Groups and Cultural Creation: The Idioculture of Little League Baseball Teams." *American Sociological Review* 44:733–45.

Fine, Gary Alan and Ugo Corte. 2017. "Group Pleasures: Collaborative Commitments, Shared Narrative, and the Sociology of Fun." *Sociological Theory* 35:64–86.

Fine, Gary Alan and Philip Manning. 2003. "Erving Goffman." Pp. 34–62 in *The Blackwell Companion to Major Contemporary Social Theorists*, edited by G. Ritzer. Malden, MA: Blackwell.

Fischer, Claude S. 1975. "Toward a Subcultural Theory of Urbanism." *American Journal of Sociology* 80:1319–41.

Fligstein, Neil and Doug McAdam. 2011. "Toward a General Theory of Strategic Action Fields." *Sociological Theory* 29:1–26.

Forstie, Clare. 2020. "Disappearing Dykes? Post-Lesbian Discourse and Shifting Identities and Communities." *Journal of Homosexuality* 67:1760–78.

Francis, Megan Ming and Leah Wright-Rigueur. 2021. "Black Lives Matter in Historical Perspective." *Annual Review of Law and Social Science* 17:441–58.

Frost, Tom. 2014. "The Hyper-Hermeneutic Gesture of a Subtle Revolution." *Critical Horizons* 14:70–92.

Gamson, Joshua. 1997. "Messages of Exclusion: Gender, Movements, and Symbolic Boundaries." *Gender & Society* 11:178–99.

Ghaziani, Amin. 2005. "Breakthrough: The 1979 National March." *Gay and Lesbian Review* 12:31–33.

——. 2008. *The Dividends of Dissent: How Conflict and Culture Work in Lesbian and Gay Marches on Washington*. Chicago: University of Chicago Press.

——. 2009. "An 'Amorphous Mist'? The Problem of Measurement in the Study of Culture." *Theory and Society* 38:581–612.

——. 2010. "There Goes the Gayborhood?" *Contexts* 9:64–66.

——. 2011. "Post-Gay Collective Identity Construction." *Social Problems* 58:99–125.

——. 2014a. "Measuring Urban Sexual Cultures." *Theory and Society* 43:371–93.

——. 2014b. *There Goes the Gayborhood?* Princeton, NJ: Princeton University Press.

——. 2015a. "'Gay Enclaves Face Prospect of Being Passé': How Assimilation Affects the Spatial Expressions of Sexuality in the United States." *International Journal of Urban and Regional Research* 39:756–71.

——. 2015b. "Lesbian Geographies." *Contexts* 14:62–64.

——. 2018. "Queer Spatial Analysis." Pp. 201–15 in *Other, Please Specify: Queer Methods in Sociology*, edited by D. L. Compton, K. Schilt, and T. Meadow. Berkeley: University of California Press.

——. 2019a. "Cultural Archipelagos: New Directions in the Study of Sexuality and Space." *City & Community* 18:4–22.

——. 2019b. "Culture and the Nighttime Economy: A Conversation with London's Night Czar and Culture-at-Risk Officer." *Metropolitics* 12, November. Available online at: https://www.metropolitics.org/Culture-and-the-Nighttime-Economy-A-Conversation-with-London-s-Night-Czar-and.html.

——. 2019c. "Methodological Problems and Possibilities in Gayborhood Studies." Pp. 103–18 in *Imagining Queer Methods*, edited by A. Ghaziani and M. Brim. New York: New York University Press.

——. 2021. "Why Gayborhoods Matter: The Street Empirics of Urban Sexualities." Pp. 87–113 in *The Life and Afterlife of Gay Neighborhoods*, edited by A. Bitterman and D. B. Hess. New York: Springer.

——. 2022. "Belonging in Gay Neighborhoods and Queer Nightlife." Pp. 540–50 in *Introducing the New Sexuality Studies*, edited by S. Seidman, N. Fischer, and L. Westbrook. New York: Routledge.

Ghaziani, Amin and Matt Brim. 2019a. *Imagining Queer Methods*. New York: New York University Press.

——. 2019b. "Queer Methods: Four Provocations for an Emerging Field." Pp. 3–27 in *Imagining Queer Methods*, edited by A. Ghaziani and M. Brim. New York: New York University Press.

Ghaziani, Amin and Thomas D. Cook. 2005. "Reducing HIV Infections at Circuit Parties: From Description to Explanation and Principles of Intervention Design." *Journal of the International Association of Physicians in AIDS Care* 4:32–46.

Ghaziani, Amin and Ryan Stillwagon. 2018. "Queer Pop-Ups." *Contexts* 17:78–80.

Gieseking, Jen Jack. 2020. "Mapping Lesbian and Queer Lines of Desire: Constellations of Queer Urban Space." *Environment and Planning D* 38:941–60.

GLA Economics. 2018. "London at Night: An Evidence Base for a 24-hour City." London: Greater London Authority.

Goffman, Erving. 1967. *Interaction Ritual*. Garden City, NY: Doubleday.

Goldberg, Shoshana K., Esther D. Rothblum, Stephen T. Russell, and Ilan H. Meyer. 2020. "Exploring the Q in LGBTQ: Demographic Characteristic and Sexuality of Queer People in a U.S. Representative Sample of Sexual Minorities." *Psychology of Sexual Orientation and Gender Diversity* 7:101–12.

Granovetter, Mark S. 1973. "The Strength of Weak Ties." *American Journal of Sociology* 78:1360–80.

Grazian, David. 2008. *On the Make: The Hustle of Urban Nightlife*. Chicago: University of Chicago Press.

——. 2009. "Urban Nightlife, Social Capital, and the Public Life of Cities." *Sociological Forum* 24:908–17.

Greater London Authority. 2017. "Culture and the Night-time Economy." London: Greater London Authority.

——. 2019. "Cultural Infrastructure Plan." London: Greater London Authority.

Green, Adam Isaiah. 2014. "The Sexual Fields Framework." Pp. 25–56 in *Sexual Fields: Toward a Sociology of Collective Sexual Life*, edited by A. I. Green. Chicago: University of Chicago Press.

Greene, Theodore. 2022. "'You're Dancing on My Seat!' Queer Subcultures and the Production of Places in Contemporary Gay Bars." *Studies in Symbolic Interaction* 54:137–65.

Guggenheim, Michael and Monika Krause. 2012. "How Facts Travel: The Model Systems in Sociology." *Poetics* 40:101–17.

Hagai, Ella Ben. 2023. "Changes in Lesbian Identity in the 21st Century." *Current Opinion in Psychology* 49:1–5.

Halberstam, Jack. 2011. *The Queer Art of Failure*. Durham, NC: Duke University Press.

Halberstam, Judith. 1998. *Female Masculinity*. Durham, NC: Duke University Press.

Harry, Joseph. 1974. "Urbanization and the Gay Life." *Journal of Sex Research* 10:238–47.

Hartless, Jaime. 2018. "Questionably Queer: Understanding Straight Presence in the Post-Gay Bar." *Journal of Homosexuality* 66:1035–57.

Hebdige, Dick. 1979. *Subculture: The Meaning of Style*. London: Routledge.

Hennen, Peter. 2008. *Faeries, Bears, and Leathermen: Men in the Community Queering the Masculine*. Chicago: University of Chicago Press.

Hilderbrand, Lucas. 2023. *The Bars Are Ours: Histories and Cultures of Gay Bars in America, 1960 and After*. Durham, NC: Duke University Press.

Hirschman, Daniel. 2021. "Transitional Temporality." *Sociological Theory* 39:48–58.

Hodkinson, Stuart. 2012. "The New Urban Enclosures." *City* 16:500–18.

Holloway, John. 2010. *Crack Capitalism*. London: Pluto Press.

hooks, bell. 2009. *Belonging: A Culture of Place*. New York: Routledge.

Hou, Jeffrey. 2020. "Guerrilla Urbanism: Urban Design and the Practices of Resistance." *Urban Design International* 25:117–25.

Houlbrook, Matt. 2005. *Queer London: Perils and Pleasures in the Sexual Metropolis, 1918-1957*. Chicago: University of Chicago Press.

——. 2017. *Queer City: London Club Culture, 1918-1967*. London: The National Archives.

Hunter, Marcus. 2010a. "All the Gays Are White and All the Blacks Are Straight: Black Gay Men, Identity, and Community." *Sexuality Research and Social Policy* 7:81–92.

——. 2010b. "The Nightly Round: Space, Social Capital, and Urban Black Nightlife." *City & Community* 9:165–86.

Hunter, Marcus Anthony and Zandria F. Robinson. 2018. *Chocolate Cities: The Black Map of American Life*. Berkeley: University of California Press.

Israelstam, Stephen and Sylvia Lambert. 1984. "Gay Bars." *Journal of Drug Issues* 14:637–53.

Johnson, Corey W. and Diane M. Samdahl. 2005. "'The Night They Took Over': Misogyny in a Country-Western Gay Bar." *Leisure Sciences* 27:331–48.

Johnson, E. Patrick. 2011. *Sweet Tea: Black Gay Men of the South*. Chapel Hill: University of North Carolina Press.

——. 2019. "Put a Little Honey in My Sweet Tea: Oral History as Quare Performance." Pp. 45–62 in *Imagining Queer Methods*, edited by A. Ghaziani and M. Brim. New York: New York University Press.

Kahn, Janet and Patricia A. Gozemba. 1992. "In and Around the Lighthouse: Working-Class Lesbian Bar Culture in the 1950s and 1960s." Pp. 90–106 in *Gendered Domains: Rethinking*

Public and Private in Women's History, edited by D. O. Helly and S. M. Reverby. Ithaca, NY: Cornell University Press.

Kampler, Benjamin and Catherine Connell. 2018. "The Post-Gay Debates: Competing Visions for the Future of Homosexualities." *Sociology Compass* 12:1–12.

Kennedy, Elizabeth Lapovsky and Madeline D. Davis. 1993. *Boots of Leather, Slippers of Gold: The History of a Lesbian Community*. New York: Routledge.

Kennedy, Tammie M. 2014. "Sustaining White Homonormativity: *The Kids Are All Right* as Public Pedagogy." *Journal of Lesbian Studies* 18:118–32.

Khubchandani, Kareem. 2020. *Ishtyle: Accenting Gay Indian Nightlife*. Ann Arbor: University of Michigan Press.

Knopp, Larry and Michael Brown. 2021. "Travel Guides, Urban Spatial Imaginaries and LGBTQ+ Activism: The Case of Damron Guides." *Urban Studies* 58:1380–96.

Knopp, Lawrence. 1990. "Some Theoretical Implications of Gay Involvement in an Urban Land Market." *Political Geography Quarterly* 9:337–52.

Krause, Monika. 2021. *Model Cases: On Canonical Research Objects and Sites*. Chicago: University of Chicago Press.

Lamont, Michele and Ann Swidler. 2004. "Methodological Pluralism and the Possibilities and Limits of Interviewing." *Qualitative Sociology* 37:153–71.

Lane, Nikki. 2015. "All the Lesbians Are White, All the Villages Are Gay, but Some of Us Are Brave: Intersectionality, Belonging, and Black Queer Women's Scene Space in Washington D.C." Pp. 219–42 in *Lesbian Geographies*, edited by K. Browne and E. Ferreira. New York: Routledge.

Lang, Nico. 2017. "How Racism in LGBT Nightlife Birthed a New Pride Flag." *The Advocate*. Available online at: https://www.advocate.com/pride/2017/6/29/how-racism-lgbt-nightlife-birthed-new-pride-flag.

Lefebvre, Henri. 1968. "The Right to the City." Pp. 147–59 in *Writings on Cities: Henri Lefebvre*, edited by E. K. Kofman and E. Lebas. Oxford: Blackwell.

Liddle, Kathleen. 2005. "More than a Bookstore." *Journal of Lesbian Studies* 9:145–59.

Lindert, Peter H. 2017. "The Rise and Future of Progressive Redistribution." New Orleans: The CEQ Institute at Tulane University.

Livingston, Jennie. 1990. "Paris Is Burning." United States: Off-White Productions (Prestige Pictures).

Lizardo, Omar. 2022. "Solving the Problem of the Permanent Social: On Isaac Ariail Reed's *Power in Modernity*." *American Journal of Cultural Sociology*. doi:10.1057/s41290-022-00156-3.

Lloyd, Richard. 2006. *Neo-Bohemia: Art and Commerce in the Postindustrial City*. New York: Routledge.

Lloyd, Richard and Terry Nichols Clark. 2001. "The City as an Entertainment Machine." *Critical Perspectives on Urban Redevelopment* 6:357–78.

Lovatt, Andy. 1996. "The Ecstasy of Urban Regeneration: Regulation of the Night Time Economy in the Transition to a Post-Fordist City." Pp. 141–68 in *From the Margins to the Centre: Cultural Production and Consumption in the Post-industrial City*, edited by J. O'Connor and D. Wynne. London: Routledge.

Love, Heather. 2016. "Queer Messes." *WSQ: Women's Studies Quarterly* 44:345–49.

Lydon, Mike and Anthony Garcia. 2015. *Tactical Urbanism: Short-term Action for Long-term Change*. London: Island Press.

Madanipour, Ali. 2017. *Cities in Time: Temporary Urbanism and the Future of the City*. London: Bloomsbury.

Madden, David J. 2018. "Pushed Off the Map: Toponymy and the Politics of Place in New York City." *Urban Studies* 55:1599–1614.

Mahoney, James. 2000. "Path Dependence in Historical Sociology." *Theory and Society* 29:507–48.

Martel, Frédéric. 2018. *Global Gay*. Cambridge, MA: MIT Press.

Mattson, Greggor. 2015. "Bar Districts as Subcultural Amenities." *City, Culture, and Society* 6:1–8.

——. 2019. "Are Gay Bars Closing? Using Business Listings to Infer Rates of Gay Bar Closure in the United States, 1977–2019." *Socius* 5:1–2.

——. 2023. *Who Needs Gay Bars?* Stanford, CA: Redwood Press.

Maxwell, Joseph A. 2010. "Using Numbers in Qualitative Research." *Qualitative Inquiry* 16:475–82.

McCormack, Mark and Fiona Measham. 2022. "Building a Sustainable Queer Nightlife in London: Queer Creatives, COVID-19 and Community in the Capital." London: Arts Council England.

McPherson, J. Miller and James R. Ranger-Moore. 1991. "Evolution on a Dancing Landscape: Organizations and Networks in Dynamic Blau Space." *Social Forces* 70:19–42.

McPherson, Miller. 1983. "An Ecology of Affiliation." *American Sociological Review* 48:519–32.

Mears, Ashley. 2020. *Very Important People: Status and Beauty in the Global Party Circuit*. Princeton, NJ: Princeton University Press.

Meyer, Alan D. 1982. "Adapting to Environmental Jolts." *Administrative Science Quarterly* 27:515–37.

Miles, Matthew B. and A. Michael Huberman. 1994. *Qualitative Data Analysis*. Thousand Oaks, CA: Sage.

Miles, Sam, Jack Coffin, Amin Ghaziani, Daniel Baldwin Hess, and Alex Bitterman. 2021. "After/Lives: Insights from the COVID-19 Pandemic for Gay Neighborhoods." Pp. 393–418 in *The Life and Afterlife of Gay Neighborhoods*, edited by A. Bitterman and D. B. Hess. New York: Springer.

Mills, Charles. 2017. *Black Rights/White Wrongs: The Critique of Racial Liberalism*. New York: Oxford University Press.

Mitchell, J. Clyde. 1983. "Case and Situation Analysis." *Sociological Review* 31:187–211.

moore, madison. 2016. "Nightlife as Form." *Theater* 46:48–63.

——. 2018. *Fabulous: The Rise of the Beautiful Eccentric*. New Haven, CT: Yale University Press.

Moore, Mignon. 2012. "Intersectionality and the Study of Black, Sexual Minority Women." *Gender & Society* 26:33–39.

Morandini, James S., Alexander Blaszczynsky, and Ilan Dar-Nimrod. 2017. "Who Adopts Queer and Pansexual Sexual Identities." *Journal of Sex Research* 54:911–22.

Morgan, Richard. 2019. "The American Gay Bar Is Down, But Don't Count It Out Just Yet." *BNN Bloomberg* vol. 2021. Available online at: https://www.bnnbloomberg.ca/the-american-gay-bar-is-down-but-don-t-count-it-out-just-yet-1.1280367.

Morris, Aldon. 2022. "Alternative View of Modernity: The Subaltern Speaks." *American Sociological Review* 87:1–16.

Muñoz, José Esteban. 1996. "Ephemera as Evidence: Introductory Notes to Queer Acts." *Women & Performance: A Journal of Feminist Theory* 8:5–16.

——. 1999. *Disidentifications: Queers of Color and the Performance of Politics*. Minneapolis: University of Minnesota Press.

——. 2009. *Cruising Utopia: The Then and There of Queer Futurity*. New York: New York University Press.

Nagel, Joane. 2003. *Race, Ethnicity, and Sexuality*. New York: Oxford University Press.

Nero, Charles. 2005. "Why Are the Gay Ghettos White?" Pp. 228–45 in *Black Queer Studies*, edited by E. P. Johnson and M. G. Henderson. Durham, NC: Duke University Press.

Oakley, Kate, Daniel Laurison, Dave O'Brien, and Sam Friedman. 2017. "Cultural Capital: Arts Graduates, Spatial Inequality, and London's Impact on Cultural Labor Markets." *American Behavioral Scientist* 61:1510–31.

Oldham, Melissa, Sarah Callinan, Victoria Whitaker, Hannah Fairbrother, Penny Curtis, Petra Meier, Michael Livingston, and John Holmes. 2020. "The Decline in Youth Drinking in England—Is Everyone Drinking Less? A Quantile Regression Analysis." *Addiction* 115:230–38.

Ossei-Owusu, Shaun. 2021. "Velvet Rope Discrimination." *Faculty Scholarship at Penn Carey Law*. 2838. Available online at: https://scholarship.law.upenn.edu/faculty_scholarship/2838.

Podmore, Julie A. 2013. "Lesbians as Village 'Queers': The Transformation of Montreal's Lesbian Nightlife in the 1990s." *ACME: An International E-Journal for Critical Geographies* 12:220–49.

Podmore, Julie A. and Alison L. Bain. 2020. "'No Queers Out There?' Metronormativity and the Queer Suburban." *Geography Compass* 14(9):1–16.

Polletta, Francesca. 2006. *It Was Like a Fever: Storytelling in Protest and Politics*. Chicago: University of Chicago Press.

Putnam, Robert D. 2000. *Bowling Alone: The Collapse and Revival of American Community*. New York: Simon & Schuster.

Roberts, Marion. 2016. "What a 'Night Czar' Can Do to Help Nightlife Survive." *The Conversation*, October 19. Available online at: https://theconversation.com/what-a-night-czar-can-do-to-help-nightlife-survive-67253.

Roberts, Marion and Chris Turner. 2005. "Conflicts of Liveability in the 24-hour City: Learning from 48 Hours in the Life of London's Soho." *Journal of Urban Design* 10:171–93.

Robinson, Cedric J. 1983. *Black Marxism: The Making of the Black Radical Tradition*. Chapel Hill: University of North Carolina Press.

Roestone Collective. 2014. "Safe Space: Towards a Reconceptualization." *Antipode* 46:1346–65.

Rosenberg, Rae. 2021. "Negotiating Racialised (Un)belonging: Black LGBTQ Resistance in Toronto's Gay Village." *Urban Studies* 58:1397–1413.

Rosser, B. R. Simon, William West, and Richard Weinmeyer. 2008. "Are Gay Communities Dying or Just in Transition? Results from an International Consultation Examining Possible Structural Change in Gay Communities." *AIDS Care* 20:588–95.

Rubin, Gayle S. 1998. "The Miracle Mile: South of Market and Gay Male Leather, 1962–1997." Pp. 247–72 in *Reclaiming San Francisco: History, Politics, Culture*, edited by J. Brook, C. Carlsson, and N. J. Peters. San Francisco: City Lights Book.

Rupp, Leila J. and Verta Taylor. 2003. *Drag Queens at the 801 Cabaret*. Chicago: University of Chicago Press.

Rupp, Leila J., Verta Taylor, and Eve Llana Shapiro. 2010. "Drag Queens and Drag Kings: The Difference Gender Makes." *Sexualities* 13:275–94.

Rushbrook, Dereka. 2002. "Cities, Queer Space, and the Cosmopolitan Tourist." *GLQ: A Journal of Lesbian and Gay Studies* 8:183–206.

Salkind, Micah E. 2019. *Do You Remember House? Chicago's Queer of Color Undergrounds*. New York: Oxford University Press.

Sassen, Saskia. 2001. *The Global City*. Princeton, NJ: Princeton University Press.

——. 2016. "The Global City: Enabling Economic Intermediation and Bearing Its Costs." *City & Community* 15:97–108.

Savin-Williams, Ritch C. 2005. *The New Gay Teenager*. Cambridge, MA: Harvard University Press.

Scott, W. Richard. 1994. "Conceptualizing Organizational Fields: Linking Organizations and Societal Systems." Pp. 203–21 in *Systems Rationality and Partial Interests*, edited by H.-U. Derlien, U. Gerhadt, and F. W. Scharpf. Baden-Baden: Nomos.

Seidman, Steven. 2002. *Beyond the Closet: The Transformation of Gay and Lesbian Life*. New York: Routledge.

Seijas, Andreina and Mirik Milan Gelders. 2021. "Governing the Night-time City: The Rise of Night Mayors as a New Form of Urban Governance After Dark." *Urban Studies* 58:316–34.

shuster, stef and Laurel Westbrook. 2022. "Reducing the Joy Deficit in Sociology: A Study of Transgender Joy." *Social Problems*. doi: https://doi.org/10.1093/socpro/spac034.

Singh, Sejal and Laura E. Durso. 2017. "Widespread Discrimination Continues to Shape LGBT People's Lives in Both Subtle and Significant Ways." Center for American Progress.

Slavin, Sean. 2004. "Drugs, Space, and Sociality in a Gay Nightclub in Sydney." *Journal of Contemporary Ethnography* 33:265–95.

Small, Mario. 2009. "How Many Cases Do I Need?" *Ethnography* 10:5–38.

Small, Mario Luis and Jessica McCrory Calarco. 2022. *Qualitative Literacy: A Guide to Evaluating Ethnographic and Interview Research*. Oakland: University of California Press.

Smith, Neil Thomas. 2022. "Concrete Culture: The Planning Hearing as a Stage for Cultural Debates." *Cultural Sociology* 16:147–64.

Souza, Marcelo Lopes de. 2006. "Social Movements as 'Critical Urban Planning' Agents." *City* 10:327–42.

Spivak, Gayatri Chakravorty. 1988. "Can the Subaltern Speak?" Pp. 271–313 in *Marxism and the Interpretation of Culture*, edited by C. Nelson and L. Grossberg. Urbana: University of Illinois Press.

Spring, Amy L. 2013. "Declining Segregation of Same-Sex Partners: Evidence from Census 2000 and 2010." *Population Research and Policy Review* 32:687–716.

Stillwagon, Ryan and Amin Ghaziani. 2019. "Queer Pop-Ups: A Cultural Innovation in Urban Life." *City & Community* 18:874–95.

Sun, Hua and Lei Gao. 2019. "Lending Practices to Same-Sex Borrowers." *Proceedings of the National Academy of Sciences* 116:9293–9302.

Swidler, Ann. 1986. "Culture in Action: Symbols and Strategies." *American Sociological Review* 51:273–86.

Taylor, Verta and Nancy E. Whittier. 1992. "Collective Identity in Social Movement Communities." Pp. 104–29 in *Frontiers in Social Movement Theory*, edited by A. D. Morris and C. McClurg. New Haven, CT: Yale University Press.

Teunis, Niels. 2007. "Sexual Objectification and the Construction of Whiteness in the Gay Male Community." *Culture, Health and Sexuality* 93:263–75.

Thomas, William Isaac and Dorothy Swaine Thomas. 1928. *The Child in America: Behavior Problems and Programs*. New York: Knopf.

Thornton, Sarah. 1996. *Club Cultures: Music, Media and Subcultural Capital*. Middletown, CT: Wesleyan University Press.

Thorpe, Rochella. 1996. "'A House Where Queers Go': African-American Lesbian Nightlife in Detroit, 1940–1975." Pp. 40–61 in *Inventing Lesbian Cultures in America*, edited by E. Lewin. Boston: Beacon Press.

Timmermans, Stefan and Iddo Tavory. 2012. "Theory Construction in Qualitative Research: From Grounded Theory to Abductive Analysis." *Sociological Theory* 30:167–86.

Tolliver, Jonathan. 2015. "Do We Need Black Gay Bars Anymore?" *LA Weekly*. Available online at: https://www.laweekly.com/do-we-need-black-gay-bars-anymore/.

Tonkiss, Fran. 2013. "Austerity Urbanism and the Makeshift City." *City* 17:312–24.

Tuck, Eve. 2009. "Suspending Damage: A Letter to Communities." *Harvard Educational Review* 79:409–27.

Valocchi, Steve. 1999. "The Class-Inflected Nature of Gay Identity." *Social Problems* 46:207–24.

Walters, Ben. 2017. "Queer Fun Matters." Pp. 4–5 in *Light After Dark*, edited by K. Hudson. London: Sutton House and Breaker's Yard.

Walters, Suzanna Danuta. 2014. *The Tolerance Trap*. New York: New York University Press.

Warren, Emma. 2023. *Dance Your Way Home*. London: Faber and Faber.

Weber, Max. [1915] 1946. "The Social Psychology of World Religions." Pp. 267–301 in *From Max Weber: Essays in Sociology*, edited by H. Gerth and C. W. Mills. New York: Oxford University Press.

Weiss, Robert S. 1994. *Learning from Strangers: The Art and Method of Qualitative Interview Studies*. New York: Simon & Schuster.

Wekker, Gloria. 2016. *White Innocence: Paradoxes of Colonialism and Race*. Durham, NC: Duke University Press.

Wirth, Louis. 1938. "Urbanism as a Way of Life." *American Journal of Sociology* 44:1–24.

Wynn, Jonathan R. 2015. *Music/City: American Festivals and Placemaking in Austin, Nashville, and Newport*. Chicago: University of Chicago Press.

——. 2016. "On the Sociology of Occasions." *Sociological Theory* 34:276–86.

Yuval-Davis, Nira. 2011. *The Politics of Belonging: Intersectional Contestations*. Thousand Oaks, CA: Sage.

Zerubavel, Eviatar. 1996. "Lumping and Splitting: Notes on Social Classification." *Sociological Forum* 11:421–33.

Zhang, Letian. 2021. "Shaking Things Up: Disruptive Events and Inequality." *American Journal of Sociology* 127:376–440.

Index

A Note on the Type

This book has been composed in Dover Serif Text, a typeface created by queer feminist designer Robin Mientjes. Dover Serif Text is a 21st-century interpretation of the 18th-century Old Style serif typefaces of English type designer William Caslon I (1692–1766). It is part of a small "superfamily" of six complimentary serif and sans-serif styles released as Dover Text by Tiny Type Co. in 2020.

Typographic display elements have been set in Monotype Grotesque Bold Extended (designed by Frank Hinman Pierpont, released by Monotype UK in 1926) and Mānuka Condensed Bold (designed by Kris Sowersby, released by Klim Type Foundry in 2021).